SECONDARY WORLDS

Open University Press

English, Language, and Education series

General Editor: Anthony Adams
Lecturer in Education, University of Cambridge

TITLES IN THE SERIES

Narrative and Argument
Richard Andrews (ed.)

The Problem with Poetry
Richard Andrews

Writing Development
Roslyn Arnold

Writing Policy in Action
Eve Bearne and Cath Farrow

Secondary Worlds
Michael Benton

Time for Drama
Roma Burgess and Pamela Gaudry

Readers, Texts, Teachers
Bill Corcoran and Emrys Evans (eds)

Thinking Through English
Paddy Creber

Developing Response to Poetry
Patrick Dias and Michael Hayhoe

Developing English
Peter Dougill (ed.)

The Primary Language Book
Peter Dougill and Richard Knott

Children Talk About Books
Donald Fry

English at the Core
Peter Griffith

Literary Theory and English Teaching
Peter Griffith

Lesbian and Gay Issues in the English Classroom
Simon Harris

Reading and Response
Mike Hayhoe and Stephen Parker (eds)

Assessing English
Brian Johnston

Lipservice: The Story of Talk in Schools
Pat Jones

Language and the English Curriculum
John Keen

The English Department in a Changing World
Richard Knott

Shakespeare in the Classroom
Susan Leach

Oracy Matters
Margaret MacLure, Terry Phillips and Andrew Wilkinson (eds)

Language Awareness for Teachers
Bill Mittins

Beginning Writing
John Nichols *et al.*

Teaching Literature for Examinations
Robert Protherough

Developing Response to Fiction
Robert Protherough

The Making of English Teachers
Robert Protherough and Judith Atkinson

Microcomputers and the Language Arts
Brent Robinson

Young People Reading
Charles Sarland

English Teaching from A–Z
Wayne Sawyer, Anthony Adams and Ken Watson

Reconstructing 'A' Level English
Patrick Scott

School Writing
Yanina Sheeran and Douglas Barnes

Reading Narrative as Literature
Andrew Stibbs

Collaboration and Writing
Morag Styles (ed.)

Reading Within and Beyond the Classroom
Dan Taverner

Reading for Real
Barrie Wade (ed.)

English Teaching in Perspective
Ken Watson

The Quality of Writing
Andrew Wilkinson

The Writing of Writing
Andrew Wilkinson (ed.)

Spoken English Illuminated
Andrew Wilkinson, Alan Davies and Deborah Berrill

SECONDARY WORLDS

Literature teaching and the visual arts

Michael Benton

Open University Press
Buckingham · Philadelphia

Open University Press
Celtic Court
22 Ballmoor
Buckingham
MK18 1XW

and
1900 Frost Road, Suite 101
Bristol, PA 19007, USA

First Published 1992

A catalogue record of this book
is available from the British Library

Library of Congress Cataloging-in-Publication Data

Benton, Michael, 1939–
Secondary worlds: literature teaching and the visual arts/Michael Benton.
p. cm. – (English, language, and education series)
Includes bibliographical references and index.
ISBN 0–335–09797–9 (pbk.)
1. English literature – Study and teaching. 2. Art and literature – Great Britain. 3. Art – Study and teaching. 4. Art in education.
II. Title. III. Series.
PR35.B45 1992
820′.7 – dc20 91–45907
CIP

Typeset by Type Study, Scarborough
Printed in Great Britain by Biddles Limited
Guildford and Kings Lynn

For my mother
and in memory of my father

Present in every human being are two desires, a desire to know the truth about the primary world, the given world outside ourselves in which we are born, live, love, hate and die, and the desire to make new secondary worlds of our own or, if we cannot make them ourselves, to share in the secondary worlds of those who can.

W. H. Auden, *Secondary Worlds* (1968: 49)

Contents

Part Two Poetry

Part Three Literature, painting and picture-books

List of illustrations

Acknowledgements

I am grateful to a number of editors and publishers who have granted me permission to reproduce revised versions of pieces that have had an earlier incarnation in article or book form. In particular, I am indebted to:

- Oxford University Press for 'Reading fiction – ten paradoxes' which originally appeared in *The British Journal of Aesthetics*, **22** (4), Autumn 1982 and now forms part of Chapter 1;
- The Editor, *Journal of Research and Development in Education*, University of Georgia, for 'Secondary worlds' which originally appeared in the *Journal*, **16** (3), 1983, and now forms part of Chapter 2;
- Ablex Publishing Corporation for parts of Chapter 3 which appeared under the chapter title, 'Possible worlds: narrative voices' in *Reader Stance and Literary Understanding*, ed. J. Many and C. Cox (1991);
- Routledge Publishers for parts of Chapter 5 which appeared under the section heading 'The aesthetic perspective' in my *Young Readers Responding to Poems* (1988);
- The National Association for the Teaching of English for Chapter 6, 'The Importance of Poetry in Children's Learning', which was first published in *Lessons in English Teaching and Learning*, NATE (1988), evidence submitted to the English Working Group chaired by Professor C. B. Cox;
- APS Publications Inc. for parts of Chapter 7 which originally appeared in *Children's Literature in Education*, **7** (2), 1978 under the title 'Poetry for children: a neglected art'.

I am indebted to the following galleries and publishers for permission to reproduce paintings, engravings, and pictorial material:

- The Tate Gallery, London, for *Coming from Evening Church*, by Samuel Palmer, and *The Siesta*, by J. F. Lewis;
- Yale Center for British Art, Paul Mellon Collection, for *The Beggar's Opera* by William Hogarth;

- Salford City Museum and Art Gallery for *Man Lying on a Wall* by L. S. Lowry;
- The British Museum, London, for prints of the following works by William Hogarth: *Marriage à la Mode*, plates 1–6, *A Rake's Progress*, plate 8, and *Gin Lane*;
- Sir John Soane's Museum, London, for *A Rake's Progress*, plate 8, by William Hogarth;
- The National Gallery, London, for *The Shrimp Girl* by William Hogarth;
- The Bodley Head for the picture 'Capture by the balloonist' from *Up and Up* by Shirley Hughes;
- Oxford University Press for 'The gagging scene' from *The Highwayman* by A. Noyes and C. Keeping;
- Julia MacRae Books for the picture 'Gorilla at the end of the bed' from *Gorilla* by Anthony Browne.

In addition, I am grateful to the following writers and publishers for permission to quote from work on which they hold copyright:

- Jonathan Cape Ltd for an extract from *The Cement Garden* by Ian McEwan;
- The Bodley Head for an extract from *The Otterbury Incident* by C. Day Lewis;
- William Collins Ltd for an extract from *Red Shift* by Alan Garner and for extracts from *Cascades Coursework Folder 14–16* by Pam Barnard and Geoff Fox;
- Phoebe Hesketh and The Enitharmon Press for the poem 'Paint Box';
- Jonathan Cape Ltd for 'The Lockless Door' from *The Poetry of Robert Frost* by Robert Frost;
- Gareth Owen and The Tate Gallery, London, for the poem '*Siesta*' from *With a Poet's Eye*, ed. Pat Adams;
- Michael Longley for '*Man Lying on a Wall*: Homage to L. S. Lowry'.

Every effort has been made to contact the publishers of Edward Storey's 'Song of a Church Visit with Children'.

Finally, I owe a personal debt of gratitude to many friends and colleagues who have helped me in the composition of this book, directly through conversations or indirectly through their writings, and, in particular, to my editor Tony Adams for his advice and encouragement. My largest debt is to my students, from whom I continue to gain more than I can offer, especially to those who have allowed me to draw upon aspects of their own work in literature and learning carried out at Southampton University. I would like to thank Mr Mark Gibbons, Headmaster of Hounsdown School, Totton, for enabling me to become a 'recent and relevant' English teacher at his school and, particularly, Ms Caroline Buckingham and her colleagues who, during the Spring Term 1990, allowed me to develop many of the materials and approaches described in Part Three of this book. My special thanks are to Ms Maggie Miller of Hounsdown School for allowing me to use extracts from her M.A.(Ed.) dissertation in Chapter 4 and for her enquiries into students' responses to paintings and poems in Chapters 9 and 10; her skill and insight in this work have been invaluable. I am grateful, too, to Mr John Teasey, Head of English at Robert Mays School, Odiham, Hampshire, for allowing me to reproduce his pupils' work (Chapter 8) and examples of his reading log (Chapter 4) and poetry journal (Chapter 8); to Ms Ros Sutton, formerly of Swanmore School, Hampshire, now Head of English at St Augustine's School, Oxford, for her pupils' writing about poetry and paintings in Chapters 6 and 10; to Mr Andy Revell of Totton College, Southampton, for help with the narratological analysis in Chapter 10; to Mr Roland Lopez for permission to use extracts from his M.A.(Ed.) dissertation on the work of Charles Keeping (Chapter 12); and to Mr Mark Dawkins, formerly of The Arnewood School, Hampshire, now Senior Teacher at The Hugh Christie School, Tonbridge, for permission to use his outline of a picture-book project (Chapter 12).

I would like to thank Rita Corbidge and Hazel Paul for supplying the word-processing skills that I lack; the University of Southampton for granting me sabbatical leave to write this book; and, of course, Jette Kjeldsen for her critical reading of the MS and for her support in enabling me to complete the work more or less on time.

General editor's introduction

Michael Benton is well known to most teachers of English especially because of the series of anthologies he has edited with his brother, Peter, beginning many years ago with the very influential *Touchstones* (2nd edn 1988). He has also written extensively on both the theory and practice of English teaching. One of the things that has come increasingly to cause his anthologies to stand out from their competitors is the strong visual sense that they show both in the selection of illustrations and the presentation of the texts. It is, therefore, wholly consistent with the development of Michael Benton's interests that the present volume should bring together his concerns with literature teaching in the fields of fiction and poetry, and with the visual arts.

There is much that is new and stimulating in each of the three sections of this book but Part Three (Literature, painting and picture-books) is the part of the book that is likely to prove most challenging to English teachers. Many have already discovered the value of picture-books in the classroom at all levels: the days of a belief that students should have outgrown such books by the time they reach secondary school are long since passed. But in this respect, as with much of the other conventional uses of visual material in the English classroom, there is a tendency for such books to be used simply as 'stimulus' materials rather than integrated into a total scheme of work. The detailed account of the 'picture-book project' given in Chapter 12 shows how much more can be done in this respect in the way in which 'such books can be exploited more fully than at present with older children'. The account given of an extended piece of teaching is in itself convincing and provides a suitable model for emulation by others. However one of its most important features for me was not just the work itself but the wide range of agencies who became involved in the work. Readers might like to compare the account given here with some not dissimilar work described in an earlier book in the series, Morag Styles's *Collaboration and Writing* (1989). With a correct, and ever-increasing, emphasis on cross-phase work in schools, programmes of this kind become very important and we need more such detailed case-studies to help us to break down the barriers that have all too often, in the past, existed between the primary and secondary stages of education. Picture-books, with their universal appeal, are one excellent means of bridging this gap. Apart from anything else it might be that the use of more material of this kind in the secondary classroom will lead to a greater attention to making the classrooms themselves more stimulating visually. Still all too often the world of rich visual display is limited to the primary sector, secondary teachers in both their training and sensibilities lacking this area of concern.

The emphasis in the present book on the visual arts is, therefore, of great importance in redirecting our attention to the central part played by the visual imagination and the way in which pictures, too, may be regarded as 'text' in the modernist sense of the term. I found the detailed account of Hogarth's *Marriage à la Mode* very helpful in its account of how to 'read' a 'visual text' of such complexity; it also provides an alternative means into an understanding of narrative and structure that may be helpful to some pupils less attuned by temperament to literary analysis.

Michael Benton's own discussion of Hogarth's work here is a good example of subtle and committed criticism showing how the skills of sensitive reading can be turned also to the demands of sensitive viewing. It has been something of an experiment in preparing the present volume to include so much in the way of visual material, and we hope that the quality of the illustrations will convey, at least in part, something of the power of the originals – and send readers back, where possible, to the originals themselves. In its own way this is this series's own contribution to the rehabilitation of the visual within the English classroom that is urged above.

It is interesting also to see how the often complex nature of much of the discussion embedded in the main text is illuminated by the diagrams that the author has prepared. These are themselves an integral part of the text, not merely embellishments or illustrations, but important contributions to the thinking and progress of the argument.

This concern with the visual becomes, in England and Wales at least, all the more important as our National Curriculum settles down and there seems increasing likelihood that the instrumental demands of much of what is called for will drive the creative arts further into the periphery of what receives attention in school.

I have dealt at some length with the final part of the book because it seems to me the section that is least likely to contain material that will immediately awake a sign of recognition in the average English teacher, but this should not lead us to underestimate the originality and contribution of the two earlier sections. That on poetry will probably be the most familiar, especially to the many users of the already established anthologies by the Bentons. Any anthologist must necessarily have a 'theory' of some kind that underpins the principles of selection that are operating: as often in classroom activity, this area of theory may be implicit. The value of the present Chapter 5 ('Thirteen ways of looking at a poem') is to make highly explicit a series of ideas concerning poetry that must have informed the making of the anthologies. They provide a clear digest of a professional lifetime's involvement in thinking about the role of poetry and the nature of the reader's response. In doing this Michael Benton's '[at least] thirteen ways', different in stance though they are, provide a kind of 1990s updating of the famous analysis by I. A. Richards in *Practical Criticism* (1929) of the problems that may arise when the reader attempts to read an unfamiliar text.

It is interesting that one of the starting points for the author's own journey into poetry is the work of Louise Rosenblatt. (See his discussion of her concept of 'aesthetic' and 'efferent' reading in Chapter 5.) It is a startling thought that her first beginnings in this area of what became her lifetime's work were published, in *Literature as Exploration*, as early as 1938, less than ten years after Richards had published *Practical Criticism*. While it would be both unfair and unwise to polarize here, we might well see these as two seminal books that have spearheaded different ways of exploring literature in the classroom until the present day.

There is, therefore, as a glance at the bibliography will confirm, a wealth of scholarship buried in the pages of this book. But the scholarship never gets in the way of a strong sense of the classroom. The practising teacher will find in these pages ideas that can immediately be translated into practice, in the fields of fiction, poetry, and painting – while the book eschews superficiality, there are plenty of ideas here for 'what to do on Monday', as one would expect from an author who called *Touchstones*, a 'teaching anthology'.

I know as editor, from my discussions with the author while this book was in preparation, that Michael Benton was very anxious to preserve the balance between the three sections into which it is divided. A glance at the contents list will show that it has been very carefully crafted to preserve this balance both between and within the individual sections. Taken together they attempt, and in my view achieve, something very ambitious: nothing less than a theory of aesthetics that is both psychologically and philosophically sound while still of immense practical value to the classroom teacher. The last real attempt to do this was Robert Witkins's highly influential, *The Intelligence of Feeling* (1974), and I have every confidence that the present volume will make an equally relevant and influential contribution to arts education in the 1990s.

Anthony Adams

Introduction. Reading and teaching literature: an overview

The writer's first love and final loyalty are to language. This book is written out of the conviction that English teachers share the same responsibilities and that a love of literary language is the single most important thing we can inculcate in our pupils.

Apart from their inherent appeal, stories and poems confer two vital benefits in respect of literature and learning. Firstly, they are the most powerful language *motivator* available to us in school. Narrative, as Susanne Langer (1953) tells us, is a primary act of mind. We all use narrative to shape each day; it is the organizer of individual consciousness and the main means by which we negotiate with others. This 'storying' is refined and given significance and point by those who compose those stories that become bound between the covers of books. It is natural, therefore, that, in school and out, telling and listening to stories should be the principal element in communication. Secondly, stories and poems are the most powerful means of *learning about language* that we have. When children are lost in a book, 'trying on' a character for size, as it were, by measuring their values and feelings against those of the fictional figure – or when pupils are caught up in that most precise and concrete use of words, poetry, and become aware that words can carry meanings by their sounds, rhythms and associations as well as by lexical definition – then they are learning more about what language is and does than they will through any number of textbook exercises.

If literature teaching falls short of these high claims, it is not the fault of the literature or the pupil but rather of our priorities and methods. I have diagnosed and defined the problem previously as the tyranny of the two Cs over the two Rs (Benton *et al.* 1988), by which I mean that, largely due to the pressure English studies experienced in establishing their credentials at the centre of modern education, there has always been a tendency to elevate what was measurable against recognized norms above what was actually felt and thought during the experience of literature. Comprehension skills and critical skills became valued by an examination system that largely bypassed literary experience as such and certainly paid scant attention to the role of the reader and the nature of literary

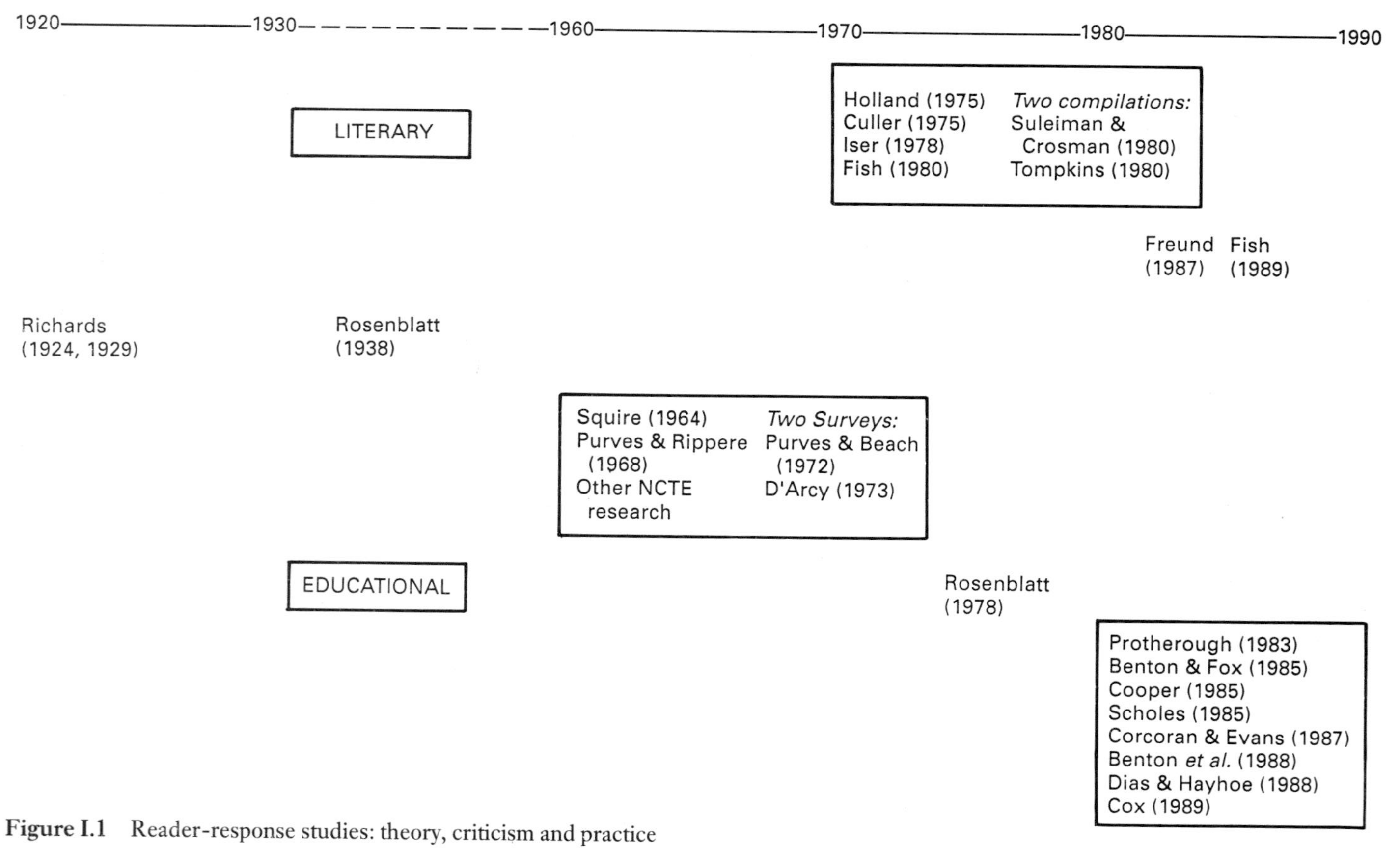

Figure I.1 Reader-response studies: theory, criticism and practice

response. The emphasis has now changed such that there is a much closer relationship discernible between reading and teaching literature. Without launching into a full historical survey, an outline of the main developments that have produced this state of affairs will help.

The diagrammatic outline in Figure I.1 indicates how the professional dialogue has developed during the last seventy years. (Details of the books are given in the Bibliography.) The quality that Richards and Rosenblatt share is a concern for both literature and learning. Thereafter, in the 1940s and 1950s, the reader was hidden from view as the critical landscape was dominated by the American New Criticism, whose adherents took a determinedly anti-reader stance to the extent that, despite a concern for 'close reading', the major statement of New Criticism views – Wellek and Warren's *Theory of Literature* (1949) – makes no mention of the reader and includes only two brief references to 'reading'. In effect, New Criticism invented 'the assumed reader'! Subsequently, the development of reader-response studies has seen the momentum shift periodically from literary theory to educational enquiry and practice almost decade by decade, as indicated in the three boxed phases in Figure I.1.

The 1960s were dominated by education, with the most influential work published by The National Council of Teachers of English (Squire 1964; Purves and Rippere 1968), culminating in two surveys, one English and the other American (D'Arcy 1973; Purves and Beach 1972). The 1970s saw the full bloom of reader-response theorizing by literary critics of whom Holland (1975), Culler (1975), Iser (1978) and Fish (1980) were perhaps the most notable figures, all of whom were well represented in the two compilations of papers that stand as a summary of work in this area at the end of the decade (Suleiman and Crosman 1980; Tompkins 1980). During the 1980s the emphasis moved back to education, where the main concern has been to translate what we have come to know about response – both from literary theory and from classroom enquiry – into principles of good practice. Protherough (1983), Cooper (1985), Benton and Fox (1985), Scholes (1985), Corcoran and Evans (1987), Benton *et al.* (1988), Dias and Hayhoe (1988) have all, in their different ways, considered the implications for practice of a philosophy of literature and learning based upon reader-response principles. In Britain, one of the more heartening results of this development is that the importance of the reader's response to literature is fully acknowledged in the new National Curriculum as embodied in the Cox Report (1989).

Reader-response criticism is a very broad church, as a reading of the two compilations in 1980 or Freund's (1987) overview demonstrates. None the less, a number of principles can be said to characterize this critical stance. Rejecting the 'Affective Fallacy' of New Criticism, all reader-response critics of the 1970s describe the relation of text to reader. This 'fallacy', in Wimsatt and Beardsley's famous description, is a confusion of the poem and its results: 'It begins', they say, 'by trying to derive the standard of criticism from the psychological effects of the poem and ends in impressionism and relativism' (1954: 21). Reader-response critics, on the other hand, operate from a different philosophical basis, one that displaces from the centre of critical discussion the notion of an autonomous text to be examined in and on its own terms and substitutes the reader's re-creation of that text. All share the phenomenological assumption that it is impossible to separate perceiver from perceived, subject from object. Thus, with the reader's creative participation as the central tenet, perception is viewed as interpretive; reading is not the discovering of meaning (like some sort of archaeological 'dig') but the creation of it. Hence, in reader-response criticism, examination of a text for itself is replaced by a discussion of the reading process, the interaction of reader and text. Stanley Fish (1980: 152) puts it succinctly: 'It is the structure of the reader's experience rather than any structures available on the page that should be the object of description.'

This shift of critical emphasis reflects a sea change in literary studies which is nowhere more apparent than when we ask what constitutes the source of literary meaning. The tabulation in Figure I.2 attempts to indicate some of the critical stances that have been adopted when the authority for a reading of a literary work is transferred from the author's words to the reader's response. Three stances are identified: Fish's oppositional view; the synthesis represented by Iser and Rosenblatt, which tries to reconcile the roles of text and reader; and the dualism of Culler, who rejects such a reconciliation.

Whatever the merits of these three positions in theoretical terms, this is clearly not the place to pursue them. The most fruitful ideas for the teaching of literature derive from the work of Iser on fiction and Rosenblatt on poetry, and their views of how readers make literary meanings underpin Parts One and Two of this book respectively. Behind each lies the concept of story with which we began. As Culler (1983: 35) puts it, 'To speak of the meaning of the work is to tell a story of the reading.' The present volume is an anthology of such stories.

The book is organized in three parts, dealing with fiction, poetry, and literature and the visual arts, respectively. Each part opens with a chapter which discusses the nature of the aesthetic experiences offered by these different art forms and argues from a position that assumes that statements about such experiences are often paradoxical and rarely susceptible to linear argument. The character of these chapters, therefore, is elliptical, maybe self-referential, in the way that art itself is, in an effort to capture the qualities that distinguish artistic experiences from others.

In Part One, ten paradoxes are offered as a description of fiction-reading, the superordinate one of which is the notion of the secondary world – a topic taken up and theorized in Chapter 2. Chapter 3 considers the implied dialogue between the author, reader, narrator and characters in fiction through a close scrutiny of readings of the openings of three novels. The aim here is to expose the nature of fiction-reading as a necessary prelude to considering the implied classroom dialogue when fiction is discussed in school (Chapter 4).

Part Two concerns poetry and begins with 'Thirteen ways of looking at a Poem', which attempts to characterize the experience of engaging with a poem.

LITERARY MEANING

AUTHORITY :	Author's creation/words	*v.*	Reader's recreation/ response
CRITICAL STANCE :	Objective criticism	*v.*	Subjective criticism
CRITICS :	*E. D. Hirsch . . .*		*S. Fish . . .*
1 Opposition	Concern with '. . . the author's aims and attitudes in order to evolve guides and norms for construing the meanings of his texts'. *Validity in Interpretation* (1969)	*v.*	'Interpretation is not the art of construing but the art of constructing. Interpreters do not decode poems; they make them.' *Is There a Text in this Class?* (1980)

W. Iser

2 Synthesis

Concern with: 'an analysis of what actually happens when one is reading a text, for that is when a text begins to unfold its potential; it is in the reader that the text comes to life . . .' (1978).

L. Rosenblatt

'The transactional phrasing of the reading process underlines the essential importance of both elements, reader and text, in any reading event' (1978).

J. Culler

3 Dualism

The dichotomy of text and reader, object and subject, refuses to go away. Synthesis is impossible because, 'For the reader the work is not partially created but, on the one hand already complete and inexhaustible – one can read and re-read without ever grasping completely what has already been made – and on the other hand, still to be created in the process of reading, without which it is only black marks on paper. The attempt to produce compromise formulations fails to capture this essential, divided quality of reading' (1983).

Figure I.2 Views of literary meaning

Chapter 6 argues that the power of poetry lies in our recognition of the importance of the narrative imagination, the need for cultural continuity and the role that poems play in the development of children's mastery of language. It identifies qualities of language, form, observation and feeling as particularly significant elements in the way poems work and suggests that poetry is uniquely well placed to encourage them in children's learning. The second part of the chapter argues that the processes of reading and responding should be at the heart of classroom methodology and illustrates how comprehension and criticism need to be rooted in a proper awareness of the reading event if the importance of poetry in children's learning is to be realized.

Chapter 7 diagnoses why, until recent times, poetry for children has been neglected and urges that there are now plenty of opportunities to exploit the rich resources of this area of literature teaching. Finally, Chapter 8 considers poetry in the classroom more explicitly and outlines the principles, methodology and practices that are most likely to win pupils' enthusiasm.

Part Three focuses upon literature, painting and picture-books. As with Parts One and Two, the first chapter raises questions which run through all the others. In this case, the issues are of visual representation and the nature of viewer response. These are considered both from the viewpoint of visual theory and in relation to how students viewed a particular painting. Chapter 10 discusses the 'sister arts' of poetry and painting and, through looking at pairs of paintings and poems, explores the viewing/reading process in relation to the two arts. The case is argued for a greater integration of literature with the visual arts, particularly painting, and practical guidance is given upon how to develop an appropriate programme of study. Chapter 11 concerns a single artist: William Hogarth. It looks at his work from the point of view of its literary and educational significance and draws many parallels between his paintings and engravings and modern concerns such as the nature of narrative; didacticism, protest and satire in the arts in relation to contemporary social issues; and the role of visual media in popular art and culture. Ample guidance is offered to teachers wishing to pursue such work with their classes. Finally, Chapter 12 deals with picture-books. It suggests a classification of picture-books into five groupings; it gives an account of three such texts, using principles of image analysis derived from Media Studies; and it offers ways in which such texts can be used in the literature classroom in both short- and long-term projects.

It can be seen from the above outline that the main thrust of this book avoids giving mere recipes. There are plenty of excellent handbooks for literature teachers already available which contain classroom-tested activities for daily use: my principal concern is to theorize the nature of such practices and to understand the sorts of aesthetic experiences that are shared in these classrooms. For, unless we develop a working theory of why we do what we do with books, we have no sure grounding for knowing how to transfer our approaches from one text or class to another.

The debate about the aesthetic dimension of education has taken on an embattled character in recent years. This is to be expected, given a nineteenth-century legacy that portrayed it as concerned primarily with the pursuit of 'exquisite sensations', and the institutional marginalization of literature and the arts that has occurred in the National Curriculum. Its main defenders (Abbs 1989) make their stand upon a 'conservationist aesthetic' and target the twin enemies of Progressivism and Modernism with impressive fire-power. The stance of the present volume, if not identical, is on nearby ground. I share the belief that working in the arts is a rigorous and exacting business which demands the commitment of the whole person, not just mental labour 'from the neck up'. I share the view that it is necessary to rehabilitate the term 'aesthetic' and to argue for a more prominent role for this particular form of sensuous understanding. It will be apparent, too, from the outline of the three parts of this book, that I agree the need to affirm, examine and illustrate the nature of literary experience in the development of young readers and to relate this to its nearest neighbour – the visual arts.

Yet the conservationist position, however keenly focused, is prone to viewing the past through the lens of nostalgia and the present through blinkers. There *are* developments in modern literary and visual theory that need to be examined and related to work in the arts in schools. The stance of the present volume is that reader-response theory and practice offers English teachers the most coherent position in relation to their work not only because of their inherent appropriateness but because of their inclusive character. They find no difficulty in accommodating both the historical continuity of Abbs and his contributors while remaining open to the insights afforded by recent thinking, for example, in narratology and feminist theory. Several areas of this book (Chapters 4 and 10 particularly) make this explicit connection. In the end, whatever the differences of emphasis, aesthetic education must be concerned with how we come to know and value those characteristics of the language and visual arts, experienced primarily through the senses, in which we locate beauty. As Greene (1989: 218) describes, 'What is important is the event, the situation out of which the aesthetic object emerges. It is not *there*, hanging on the wall; it is not *here*, in the attending mind. The situation is created by the transaction . . .' In exploring such transactions, pupils' experiences of stories, poems and pictures are the raw materials with which English teachers are fortunate enough to operate.

PART ONE

Fiction

1 Reading fiction: ten paradoxes

Stories about stories

Fiction has a narcissistic tendency. Perhaps more than the other arts, it is, if not self-regarding, then self-exploratory. There are stories about stories, about those shared intimacies of writers and readers that make them indivisible, in both children's literature and mainstream fiction.

Jan Mark's 'William's Version' (1980), told in dialogic mode between William and his Granny, enacts the processes of telling and listening and, in so doing, re-enacts the exploration made by Mary Norton in 'Paul's Tale' (1958), where Paul makes a successful take-over bid for his Aunt's storytelling with a far more exciting narrative of his own in order to show her what he means by stories. The interplay of teller and listener *within* each story, and the intertextual references they share, hold powerful reading lessons for young children, as Margaret Meek (1988) has argued in relation to Jan Mark's tale. Intertexuality – that growing mental warehouse of verses, stories, jokes, puns, sayings, 'snatches of old tunes' and the conventions and language in which they are cast – is the reader's private and public property: an asset to be cultivated as a source of personal growth in literary competence, but also one to be shared and enjoyed with other readers. It is the salient feature of the Ahlbergs' *The Jolly Postman or Other People's Letters* (1986), where the reader's appreciation of the literary jokes relies upon an awareness of traditional tales and characters and the linguistic registers in which their stories are told. Indeed, as Stephens wryly speculates (1990: 170), the structure of the text could be 'read as a gentle send-up of certain reader-response concerns . . . as an exaggerated mime of the "shifting viewpoint", [via which] the reader is required to seesaw between interpretive standpoints, in the interests of an activity pronounced as furtive in the subtitle of the book.' The balance between public and private, between social jokes and personal secrets, is perfectly struck.

Haroun, too, experiences the intertextual power of stories, by drinking from the Ocean of the Streams of Story which Iff, the Water Genie, shows him. Rushdie (1990: 72) describes the image:

> Different parts of the Ocean contained different sorts of stories, and as all the stories that had ever been told and many that were still in the process of being invented could be found here, the Ocean of the Streams of Story was in fact the biggest library in the universe. And because the stories were held here in fluid form, they retained the ability to change, to become new versions of themselves, to join up with other stories and so become yet other stories; so that unlike a library of books the Ocean of the Streams of Story was much more than a storeroom of yarns. It was not dead but alive.

Haroun drinks the 'magic of story' from the golden cup that the Water Genie offers him, and instantly, in an Alice-like transformation, becomes the hero in 'Princess Rescue Story Number S/1001/ZHT/420/41(r)xi'!

> He found himself standing in a landscape that looked exactly like a giant chessboard . . . He was, so to speak, looking out through the eyes of the young hero of the story.
> (p. 73)

Haroun and The Sea of Stories celebrates, in light-hearted, modern vein, the ancient interdependence of one story and all other stories, of writers and readers, tellers and listeners, all within the rules and conventions of a brilliantly played game of imagination.

In mainstream fiction, the self-consciousness of story-making was there from the outset. Sterne's *Tristram Shandy* (1767) has many of the narrative features that modern critics write about: 'indeterminancy gaps', diagrams of plot lines, temporal playfulness with 'story-time' and 'discourse-time' and so on. A century or so later, Henry James's 'The Figure in the Carpet' (1896) dramatized the issue of the interpretation of meaning in stories. And, recently, readers find they can open a new novel and be addressed thus:

> *Chapter One*
> You are about to begin reading Italo Calvino's new novel, *If on a Winter's Night a Traveller*. Relax. Concentrate. Dispel every other thought. Let the world around you fade . . .
> (Calvino 1982: 9)

After four or five pages of solicitous concern for the supposed 'real' reader's comfort, the supposed 'real' author starts his tale through the voice of a narrator who seems to be having trouble seeing the story he has to tell:

> The novel begins in a railway station, a locomotive huffs, steam from a piston covers the opening of the chapter, a cloud of smoke hides part of the first paragraph.
> (p. 14)

A man comes and goes between the bar of the station café and the telephone booth. The novel announces solemnly, 'I am the man . . . Or, rather: that man is called "I", and you know nothing else about him . . .' 'Watch out!' the reader is warned a few sentences later, for this is all a method of 'capturing you in the story before you realize it – a trap' (p. 15). Secrets, playfulness, assumed complicity, trust in fictions – these are the features of the author–reader relationship that Calvino explores. So he mesmerizes the hapless reader by focusing attention upon the 'I', to-and-froing between bar and telephone, knowing that 'this alone is reason enough for you (the reader) to invest a part of yourself in the stranger "I".' By the same token, the author stays concealed behind the 'I' yet, 'by the very fact of writing "I", the author feels driven to put into this "I" a bit of himself, of what he feels or imagines he feels' (p. 17).

If on a Winter's Night a Traveller is a story about stories. Its protagonists are its author and his reader. Its plot traces the reading of a novel and the consummation of a love affair between the Reader and the Other Reader who read both literature and each other with passionate intensity. They begin but never finish reading ten novels, all for playfully plausible reasons, so that the characters of the book are the many figures engaged in writing, making, distributing and reading fiction. Throughout, you and I as actual readers are teased about our relationship with Calvino's text: 'This book so far has been careful to leave open to the Reader who is reading the possibility of identifying himself with the Reader who is read . . .' (p. 13).

At the end, the Reader goes to a great library in the hope of completing the ten novels he has started. None is available and, while the librarian searches for them, the Reader encounters several other people who, in turn, tell him about how they read. There is the fantasist, for whom books are a catalyst to the imagination; the literal reader, who is obsessed by the words on the page; the reader for whom 'the promise of reading is enough' stimulation in itself; the reader for whom 'the sense of the ending' is all that counts; the intertextual reader, for whom each new fiction enters into a relationship with all others that have been read; the retrospective reader, who nostalgically seeks echoes of the book of a lost childhood; and the rereader, who says:

> at every rereading I seem to be reading a new book, for the first time. Is it I who keep changing and seeing new things of which I was not previously aware? Or is reading a construction that assumes form, assembling a great number of variables, and therefore something that cannot be repeated twice according to the same pattern? . . . The conclusion I have reached is that reading is an operation without object; or that its true object is 'itself'.
>
> (pp. 200–3)

It is this aesthetic experience that the remainder of this chapter sets out to explore.

Ten paradoxes

> Some books are to be tasted, others to be swallowed, and some few to be chewed and digested: that is, some books are to be read only in parts; others to be read, but not curiously; and some few to be read wholly, and with diligence and attention.
>
> (Bacon 1625/1890: 342)

If the commonest metaphor for the writing process is to do with birth (writers speak of conceiving and incubating ideas), the most frequent figure for reading concerns food. True, recent French criticism has preferred to stress the sexual appetite, to speak of an erotics, rather than a poetics or even a dietetics, of reading and to characterize (perhaps, caricature is more accurate) the act of critical reading as a form of perversion, as voyeurism rather than serious study or innocent pleasure (Barthes, 1976). These excesses apart, Francis Bacon's description of the ways in which readers and books relate is nearer to most people's experiences.

Bacon, of course, was writing well before the invention of the novel in the mid-eighteenth century, yet not only is his metaphor echoed by the early novelists (see the opening chapter of *Tom Jones*), but his sentiments about reading remind us of the diversity of ways in which fiction can be read. The distinction between reading for study and reading for enjoyment is not an absolute one, but it is important when considering the processes involved. Ends do affect means. At one extreme, the reader may be a literary critic with an article to write and a concern for the revaluation of a familiar text; at the other may be the child reader whose sole, unexpressed, wish is the pleasure of being engrossed in a new story as an end in itself. In practice, most readings lie somewhere between these positions, but the polarities help to focus us upon the functions and thence the processes of reading. A contemporary version of Bacon's metaphor distinguishes critic from reader thus:

> The critic reads in order to reach a judgement of value: the reader reads in order to receive the value of what the work offers. The judge in a baking competition may award the prize to a loaf on account of its texture, lightness, crustiness, and so on. But a man does not normally eat bread in order to judge it. He eats it in order to satisfy his hunger and his palate.
>
> (Langman 1967: 93–4)

The critic will be rereading, backtracking, noting and interpreting the minutiae of a text; the ordinary reader will be performing a mental script, swept along, unquestioningly for the most part, willing to submit to the illusion, suspending judgement and withholding evaluation until the process is complete and the appetite satisfied. My concern in this chapter is less with the considered reading of the critic and more with the experience of the naïve reader; not with study but with performance. In Bacon's terms, I am interested more in the processes of swallowing than in those of chewing and digesting.

What happens when we become 'lost' in a book? Despite a number of attempts to formulate what is variously called a poetics of reading (Barthes 1976), a poetics of fiction (Spilka 1977) or a theory of aesthetic response (Iser 1978), no convincing explanation has yet emerged, quite probably because the delicacy of the phenomenon itself becomes 'lost' under the pressure to propound a favourite theory. For the crucial recognition we must make about being in the reading state is that it is an essentially *creative* process. Once this is acknowledged, it becomes possible to reflect the nature of engrossed reading in a way that honours the character of creative activity rather than argues from the entrenched standpoint of a committed position. In short, it is appropriate to formulate some answers to the question not as a set of principles derived from sequentially reasoned argument but as a series of paradoxes.

1962 was a good year for paradoxes: it saw the publication of Bruner's *On Knowing* and the appearance of what is now judged to be a classic essay on the reading of fiction by D. W. Harding. In characterizing the reader's mental state, I have in mind both the manner in which Bruner considers the conditions of creativity and the insights afforded by Harding in his description of the paradoxical participant/spectator role that the reader adopts. What follows might be seen as a counterpart to Bruner's essay, as antinomies that describe the conditions of re-creativity as it is experienced in reading fiction.

I should like to propose ten notions about the nature of participatory reading. It would be false to suggest that there is a logical order. Clearly, in such formulations many of the ideas will be interdependent and, in some instances, reliant upon what has preceded them. None the less, in the discussion of these notions, there is a progression of emphasis from those paradoxes that relate to the status of the literary experience to those which better describe the means by which the text is apprehended. Given these caveats, we can say the following of the process of reading a story:

1 *Reading a story is detached and committed* Only this first paradox derives directly from Bruner and Harding. In successful reading, readers detach themselves from the demands and pressure of the world around them and commit themselves to the virtual world that the text offers. All habitual readers have experienced the sensation of finding the world of the book more 'real' than that of the room in which they are reading. Time and place fade and are replaced by the fictional time and space that the story decrees. We become 'lost' in a book. To adopt a sentence of Bruner (1962/65: 24), we might say that when readers experience this shift, '. . . at one stroke they . . . are disengaged from that which exists conventionally and are engaged deeply in what they construct to replace it.' It is the 'detachment of commitment. For there is about it a caring . . .', a need to understand the world of the story.

What psychological processes prevail in such a condition of abandonment? Harding's answer (1962: 136) extends the paradox by pointing out that the day-dreamer, the child engaged in make-believe and, by extension, the reader of fiction 'normally fills the dual role of participant and spectator'. To stress merely the spectator role and to describe it in terms of identification and vicarious experience . . .

> neglects the fact that the onlooker not only enters into experience of the participants but also contemplates them as fellow-beings. It is an elementary form of onlooking merely to imagine what the situation must seem like and to react *with* the participant. The more complex observer imagines something of what the

> participant is experiencing and then reacts *to* him, for instance with pity or joy on his account.
>
> (1962: 145)

Empathic insight implies that not only do we hold on to the intelligence of our feelings but we also exercise our feelings as quasi-participants in the fiction. During reading, we are simultaneously detached spectators and committed participants. The next paradox adds a gloss upon this phenomenon.

2 *Reading a story entails belief in an acknowledged illusion* Coleridge (1798) has dramatized for all literature the spell-binding relationship between teller and listener in his cameo of the wedding guest who 'cannot choose but hear' the mariner's tale. In *Biographia Literaria*, the twin pull of the actual world and the story world is given in Coleridge's celebrated description of 'that willing suspension of disbelief for the moment, which constitutes poetic faith' (Coleridge 1817/1949: 147). The dualism contains the paradox. For, whatever doubts we may entertain about the adequacy of Coleridge's description, there lie in the elaboration of the idea the seeds of a paradox about literary belief. Coleridge (*ibid.*) says:

> The mind of the spectator, or the reader, therefore is not to be deceived into any idea of reality . . . neither, on the other hand, is it to retain a perfect consciousness of the falsehood of the presentation. There is a state of mind between the two, which may properly be called illusion, of which the comparative powers of the mind are completely suspended; as in a dream, the judgement is neither beguiled, nor conscious of the fraud, but remains passive.

Where Coleridge notes our passivity of judgement in respect of such illusion, Koestler (1964/75: 302–3) emphasizes our willingness to submit to its power. He points out that it is a remarkable phenomenon that, when watching a film, intelligent adults should go through agonies of suspense, and display the corresponding bodily symptoms, and yet know all the time that the faces they see on the screen are mere projections by a machine and that the hero will win in the end anyway. He continues, 'It is even more remarkable that this capacity for living in two universes at once, one real, one imaginary, should be accepted without wonder as a commonplace phenomenon.' And he goes on to develop the point by reference to an account of viewers' reactions to *Coronation Street* which purports to show that many devotees of serial fictions on television actually believe in the existence of the people and places portrayed. Koestler comments (ibid., p. 302) that, of course, there is no straight logical answer to the question of fictional belief:

> The answer is neither yes nor no, but yes and no. The so-called law of contradiction in logic – that a thing is either A or not-A but cannot be both – is a late acquisition in the growth of individuals and cultures. The unconscious mind, the mind of the child and the primitive, are indifferent to it. So are the Eastern philosophies which teach the unity of opposites, as well as Western theologians and quantum physicists.

> The addicts of *Coronation Street* who insist on believing in the reality of Ena Sharples have merely carried one step further the momentary split-mindedness experienced by a sophisticated movie-audience at the climax of a Hitchcock thriller; they live in a more or less permanently bisociated world.

Koestler's notion of bisociation serves as the vehicle for the paradox that, in willingly believing in both the meanings of illusions and the meanings of the actual, the watcher of a film and the reader of a story are enjoying a sort of literary schizophrenia. Granted that there are differences of degree rather than of kind, according to the medium involved, the principle remains the same. The bisociated mind edits from both the illusory and the actual, mixing elements of the primary and secondary worlds together, varying its degree of attachment to each as the fiction unravels.

3 *Reading a story is individual yet cooperative* Reading is private and singular. It is highly individual with no observable outcome, no finished product for us to examine. The story happens inside the reader's head. The activity of 'storying' from the printed pages of a book lies within; it is over before it can be articulated. The individuality of reading is axiomatic. Yet reading is also cooperative. The experience of reading fiction is a compound of what the text offers and what the reader brings. If writing is a 'one-headed' job (the author with his pen and blank sheet of paper), reading is a 'two-headed' experience. The reader creates with the products of two imaginations, his or her own and the writer's.

The ramifications of this paradox are startling. For, given that no two readers re-create the same story and no one reader can ever repeat the experience a second time, this leaves what we can call each unique 'textual performance' in a curious limbo, for it belongs wholly neither to the author nor to the reader but hovers somewhere between them, partaking of both. Whether looked at through the author's or the reader's inward eye, its status is that of a 'virtual experience'.

4 *Reading a story is simultaneously monologue and dialogue* In the effort to bring this virtual world into being, readers process the text in both individual and cooperative ways. On the one hand, the text is experienced as a *mechanical monologue* as readers decode signs into meanings as they track back and forth across the page; on the other, it is simultaneously experienced as an *imaginative dialogue*, of the sort that has been described by Wayne Booth (1961: 155). 'In any reading experience', he says, 'there is an implied dialogue among author, narrator, the other characters and the reader.' Books are embalmed voices. The reader's job is to disinter them and to breathe life into them.

5 *Reading a story is active and passive* As the first paradox implies, there are both constructive and receptive elements in the process of reading fiction. The former are readily recognized, for it is a commonplace in any reader's experience (and in books about reading) that the mental activity set going when reading a story involves the reader in making meaning from signs. When we are engrossed in a

book, we are conscious not of words on the page but of meanings made. E. H. Gombrich has argued that the perception of such meanings is achieved through the reader's projection from the textual cues. He says (1962: 170):

> All representation relies to some extent on what we have called 'guided projection' . . . Psychologists class the problem of picture reading with what they call 'the perception of symbolic material'. It is a problem which has engaged the attention of all who investigate effective communication, the reading of texts or displays or the hearing of signals.

Yet, together with this active role, there coexists the traditional notion that the condition of literary belief, that accompanies the reader's involvement in story, demands passivity. Auden (1973a) speaks of the 'total surrender' of the reader to the world of the tale. C. S. Lewis (1961: 19) catches the paradox when he talks of the 'positive effort' involved in reading, of which the first demand is 'Surrender. Look. Listen. Receive. Get yourself out of the way.' The process, as we have seen, is one that requires readers to invent an illusion in which they will willingly believe for the duration of its existence. They are active in its construction, insistent about the coherence of the secondary world they make; yet they are passive recipients of the effects of this world, essentially submissive to its power. The reader's mind both *makes* things happen and *lets* things happen.

6 *Reading a story is recreative and re-creative* The idea of reading as recreation has a useful ambiguity, for recreation betokens play, where reading is the proper indulgence of a pleasurable pastime; whereas re-creation suggests work, where reading is the proper effort involved in remaking the story. If we are to understand the recreative act of reading fiction, both facets of this ambiguity must be allowed. The interaction of play and discipline which is so much part of the writer's process of making finds its corollary in reading. Tolkien's (1938/64: 36) often quoted statement about the writer as a 'sub-creator' of a 'secondary world' has implications for the reader too. For, in remaking a story from a text, readers generate a 'secondary world' in their own imaginations. They are performers, interpreters of a text. Granted they do not have the expressive outlet of a stage and an audience but, instead, they build a mental stage and fill it with the people and scenes and events that the text offers and, as will be indicated in the eighth paradox, with other images generated by their own individual inclinations and limitations. Reading is a sort of 'armchair acting'.

7 *Reading a story is unique yet repetitive* As with the performance of a play or a symphony, each 'reading' is a unique experience. To take an extreme example, this includes rereadings of the same text by the same person. Most people have had the experience of finding different things in the story world on reading a book for the second time. The book has not changed: the same words are in the same order. It is the reader who has changed; or, more precisely, the nature of the reader's imaginative participation has changed – and will change every time he or

she reads. Undeniably, there will be a large measure of 'sameness' about each performance: repeated readings, even allowing for marginal variations due to error, are all bound by the criterion of faithfulness to the text. Yet, although each reading has to follow the same 'score', as it were, none the less, there are unique elements of interpretation that occur each time the textual performance is set going. Frank Kermode (1975: 17) has argued that, when reading fiction, there is 'always a requirement that the reader should be a more or less sophisticated interpreter . . .' and, a few sentences later, he signals the nature of the reading process by using three words we have frequently employed and treating them as synonymous factors. He says, 'Another word for performance is interpretation; and interpretation is another word for reading'. Reading is performance is interpretation: a commonplace remark when used about the director of a play or the conductor of a symphony but an unfamiliar one when applied to the reader of a story.

8 *Reading a story entails both abstraction and filling in* In his book *How to Read a Page*, I. A. Richards (1943: 93) identifies three characteristics of 'educated human experience' and sees them as central to the reading process. They are 'approximate understanding, a sense of the diversity of word-senses [and] . . . essential omission'. These three elements, Richards says, 'constitute the focus of consciousness in the reading experience'. All derive from the process of abstraction that he regards as crucial, for 'In all readings we *abstract*, we take only some of the possibilities of the words' meanings into account.'

Yet the literary and life experiences that a reader brings to this task provide a context for the process that is as vital as the abstraction itself. Richards tacitly acknowledges this, for, although he stresses the importance of abstraction, the terms in which he goes on to describe the way abstraction varies according to the nature of the text clearly indicate the presence of a complementary process of filling in from the reader's own imagination. He continues (*ibid.*):

> We let in (or should let in) less in reading such prose as this than we let in with most poetry. But in all reading whatsoever much must be left out. Otherwise we could arrive at no meaning. The omission is essential in the twofold sense: without omission no meaning would form *for us*; and through the omission what we are trying to grasp becomes *what it is* (gets its essential being).

Richards prefers to stress the 'leaving out' rather than the 'letting in'. Recent criticism, notably that of Slatoff (1970) and Iser (1978), has favoured the contrary emphasis and in so doing has caught something of the spirit of Fielding and Sterne. Slatoff comments upon the 'inevitable and valid imaginative filling in and fleshing out which we perform as we read . . .', pointing out that '. . . if we did not do something of the sort, fictional characters would in fact be no more than verbal structures or anatomical and psychological freaks . . .' (1970: 17).

9 *Reading a story is both ordered and disordered* The continuous effects of a story on an engrossed reader's mind are analogous to those which Virginia Woolf

urged her contemporary novelists to make their main concern. Impatient with what she judges to be the superficialities of Wells, Bennett and Galsworthy, she prepares us for her praise of Joyce with this exhortation (1925: 189):

> Examine for a moment an ordinary mind on an ordinary day. The mind receives a myriad impressions – trivial, fantastic, evanescent, or engraved with the sharpness of steel. From all sides they come, an incessant shower of innumerable atoms; and as they fall, . . . they shape themselves into the life of Monday or Tuesday . . . Life is not a series of gig lamps symmetrically arranged; life is a luminous halo, a semi-transparent envelope surrounding us from the beginning of consciousness to the end. Is it not the task of the novelist to convey this varying, this unknown and uncircumscribed spirit?

And is it not, we might also ask, the nature of the reader's collaboration to apprehend this same spirit? The streams of impressions triggered by the text during the reader's experiencing of the secondary world are similar in kind to those that Virginia Woolf sees as the writer's raw material in the primary world. They are characterized by their variety and unpredictability. Yet, if such disorder is a condition of the mind's fertility, a complementary need for order is the way in which the mind makes sense of this 'incessant shower of innumerable atoms'. The reader's search for coherence and the need for form are as necessary to the patterning, and thence to the comprehending, of the secondary world of story as the shaping that takes place in the mind to make sense of Monday or Tuesday. Bruner has noted the paradox of vitality and decorum in creative activity. Here we have the corresponding antinomy of re-creative reading: the streams of images, ideas, memories and associations that flood the consciousness are controlled and channelled by the mind's drive towards order – by, to adopt Bruner's words, 'a love of form, an etiquette toward the object of our efforts . . .' (1962/65: 24).

10 *Reading a story is anticipatory yet retrospective* First, let us grant that there is an important retrospective element in reading, in that the reader's span of attention lags behind the point to which the eye has travelled and the transformations that the mind makes upon the text accumulate towards a growing sense of coherent form. Mechanically and imaginatively, retrospection is crucial. Nevertheless, the main thrust of the *engrossed* reader of fiction is forwards, anticipating what is to come. The 'textual performance' proceeds through the impetus of the reader's imaginative anticipation which forms the driving edge of each 'reading'. The twin processes of anticipation and retrospection are thus complementary and oscillate together as the reader moves through a narrative and reconstitutes a form of the story inside his or her head. As Coleridge puts it with great precision and charm (1817/1949: 50):

> The reader should be carried forward, not merely or chiefly by the mechanical impulse of curiosity, or by a restless desire to arrive at the final solution; but by the pleasurable activity of mind excited by the attractions of the journey itself. Like the motion of a serpent, which the Egyptians made the emblem of intellectual power; or like the path of sound through the air; at every step he pauses and half recedes, and from the retrogressive movement collects the force which again carries him onward.

Two steps forward and one step back is not a bad description of how we read stories.

A collection of paradoxes lacks the solidity of a set of principles, at least where developing an argument is concerned. Instead of the carefully constructed building there appears to be only the façade. Rather than offering underlying ideas to which constant reference can be made, antinomies tend to beg questions or, at any rate, to leave issues open for further exploration. Yet, as was mentioned at the outset, the creative character of the reading process dictates that it should be conveyed in a manner that befits its plural and contradictory nature.

Finally, even if we lack the neat coherence of a set of principles, there is the phenomenon of the reader's mood enveloping the whole experience and tending to unify the sometimes disparate elements that make up the process. What is this state of being that characterizes the reader's engrossment in the fictional world? Wallace Stevens (1963: 90–1) captures what we have called the 'reading state' in his poem 'The House was Quiet and the World was Calm'. The poem begins

> The house was quiet and the world was calm.
> The reader became the book; and summer night
>
> Was like the conscious being of the book.

and steadily creates the mood of absorption that most experienced readers of novels will recognize. The poem evokes it as much by the measured repetitions of certain phrases that seem to pad the house with their dull monotones, merging its reality with the unreality of the book, as by the explanation of what happens when 'The reader became the book'. The four key words of the title are permutated with other monosyllables – 'night', 'book', 'lean', 'page' and so on – to create a rhythmical pattern that is flat and steady, and to reflect a safe, enclosed, inviolable experience. Stevens explains the sense of 'becoming the book' in terms of a transformation: the summer night around the reader is 'like the conscious being of the book'. Primary and secondary worlds coalesce. The physical nature of the book recedes and the atmosphere of quiet enveloping the reader is so pervasive as to become 'part of the meaning, part of the mind' that is re-creating the story.

Yet, for all its subtlety in characterizing the experience of being in the reading state, there is also a strong sense of the impermanence of such engrossment, reminding us of Coleridge's phrase 'for the moment' quoted earlier. This derives partly from the emphasis upon perfection, from the sense that the reading Stevens is describing is an ideal experience under optimum conditions for total immersion, whereas much reading takes place at other seasons when the mood is less easily sustained; and partly from the self-regarding quality of the poem, from the feeling that the poet is both absorbed and detached, both reader and onlooker, both 'lost' in the secondary world yet present in the primary one. This, of course, is the ultimate paradox: we cannot, as Ryle (1949: 158) says, 'attend twice at once'. In order both to read and to attend to ourselves reading, we are asking for the best of both worlds.

2 Secondary worlds

We cannot discuss reading and writing in isolation, for in both we are makers. Tolkien (1938/64) implies as much in his well-known essay 'On Fairy Stories'. In a celebrated passage (p. 36), he writes:

> Children are capable, of course, of *literary belief*, when the story-maker's art is good enough to produce it. That state of mind has been called 'willing suspension of disbelief'. But this does not seem to me a good description of what happens. What really happens is that the story-maker proves a successful 'sub-creator'. He makes a Secondary World which your mind can enter. Inside it, what he relates is 'true': it accords with the laws of that world. You therefore believe it, while you are, as it were, inside. The moment disbelief arises, the spell is broken: the magic, or rather art, has failed. You are then out in the Primary World again, looking at the little abortive Secondary World from outside.

What do the secondary worlds of writers and readers have in common? At first sight, the processes that create such worlds appear to be so different that we might expect their psychic products to show few similarities. Writing is slow, laborious and deliberate; reading is fast, light-footed, cavalier. Writing is concerned with *le mot juste*, and to fix words so that they will not slip and slide out of place; reading skips over words to meanings, slipping and sliding all the time in order to make a unique analogue of the given text. Writing uses reading and rereading as a means to its own ends; reading is 'a free spirit' that uses writing only when it turns into study. However, the single, overriding concept that writers and readers agree upon is the creation of 'a world', one that is variously described as 'virtual', 'alternative', 'three-dimensional', 'story' and so forth. The clearest and most fully explained adjective is Tolkien's 'secondary', and this will be adopted as the preferred term since it invites the development of the conceptual model that is required to link both writing and reading and the world of the book to the world around us.

W. H. Auden found the distinction between the primary and secondary world a helpful one. Acknowledging his debt to Tolkien for these terms, Auden says (1968: 49):

> Present in every human being are two desires, a desire to know the truth about the primary world, the given world outside ourselves in which we are born, live, love, hate and die, and the desire to make new secondary worlds of our own or, if we cannot make them ourselves, to share in the secondary worlds of those who can.

He goes on to characterize this making and sharing of secondary worlds in terms of our dissatisfaction with the primary world. Secondary worlds, embodied in verbal, visual or auditory objects, are people's efforts to complement the primary world we all inhabit. They are not given, we must *choose* to make them; they are not subject to natural death, their sub–creators are omnipotent and omniscient, so that they can exclude everything except that which is deemed to be sacred, important and enchanting. Within a secondary world, even evil and suffering can be made comprehensible. What Auden does not do, because it is not to his purpose, is to ask questions such as: Where does this secondary world exist? What is its structure? What is it made of? How is it brought into being? What is the viewpoint from which writers and readers see it?

The purpose of this chapter is to develop the concept of the secondary world and to attempt some tentative answers to these questions. This will entail discussion, in turn, of four aspects of the secondary world: its location and nature, its three-dimensional structure, the viewpoint that brings it into existence, and the substance of which it is composed.

The space between

The secondary world exists in the limbo between the author or reader and the text. The burden of much recent literary criticism is that a proper attention to the act of reading demonstrates that the compelling power of literature lies neither in the individual nor in the text but in their interaction in what we shall call 'the space between'. The phrase is Craig's (1976: 35–6), and by it he conceives of something similar to Winnicott's (1974: 102–3) 'third area', that highly variable factor (from one individual to the next) which exists between the personal or psychic reality that is biologically determined for each of us and the actual world that is our common property.

Craig sees writer and reader meeting in a literary no-man's-land. The writer works in a 'third area', the space between 'the subject (his whole self, forever unknowable)', and the external world as it is apprehended according to the needs and motivations of 'the "I" that he knows (writer, reader, comparer, aspirer) . . .' The result is the language of the text. The literary work is a dialogue with self, a 'dialogue across the space between'. In its turn it forms the external reality to which the reader must respond, thus setting up the reader's 'third area' between his or her whole self and the world in the text. Craig concludes (p. 36):

> Whether he is swept away, brought up short, briefly amused or gradually repelled

> will depend on how far, in no-man's-land, the writer's 'dialogue' creates the conditions of a corresponding 'dialogue' in the reader. Only when each has had to forgo direct sight of the other can relation be established. To the form of one man's venture responds the form of another's: the unimaginable contact is made across the ground of fiction.

The virtual world of the text is thus central, created in the space between the writer's inner self and outer reality, re-created in the space between the reader's inner self and the words on the page.

If the secondary world is thus notionally located, what is its nature? Huizinga (1949/70), Winnicott (1974) and others describe it in terms of mental play activity: '. . . the construction of any secondary world', as Auden (1970) reminds us, 'is a gratuitous not a utile act, something one does not because one must, but because it is fun.' This 'play' or 'fun' takes its nature from the individual's need to relate the world of 'inner necessity', to use Britton's (1977) gloss upon Winnicott, with the demands of the external world. It is a need that may be met both by writing and by reading. Yet, to equate the secondary worlds of writers, readers and dreamers is clearly fallacious, as Freud acknowledges, even though they may have some elements in common. Freud's (1908/70) classic essay on 'Creative writers and day dreaming' sees the adult writer engaged in essentially the same activities as the child at play. Both create a secondary world that they take seriously, invest with large amounts of emotion, govern with certain rules and laws and thus separate sharply from reality. Furthermore, he argues that 'a piece of creative writing, like a daydream, is a continuation of, and a substitute for, what was once the play of childhood.' And, we could add, re-creative reading stands in a similar relationship with childhood play. Even so, despite their common derivation, the secondary worlds of the daydreamer, the writer and the reader will be very different. Freud points out that the fantasies of the first would merely embarrass or bore us. The contrivance is the writer's 'innermost secret', the 'essential ars poetica', which Freud explains in terms of the transmutation of the writer's inner fantasies through the disguise of symbol, allegory, story-line and the like. Post-Freudian critics like Lesser (1957) and Holland (1968) have seen the reader's secondary world as the product of a complementary activity, one involving the management of his or her own fantasies and those embedded in the text.

Even when we prefer to stop short of embracing these psychoanalytic interpretations of writing and reading, Freud and his followers are helpful in stressing both the continuity that links these different manifestations of play activity and the characteristics of particular manifestations, such as writing and reading, that are controlled by the presence of the text. For it is the writer's and reader's consciousness of the controlling text that separates their secondary worlds from that of the dreamer. The narratives of dreams and daydreams consist of temporary, evanescent, airy images, unstable in form and direction, whose source, if we are to believe Freud, is largely dependent upon the perceptual experiences of the previous day. The narratives of the maker and reader of stories may draw upon such involuntary, autistic content, but their orientation is towards the objectifying of images and the arrangement of them in a permanent and significant form.

Yet, while the secondary worlds of writer and reader may be similar in location and nature, they are never identical. This is obvious not only because of the idiosyncratic experience that they bring to their respective tasks but also because of the different psychic operations these tasks involve. For writing grows out of the fertility of the author's unconscious into conscious realization; reading works in the opposite direction, beginning with the conscious perception of the text which, in turn, leads to effects on the reader's unconscious. While these processes are complementary and have characteristics in common, they are not the same. To account for these likenesses and differences between writing and reading and to explore the relationship between the secondary and the primary world, a structural model is helpful.

The three-dimensional structure

In the passage quoted at the beginning of this chapter, Tolkien describes the writer as a 'successful "sub-creator"' of a secondary world which the reader's mind imaginatively enters. 'Belief' in it entails two factors: the condition of being 'inside', the surrender of the self to the book, and, secondly, the recognition that this world, like any other, is governed by certain laws. The first condition indicates the viewpoint we adopt in relation to the secondary world and is discussed presently. The second idea, the literary need for rules and conventions, suggests that, in both its structure and its substance, the secondary world can be conceptualized as an analogue of the primary one. For, to make sense of the primary world, we postulate its structure and our relation to that structure in terms of the three dimensions of length, breadth and height, and we describe our perceptions of experience within this framework in terms of the information given to the brain through our five senses. These dimensions and sense perceptions comprise our spatial perspective. In the temporal perspective, memory is our crucial facility, allowing us to store experience and to speculate on the basis of this store about past, present and future. The argument can be summarized simply: the dimensions and substance of the secondary world are susceptible to an analogous description. The imaging that gives substance to this world in the head is discussed in the final part of this chapter; meanwhile, a diagram (Figure 2.1) will help us to visualize the psychic dimensions.

One other consideration that must preface our discussion of the structure of the secondary world is the fact that, although the model is developed largely from ideas about aesthetic response, it is equally appropriate in the respects for which it is used for creative activity, if for no other reason than the process of creation involves a good measure of aesthetic response simply in order to function. As was noted at the outset, writing employs reading as a means to its own end. The writer is his or her first audience, the most attentive, creative and critical audience of all.

Reading does not make a reciprocal use of writing. Since the process of reading is integral to the writer's work as well as to the reader's, it is likely that any model of the secondary world will derive from studies of aesthetic response. For this reason, the discussions of structure, viewpoint and substance which follow encompass both the writer's and the reader's experience of the secondary world.

In the course of his book *Psychoanalytic Explorations in Art* (1952/1964), Kris argues that genuine aesthetic response takes place only when, in the mind of the viewer of a painting or the reader of a poem, there occur shifts of *psychic level* and *psychic distance*. The idea is of the mind in constant movement between these two interlocking axes: 'level' conveys the continuous state of interplay between the conscious and unconscious, the controlled and regressive elements; 'distance' catches the continuous fluctuations in the degree of involvement with an art object. Together they describe two dimensions of aesthetic response. Perhaps because he is primarily concerned with the visual arts (and, when he deals with literature, mostly with poetry), Kris confines his description to these spatial dimensions. To account for the experience of writing and reading a novel, however, we need to add a third dimension, a temporal axis along which shifts

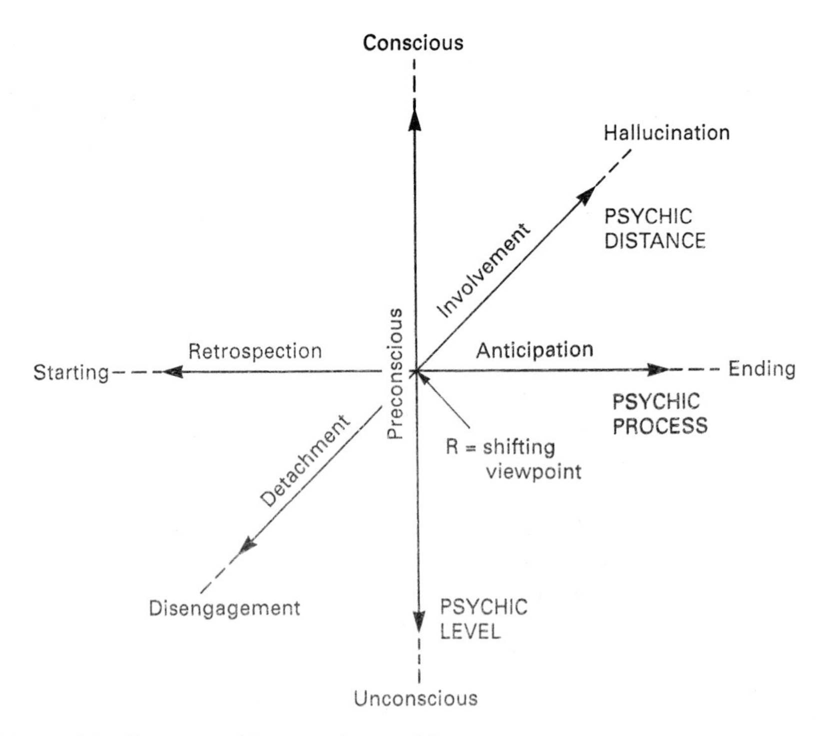

Figure 2.1 Structure of the secondary world

also occur, as Iser's (1978) work most clearly suggests. We can use the term *psychic process* to convey this third notion. Individually, each of these dimensions has been explored by other enquirers from predictable standpoints: the psychoanalytic approaches of Lesser and Holland stress the idea of 'level', a psychologist such as D. W. Harding (1962) is primarily concerned with matters of 'distance', whereas the phenomenological theory of aesthetic response, as seen in Iser, emphasizes the psychic processing that reading entails. Together, these approaches encourage the development of a composite picture. Given these three dimensions, we might visualize the structure of the secondary world diagrammatically as in Figure 2.1.

Representations of three-dimensional concepts on paper are always awkward. The diagram is conceived as a sort of literary holograph which attempts to convey our sense of the structure of the secondary world as it is experienced at any moment of engrossed writing or reading. When we are 'lost' in a book, whether in the writing of it or the reading of it, we can describe our apprehension of the world we inhabit in terms of the three dimensions of level, distance and process. The regulator is the text: it sets the limits, indicated by the arrows. Beyond the textual limits lie states that are outside the fictional experience.

Hence, the dimension of *psychic level* allows for the common view, shared by poets, critics, psychoanalysts and others, that writing and reading involve a mixture of conscious and unconscious activities. Whether couched in the pre-Freudian language of Coleridge (1817/1949) or the post-Freudian jargon of Havelka (1968) or Holland (1968), there is general agreement that the secondary world is conceived below the level of consciousness but above the unconscious. Moreover, the preconscious mind, whether viewed topographically or kinetically, is clearly an important aspect of this dimension. The axis of psychic level gives depth to the world we imagine, acknowledges the amalgam of conscious and unconscious mechanisms at work, and insists on the boundaries beyond which the secondary world disappears. Beyond the textual limits, either it vanishes into the oblivion of the unconscious or it is supplanted by the preoccupations of the conscious mind or, more particularly, by its concern for matters in the primary world.

Similarly, the dimension of *psychic distance* allows us to describe the varying degrees of involvement we experience during the composing or reading of a story. Both authors and readers undergo phases of relative absorption with and detachment from the fictional events. Writers' makings of their secondary worlds entail some periods of intense absorption during which they seem a part of the very world they are creating; at other times they are the calm carpenters, 'making things fit' in Philippa Pearce's (1975: 140–1) image, and mentally existing at a much greater distance from the world of the story. For readers, too, the onlooker role is not a constant. Their spectatorship will vary in the intensity of its commitment and attention at different phases of a novel. The axis of psychic distance expresses our sense of relationship with the fictional world, acknowledges that it is in a state of continuous change, and indicates the horizons beyond which that world ceases to exist. For, if involvement becomes obsessive and takes on psychotic characteristics, it leads to hallucination. (Koestler's (1964/75) theory of bisociation gives a plausible account of how the mind protects itself from this extreme.) Conversely, if the sense of detachment from the secondary world is taken to the limit, it is but a short distance before writers or readers become disengaged from the fiction and the story is deemed unwritable or unreadable.

Finally, the dimension of *psychic process* provides the time-axis of the secondary world. Not only is it a rough, quantitative measure of the elapsing time between our points of entry to and exit from this world; it also gives a qualitative sense of the journey being undertaken. The process of writing implies the discovering of unexplored territory: writers may know the eventual destination and some of the major landmarks *en route*, but to predict the details of the journey is not possible. Surprise, as Bruner (1962/65) rightly says, is a prime condition of creativity. The writer's exercise of 'internal memory' in respect of the secondary world under construction is a vital element in 'making' – helping to blend the details that imagination produces to take the story towards its end with those that are already fixed in the partially written text. The reader's journey is not dissimilar. To change the metaphor slightly: as readers, we make a mole-like progress through a novel, shovelling mounds of textual information behind us while simultaneously anticipating light at the end of the fictional tunnel. Like the mole too, we are all but blind to the processes we undergo. It is the lot of moles and readers to work in the half-light of other worlds. None the less, the impetus towards the assumed end is clear and operates, as Iser has argued, through the continuous oscillation between anticipation and retrospection. The axis of psychic process gives a temporal dimension to the secondary world, allows for the way in which memory deals with information during the composing and reading of a story, and defines the limits of this world as starting 'once upon a time' and ending when all 'live happily ever after'. These ritualistic formulae tell us that what is reported between them never happened, that we are operating in fictional time.

The shifting viewpoint

Both Tolkien and Iser state that we adopt an 'inside viewpoint' in our experiencing of the secondary world. Tolkien speaks of the reader imaginatively entering this world, of being 'inside'; Iser (1978: 109) describes the 'wandering viewpoint' as one which 'travels along inside that which it is to apprehend'. On the diagram, therefore, the shifting viewpoint, 'R', is situated at the junction of the three psychic dimensions described above. Its position is notional in that it is defined by the point of intersection, a point that is in continuous movement during the apprehending of the story world.

The focal point of any act of reading or composing – that is, what is happening at any moment during the processes of creating or recreating the text – is at 'R'.

At 'R' the text is in the process of being perceived in the sense that the secondary world is being made. 'R' is a constantly shifting notion to describe the existential present of a writer's 'writing' and a reader's 'reading'. At 'R' the three axes of the different dimensions interlock: this junction is in constant movement as stories are composed or read. Hence, from one moment to the next the dimensions of the secondary world depend upon shifts that occur with respect to these axes. We have noted how each of these axes operates as a continuum and how the mind moves freely along it according to the needs and provocations of the text. We vary in our degree of involvement in and detachment from the story world, the degree to which the story engages our conscious and unconscious mind through preconscious mental activities, and the degree of anticipation of what is going to happen, or what *has* to happen, based upon our retrospective knowledge of the story so far. The shifting viewpoint is the point of coherence, bringing these psychic dimensions together and allowing writer and reader to imagine the secondary world. The adoption of this viewpoint is a necessary precondition of its existence.

The two essential qualities of this viewpoint, its 'inside' position and its continuous mobility, are sometimes hinted at in other accounts. That the reader is an 'insider' is indicated in D. W. Harding's (1967) description of the 'ghostly watcher'; a similar viewpoint is conveyed in Enid Blyton's sense of having been present in the cinematic world of her stories, a phenomenon vividly documented in her letters to Peter McKellar (McKellar 1957: 136–9). Both accounts are of static viewpoints, however; personified descriptions of a moving viewpoint are rare. Holland quotes his eight-year-old daughter as saying, 'When I read a book, I sort of feel like I'm invisible and walking around unseen with the things or people in the book . . .' (1975: 65). More commonly, the mobile nature of the viewpoint is conveyed in theoretical terms, as in Iser's work (1978: 116) or in the following description by Slatoff (1970: 38–9):

> The single most important thing to observe about our emotional transactions with a literary work is that they do not occur along single continuums . . . Even the most limited reader is capable of maintaining several simultaneous states of relation and feeling toward a work . . . We can share the experience of a Gulliver, say, feel the experience, and at the same time, view him with detachment and view with detachment the part of ourselves that is identifying . . .

By all accounts, the shifting viewpoint seems to enjoy the advantages of a 'negative capability': it is located inside the secondary world amid movements and uncertainties, yet nothing is required of it, in the way of judgements or reasons, save that of being an alert observer and recorder.

Imaging

If the diagram in Figure 2.1 gives us an outline drawing or mental arena of the secondary world, what is it that brings colour, sound and movement to this arena, often with such power and immediacy that authors describe themselves as 'inspired' or readers as 'lost in a book', oblivious of the demands of the primary world? To understand this element of the analogy, we must return to the process of imaging, for images are the carriers of information about the secondary world to the brain and correspond to the functions of the five senses in our perception of the primary world.

If we accept that mental imagery is the prime coinage of the brain during the creative activity of writers and readers, for this appears to be what they themselves tell us, several caveats must be entered immediately. Firstly, that the use different people say they make of imaging in relation to fiction varies considerably, just as the strength and incidence of dream imagery varies greatly from one person to the next. Secondly, that an important aspect of this variability is in the degree of mental control that any individual exercises. The images that the mind constructs to fill the 'third area' may arrive unbidden like those of night dreams or bidden like those of daydreams to be indulged or banished at will. Writers shape their images, via the use of words, into a text; readers shape the text, via the use of images, into a meaning. The role of images, thus delimited, leads us to the third point: images are a means to an end, not the end itself. The substance of the secondary world may be conceived of in terms of images but, as Sartre (1972) and Iser make clear, it is the manner in which this substance is processed that endows it with significant meaning.

Sartre, in particular, is unhappy with the whole notion of images composing a mental world as an adequate description of the act of reading. He claims that when reading a novel, fully engrossed, there are no mental images. Rather, images occur when we cease reading and/or when we think about the story. Later, after much elaborate argument to demonstrate the essential unreality of the spatial and temporal nature of images, he rejects the term 'world' to describe a fictional setting because it is imprecise and fails to individualize objects in a balanced environment. He concludes, '. . . there is no imaginary world. We are concerned rather with a matter of mere belief' (1972: 195). In terms of strict, philosophical distinctions, this line of argument may be true (although, even on these grounds, Warnock (1972, 1976) is sceptical). In practice however, it is impossible to sustain a distinction between what actually happens and our apprehensions of what happens during the course of reading. Even Sartre is driven to acknowledge that 'in order to describe correctly the phenomenon of reading it must be said that the reader is *in the presence* of a world' (1972: 70). If this awareness is conceded, how, we might ask, is the reader to perceive this 'presence' if not through the medium of images? Throughout, Sartre adopts a tone of grudging ambivalence whenever he discusses the idea of a story world: no sooner has he deprecated the notion than he has to confess that images do *suggest* a world even if they do not embody one. He admits 'each image presents itself as surrounded by an undifferentiated mass which poses as an imaginary world', and he prefers the description 'atmosphere of the world' to anything more precise in order to convey the nature of images during reading (1972: 195).

Sartre's argument is instructive. He dismisses the term 'imaginary world' as a mere cover phrase in much the same way as Harding (1962) challenges the term 'identification'; that is, the term is still legitimately available to us only so long as we limit its meaning and avoid using it as a convenient gloss for several undifferentiated mental processes. Just as we distinguished several psychic dimensions in describing the structure of the secondary world, so also must we discriminate between various features of its substance. There are two broad areas of comment to do with the temporal and spatial characteristics of imaging respectively: the process of image-building and the variety of image manifestation.

The time-controlled nature of images is fundamental. Iser's concept of the 'snowball effect', by which he describes the way 'all images cohere in the reader's mind by a constant accumulation of references' (1978: 148), depends upon the disposition of images in the temporal flow of reading. Images are always shifting during imaginative activity, and it is this trait of continuous fluctuation that conditions the use we can make of them in our efforts towards meaning. The process of compilation is not simply additive, a series of distinct, separate images coupled together like railway carriages. Rather, the manner in which images are processed by the brain means that every image we have is restructured or modified in some way by each of its successors. For it is fundamental to the nature of image-building, as Iser, after Sartre, points out, that 'images cannot be synthesized into a sequence, but one must continually abandon an image the moment one is forced by circumstances to produce a new one. (1978: 186). Images may dissolve or be discarded; they may emerge slowly, like the shadowy outlines of a photographic negative forming in a developing-dish, or flash upon the inward eye with sudden and unpredictable vividness. During their emergence, existence and dissolution, processes of superimposition, collision and modification take place, ensuring that no single image is the same as the one that has passed or the one that is to come. These changing images of the secondary world give us the illusion of fictional time passing at a different rate from the actual time-flow of the primary world.

The substance of the secondary world, then, is composed not of a sequence of complete, discrete images of similar status and definition but rather of a series of more or less formed images of unequal importance and clarity which occur during writing or reading in a rich variety of manifestations. This variety depends upon the sensory modes in which the images are experienced, their relative precision or vagueness and whether they appear alone or in a predetermined context. Any discussion of such imaging must discriminate between, on the one hand, the significance and strength of a writer's single, controlling image, like Fowles's woman on the quay (which, according to his own account (1977), was the source of *The French Lieutenant's Woman*) and, on the other, the reader's partially glimpsed image of some fragment of a scene or a landscape. Similarly, we must be prepared for the varying durability of mental images, from the stereotyped memory images that writers and readers construct to serve as stage sets or backdrops for the inner performances of the imagination, to the vivid but momentary image of a particular idiosyncratic memory triggered by the text. If we can translate these details about the location, structure, viewpoint and substance of the secondary world from theoretical concept into an instrument for the descriptive analysis of what writers and readers actually do, then we shall go some way towards an understanding of literary processes.

The effort towards such understanding cannot be overrated in educational settings, for it entails a shift in emphasis from an existing pedagogy that values the apprehension of the text as an inevitable and necessary part of comprehension and elevates instead the creative processes of the first two 'R's' and the articulation of personal responses. Above all, the virtual nature of writing and reading experiences must be appreciated. The secondary world that each child makes when writing a story and that he or she remakes when reading or listening to one is fundamental to literature teaching. This chapter is an attempt to describe this phenomenon. It is offered in the conviction that the concept of the secondary world is central to the praxis of English teaching.

Towards practice: four elements of response

How, then, does the literature teacher make use of this secondary-world concept? Before reading my comments upon the following passage, you might first wish to carry out the same procedure that I adopted. In an effort to 'tap into' what readers experience and to describe the elements of response, read through this opening page of Ian McEwan's *The Cement Garden* (1980) and record, in 'stream of consciousness' style, all the things that go on in your head as you read – images, associations, feelings, thoughts, judgments and so on.

> I did not kill my father, but I sometimes felt I had helped him on his way. And but for the fact that it coincided with a landmark in my own physical growth, his death seemed insignificant compared with what followed. My sisters and I talked about him the week after he died, and Sue certainly cried when the ambulance men tucked him up in a bright-red blanket and carried him away. He was a frail, irascible, obsessive man with yellowish hands and face. I am only including the little story of his death to explain how my sisters and I came to have such a large quantity of cement at our disposal.
>
> In the early summer of my fourteenth year a lorry pulled up outside our house. I was sitting on the front step rereading a comic. The driver and another man came towards me. They were covered in a fine, pale dust which gave their faces a ghostly look. They were both whistling shrilly completely different tunes. I stood up and held the comic out of sight. I wished I had been reading the racing page of my father's paper, or the football results.
>
> 'Cement?' one of them said. I hooked my thumbs into my pockets, moved my weight on to one foot and narrowed my eyes a little. I wanted to say something terse and appropriate, but I was not sure I had heard them right. I left it too long, for the one who had spoken rolled his eyes towards the sky and with his hands on his hips

stared past me at the front door. It opened and my father stepped out biting his pipe and holding a clipboard against his hip.

'Cement', the man said again, this time with a downward . . .

The complex of responses to fiction defies categorization, despite the well-intentioned efforts of some (Squire 1964; Purves and Rippere 1968) to codify it. Yet, as a means of description, it is possible to characterize the broad elements of response. Typically, I want to suggest, they can be described under four headings: during reading, we engage in the processes of *anticipating/retrospecting, picturing, interacting* and *evaluating*. The concept of these four elements was developed during the late 1970s in the course of some research I carried out with ten- and eleven-year-olds into their story reading and was later refined and incorporated into *Teaching Literature 9–14* (Benton and Fox 1985). It has been gratifying since to discover that teachers and researchers find this formulation helpful in understanding young readers' responses to stories (Corcoran and Evans 1987).

Thus, with the opening of this novel, we want to know 'Why this cement?' and cannot stop ourselves speculating about its purpose. Even as early as the start of paragraph two, when we are moved back in time, we remain unsure about whether the father is alive and have to wait until the end of the paragraph to find out. At the level of discourse the movement is retrospective, while the driving edge of our reading is forward, anticipating clues, if not solutions to the problems these opening paragraphs set us – in particular, we want to know what is the relationship between the children and the father.

Mental imagery, as Iser (1978) argues, is a prime means of making meaning from fictional texts. Different readers, of course, make very different uses of such imagery; so here it might be the 'bright-red blanket' that triggers the picture in the mind's eye of the stretcher being lifted through the open rear doors of the ambulance. This, in turn may colour the scene with our awareness of the father's 'yellowish hands and face' and the pervasive grey cement dust. For some readers, these localized visual images will be set against a backdrop of an urban street, as the focus moves into the later paragraphs, with steps to the door of the house and the sense of traffic nearby. There may be auditory images (men whistling) or tactile images (cement dust). Whatever our idiosyncratic mental images, it is common for readers to experience this sort of picturing as an important element of responding to fiction.

The third activity is that of interacting with the fictional world at an affective level. Typically, we may find associations in our own lives with what is described in the text; so here the death of someone close to us and the attendant feelings evoked by such loss may be brought to mind. And we measure such feelings against the tone of this first paragraph: in particular, against the sense of unease generated by the explicit connection, made at the end of paragraph one, between the father's death and the large quantity of cement. In Piagetian terms, assimilating the textual material and accommodating it to our own experience are fundamental ways in which literary understanding operates.

Finally, during reading we are evaluating the experience we are undergoing, deciding perhaps whether we are enjoying it, aware maybe of how the author is manœuvring us as readers and conscious of how he is achieving his effects. Here we may well react first to the narrative voice, that of a first-person narrator whose detached, ironic attitude to his father's death is cast in a cold and alienating tone. The prose has clarity and precision, nowhere more so than in the arresting opening sentence, which some may judge to be self-consciously dramatic, others to be provocatively engaging. Either way, its impact cannot be ignored; indeed, it tends to lodge in the mind. Practised readers will also be evaluating how the narrative is operating and will perhaps be drawing upon modern narratological distinctions to help explain its effects. Genette (1980) distinguishes between the story ('*histoire*') which is the signified narrative content; the narrative ('*récit*'), which is the signifier or discourse, the narrative text itself; and the narrating, which is the action of producing the narrative. So here we have (in reverse order) a narrator, who appears to be a teenage boy, telling us his 'little story' of his father's death (narrating); he presents a discourse ('*récit*') which incorporates a clearly marked time-shift between paragraphs one and two; and this discourse represents events ('*histoire*') which, from the beginning of paragraph two, have taken place earlier.

During reading fiction, these elements of response will vary in their degrees of intensity and importance, but they appear to be the main activities we undergo and, taken together, they provide a helpful working description of what is involved when we become engrossed in a story. At the very least, they provide teachers of literature with the places to start. Often there is lip-service paid to the idea of 'starting where the kids are'; yet, in respect of story-reading, we have no idea where our pupils are unless we begin from some description of reader-response. If we assume that these four elements recur in fiction-reading, we can formulate our questions and approaches confident that our teaching of fiction is derived from the reading of fiction. Such questions will be very different from conventional comprehension questions with their tendencies to elicit mere factual information, suggest right and wrong answers and signal to pupils that they are the subject of an inquisition on which they will be assessed. Appropriate questions about fiction-reading might be as follows:

On anticipating/retrospecting
- How did these present circumstances arise? What do you think will happen next and why? How will it all end?

On picturing
- What pictures do you get in your mind's eye of this character, scene or event?

On interacting
- What do you feel about this character, setting or incident?

On evaluating
- What do you feel about the way the story is being told?

(Benton and Fox 1985)

Note-making and informal discussion along these lines build upon the reading experience, take the pupils back inside the story, indicate to them that their individual responses are both valid and valued and provide a sound basis for a more considered response, perhaps in essay form, when this is required.

Finally I want to indicate briefly one or two classroom practices that follow from what I have argued about the relationship of reading and teaching literature. In fiction, if time and the linearity of response are so important, then encouraging pupils to generate their own 'mental maps' of the unfolding action, to realize the 'secondary world' of story, should be a basic principle. One means of doing this is through keeping a reading-log or journal of one's progress through a story. Figures 2.2 shows a sheet developed for use with fifteen- to sixteen-year-old comprehensive-school pupils. It is self explanatory, but notice how the four elements of response to fiction which we have just been discussing are embedded in the headings.

The classroom dialogue about stories that this process encourages is

Keeping a Reading-log

You've probably had some experience of keeping a reading-diary. You might like to try something more interesting, but more demanding.

It's a record of your thoughts and feelings as you read a book. You'll find that it will contain:

QUESTIONS that you ask yourself about characters and events as you read.

MEMORIES from your own experience, provoked by the reading.

GUESSES about how you think the story will develop, and why.

REFLECTIONS on striking moments and ideas in the book.

COMPARISONS between how you behave and how the characters in the novel are behaving.

THOUGHTS AND FEELINGS about characters and events.

COMMENTS on how the story is being told – for example, words or phrases or even whole passages which make an impression on you.

We've found that by keeping a log you learn much more about the book than we can teach you!

Don't, please, rewrite the story.

Do, please, date each entry and take pleasure and pride in your log. You may decide at a later date to produce a more considered and formal piece of writing for coursework, based on your entries.

Figure 2.2 Guidelines for keeping a reading-log

quite different from that which prevails when the principles are the answering of comprehension questions and estimating of literary value. Reading and responding are places to start; ways of proceeding are further developed in Chapter 4. Meanwhile, we need to look at the narrative dialogues that readers are invited to participate in with different sorts of fictional texts.

3 Narrative voices: slow-motion readings

The ways of telling

Two concepts which appear often in discussions of fiction – the notion of an alternative world and the implied voices we encounter during reading – together offer a useful basis for theorizing our approaches to the teaching of fiction. This chapter builds upon the concept of the secondary world outlined in Chapter 2 and, through carrying out slow-motion action replays of my readings of the openings of three novels, explores the narrative dialogue in which the reader engages. The focus of concern is upon what Susanne Langer calls 'the ways of telling'. It is through reference to some of the classic tales in children's literature, Kipling's Mowgli stories in *The Jungle Book*, that Langer (1953) demonstrates

> what may, in fact, be found in any well-told story – that the whole fabric of illusory events takes its appearance and emotional value entirely from the way statements which actually compose the story are worded, the way the sentences flow, stop, repeat, stand alone etc., the concentrations and expansions of statements, the charged or denuded words. The ways of telling make the place, the action, the characters in fiction . . .
>
> (p. 298)

The voices within the narrative that do the 'telling', the generative power of the words that are chosen, the emotional charge that language carries with it: all these qualities invest both the virtual world that is created and the formal shape in which the story is cast. Potentially, then, these twin concepts indicate the site upon which literature teaching might build: the world in the head of the reader and the voices in the story that sustain this world.

In recent years, the most potent development of these concepts has come in the work of Bakhtin (1981) whose notion of 'dialogism' is helpful in rethinking the idea of the secondary world in more dynamic terms. In the Introduction to his *After Bakhtin* (1990), David Lodge notes a passage from Bakhtin which, he says, had the effect of a light-bulb being switched on in his head. The passage reads:

> The possibility of employing on the plane of a single work discourses of various

types, with all their expressive capacities intact, without reducing them to a single common denominator – this is one of the most fundamental characteristics of prose. Herein lies the profound distinction between prose style and poetic style . . . For the prose artist the world is full of other people's words, among which he must orient himself and whose speech characteristics he must be able to perceive with a very keen ear. He must introduce them in the plane of his own discourse, but in such a way that this plane is not destroyed. He works with a very rich verbal palette. (p. 9)

In Bakhtin, the dialogic imagination is described throughout in auditory terms, even though here he edges towards a painterly analogy at the end. This is not, of course, the auditory imagination of Eliot but a way of saying that the virtual world the reader experiences during reading, in all its multi-sensory variety, is activated by the voices – stated, implied, imitated and so on – embedded in text. In initiating this experience, the reader begins the aesthetic process, creating a sense of a living secondary world which is both dialogic in origin and impetus and experienced as a sensuous phenomenon whose nature, coherence and point relate intimately to the primary world and, intertextually, to other secondary worlds created in the past and yet to come.

Slow-motion readings

In order to explore 'the ways of telling', I shall focus upon the opening pages of three texts: *Tom Brown's Schooldays* (Thomas Hughes 1856/1971), *The Otterbury Incident* (C. Day Lewis 1948/61) and *Red Shift* (Garner 1973/75). The first is the most celebrated of all Victorian school stories and a classic of children's literature; the second, written by a much respected poet of the 1930s, enjoyed considerable popularity as a children's book in the postwar years; and the third, written by an author who made his name as a children's writer, is a modernist novel for older readers. Together, they provide some notable contrasts and insights into the processes I have outlined earlier. To highlight these, I have concentrated mainly on the openings and have attempted to slow the reading process down and do an 'action replay' on my 'textual performance', on the principle that performances are often best understood through the scrutiny afforded by slow-motion. The virtual world that is evoked each time, of course, is dramatically different, but so are the ways of telling. Only a reading of the whole book will show whether or not the characteristics I single out from its beginning are true throughout its length. I would claim, however, that the openings of stories are the most fruitful excerpts to examine, for, when we embark on a fiction, we adjust more or less insensibly to the demands it makes and the relevance it establishes. Martin Price (1971: 82) puts it like this:

The openings of novels serve to set the rules of the game to be played by the reader. The degree of specification in the setting, the presence or absence of a persona behind the narrative voice, the verbal density of the style . . . all these are ways of

> indicating the nature of the game, of educating the responses and guiding the collaboration of the reader . . .

Let us now see how this collaboration works in practice.

Tom Brown's Schooldays, *by Thomas Hughes*

After two paragraphs in praise of the Brown family and its history, the reader is addressed directly as follows (1856/1971: 14):

> However, gentle reader, or simple reader, whichever you may be, lest you should be led to waste your precious time upon these pages, I make so bold as at once to tell you the sort of folk you'll have to meet and put up with, if you and I are to jog on comfortably together. You shall hear at once what sort of folk the Browns are, at least my branch of them; and then if you don't like the sort, why, cut the concern at once, and let you and I cry quits before either of us can grumble at the other.

It is natural enough for a man with Thomas Hughes's belief in robust, physical exercise, to invite his reader to come 'jogging'! Nor is this such a whimsical notion as might at first appear, for notice that, in the space of this paragraph, several operations have been carried out with the reader's tacit compliance. A narrator, 'I', has appeared in the text; a narratee has been invoked (whether 'gentle' or 'simple'), with whom you, the implied reader, have been identified; and a contract has been proposed, namely that the 'jogging' shall proceed according to certain rules. The narrator is confident in his 'take-it-or-leave-it' manner because he knows that there is no danger of the reader either 'crying quits' (crying off before the contract is signed) or 'grumbling' (bickering about the small print later). Such dangers have been precluded by the neat placing of the reader. If you withdraw now, you are a 'quitter'; if you protest later, you are a 'grumbler'. The narrator has made you an offer you can't refuse. Your only option is 'to jog on comfortably together' and observe his rules, pre-eminent among which is his authorial right to give you a prod and insist on your attention. You or I or our children, coming to *Tom Brown's Schooldays* as new readers, must acquiesce then in a particular set of relationships. Already, before any characters have been introduced, we have a dramatized narrator who *seems* very close to the implied author, but we cannot be sure about that. We also have an implied reader, nominated as a narratee, whom we have just seen made into a captive audience.

The narrator is a forthright chap, patriotic, well informed, with a feel for the Vale of White Horse that he goes on to describe. After several pages of local geography and history, he chastises himself for digressing and there follows a curious passage which exposes the complex relationships that exist when the dialogic in fiction is operating in the secondary world. In what follows, I shall use a diagnostic instrument drawn from narratology to illuminate my reading of the passage. Adapting Chatman's (1978) model of narrative communication, these relationships can be represented by the diagram in Figure 3.1

The box marks the boundaries of the text. The figures within the box are all

ACTUAL AUTHOR →	IMPLIED AUTHOR ↔	NARRATOR ↔	NARRATEE ↔	IMPLIED READER	← REAL READER
Thomas Hughes	Hughes's 'second self' inscribed in the text	'I' or 'We': a shifting voice	The 'gentle' or 'simple' reader	The reader assumed by the text – 'schoolboys'	You and I

Figure 3.1 Narrative communication in *Tom Brown's Schooldays* (after Chatman 1978)

aspects of the text. With these 'personae' in mind, let us observe in slow motion what happens when we monitor the voices of the narrative in close detail. The text (1856/1971: 22) reads:

(a) 'But we must get down into the vale again, and so away by the Great Western Railway to town, for time and the printer's devil press, and it is a terrible long and slippery descent, and a shocking bad road.
(b) At the bottom, however, there is a pleasant public, whereat we must really take a modest quencher, for the down air is provocative of thirst.
(c) So we pull up under an old oak which stands before the door.
(d) "What is the name of your hill, landlord?"
(e) "Blawing STWUN Hill, sir, to be sure."
(f) (READER. "*Sturm*?"
AUTHOR "*Stone*, stupid: The Blowing *Stone*.")
(g) "And of your house? I can't make out the sign."
(h) "Blawing Stwun, Sir," says the landlord, pouring out his old ale from a Toby Philpot jug, with a melodious crash, into the long-necked glass.
(i) "What queer names," say we, sighing at the end of our draught, and holding out the glass to be replenished.'

What is happening?

First (a), the narrator moves in an authorial direction supposedly worried about meeting the printer's deadline for his story and threatening to jump on a train up to London. The concerns of the actual author, whether real or affected, are showing through the fiction. (b) In the sentences that follow, however, the narrator's 'we' is, ambiguously, both the stylistic affectation of the 'royal we' and a narrative figure to include the jogging reader. The narrator, therefore, now moves in the reader's direction and pauses at the pub. (c) Having shifted sideways back and forth, across our diagram, the narrator now steps out of its one-dimensional limits and becomes an overtly dramatized character as he speaks to the landlord (d). The rustic-landlord character is introduced (e), to be followed immediately by an odd, quasi-theatrical parenthesis (f). It is as if the narrator has stepped forward into a fully realized character part and, with the spotlight on him, the implied author and the implied reader can mutter to each other in the wings without fear of interrupting the scene. This parenthesis, however, does more than provide a little cameo in which implied author and implied reader can meet behind the narrator's back: it affirms authorial superiority and knowledge and the reader's ignorance. Moreover, it differentiates the implied author from the narrator, emphasizing both the author's 'textual control from the rear' and the shifting voice of the narrator. The narrator character continues the dialogue (g), the landlord replies and pours ale (h), and, perhaps under the influence of a swift pint, the narrator reverts to the not only ambiguous but now awkward 'we' form, seemingly befuddled about his role and identity (i). You or I, as actual readers, could be forgiven a similar uncertainty.

Our slow-motion examination of this short passage indicates the complexity of being a participatory reader of *Tom Brown's Schooldays*. A few signposts to other points of interest in the opening chapter must suffice. The paragraph following the quoted piece above continues the awkwardness of address brought about by the shifting voice of the narrator. The landlord speaks to him as a realized character, emphasizing his singularity; the narrator, for his part, sustains the ambiguous 'we' for half the paragraph, but, under the mounting tension of the landlord's preparations to sound the blowing stone, he shifts to 'I'. After several more exchanges, the narrator suddenly throws off his character part and moves in the reader's direction more purposefully than he has done so far (1856/1971: 23):

> And now, my boys, you whom I want to get for readers, have you had enough? Will you give in at once and say you're convinced, and let me begin my story . . .?

The brusque, peremptory tone suggests several points: an affectation of authorial uncertainty at whether his story is proving acceptable; a more overt, direct address to his child readers to 'sign the contract' and read on; and a voice that is distinctly more schoolmasterly. This tone is stressed a few sentences later when, referring to *The Ingoldsby Legends*, the narrator urges, 'If you haven't [read them], you ought to have.'

Of course, the story *does* go on, the readership *is* assumed and the testy narrator reverts to the quieter role of documentary historian to introduce Tom. But he will not be submerged and, within a page, he is telling us about his travels 'away from home no less than five distinct times in the last year', about his love for vagabonds and about the contradictory views he has expressed in his first chapter which he hopes will endear him to his readers. He ends as a good narrator of fiction should, by affirming his intention to tell the truth. The narrator's voice thus orchestrates the reader's response, yet plainly the secondary world the reader creates is a dialogic one in which, in Bakhtin's words quoted earlier, 'discourses of various types, with all their expressive capacities intact . . .' are blended.

The Otterbury Incident, *by C. Day Lewis*

This is the start of C. Day Lewis's story (1948/61: 11–12):

> *Chapter One The Ambush in Abbey Lane*
> Begin at the beginning, go to the end, and there stop – that's what Rickie, our English master, told me when it was settled I should write the story. It sounds simple enough. But what was the beginning? Haven't you ever wondered about where things start? I mean, take my story. Suppose I say it all began when Nick broke the classroom window with his football. Well, O.K., but he wouldn't have kicked the ball through the window if we hadn't just got super-heated by winning the battle against Toppy's company. And that wouldn't have happened if Toppy and Ted hadn't invented their war game, a month before. And I suppose they'd not have invented their war game with tanks and tommy guns and ambushes, if there hadn't been a real war and stray bomb hadn't fallen in the middle of Otterbury and made just the right sort of place – a mass of rubble, pipes, rafters, old junk, etc. – for playing this particular game. The place is called 'The Incident', by the way. But then you could go back further still and say there wouldn't have been a real war if Hitler hadn't come to power. And so on and so on, back into the mists of time. So where does any story begin?
>
> I asked Rickie about this, and he said, 'Jump right into the deep end of the story, don't hang about on the edge' – which incidentally was contradicting what he'd said first. 'Start with the morning you kids had the battle and Nick broke the window,' he said.

The narrative begins with the voice of George, Day Lewis's narrator, enlisting the sympathetic understanding of 'you', the implied reader, over his storytelling difficulties. Day Lewis's device here is clever in that it enables him to introduce several main characters, the setting and the gang situation all within a page while purporting to be stuck for an opening. It is appealing, too, not only through the colloquial voice but also through its word-game nature. The narrator is playing a 'find-the-start-of-the-story' game with us, pretending to pursue the start of his tale backwards in time, and, in doing so, reminding us of the familiar children's game, or doodle, of defining home by an ever-lengthening address which extends into the universe, space, infinity, . . . 'And so on and so on, back into the mists of time. So where does *any* story begin?' asks George at the end of the first paragraph, with a mixture of mock puzzlement and mock frustration. Both George and the implied reader know the answer: a story begins 'once upon a time' – which, essentially, is the advice George gets from his English teacher in the sentences that follow. Although Day Lewis avoids this traditional linguistic formula for starting his story, nevertheless his literary strategy here creates similar effects both in the suggestion of chronological vagueness and in the implied invitation to the reader to use his imagination.

What is the nature of the contract between author and reader here? How does it compare with the one in *Tom Brown's Schooldays*? In Hughes's story, although the distance between the narrator and the implied author changes, nevertheless they are always more closely identified than are their counterparts in *The*

Otterbury Incident. Indeed, one subtlety of Day Lewis's technique is that, by attributing the style of his work to his narrator, he can detach himself from immediate responsibility for that style. The implication is that, if we find weaknesses, they are George's limitations not Day Lewis's and we as readers tolerate them more indulgently. It is a different offering with a different end in view. Instead of an 'educational jog' with the schoolmasterly narrator of *Tom Brown's Schooldays*, here we are invited into the story as though joining the gang as friends of this humble, modest lad called George. As we have seen, in *Tom Brown's Schooldays* the author retains control through his narrator. In *The Otterbury Incident*, however, the author takes up a more detached position by handing over control to George. Where Hughes's concern is with the reader's compliance, Day Lewis's concern is with objectifying his story clearly. In other words, although the technique of dramatized narrator is a conventional one, Day Lewis uses it not to cajole and persuade the reader but as a means of expressing the objective existence of his story. Hughes's narrator is given a social role, to enlist boys as readers; Day Lewis's George has a literary problem, how best to tell the story.

The qualities that George is given in the rest of the book derive directly from this role. Having established George's concern for artistic matters, Day Lewis can now exploit his narrator in a variety of ways: to hover over the characters making choric comments and judgements (1948/61: 14 and 15 about Ted and Skinner); to make 'asides' to the reader-audience (p. 14 about Nick); to enter the action and take part in events (p. 22 about the tank ambush); and to allow us to eavesdrop on his fears and feelings (*passim*). Some of these activities take George close to the reader, others towards the author; others again see him joining the characters in the story. But the controlling purpose is an artistic one – the drive towards clarity, to help the reader to *see*. This is made explicit in a delightful passage when Johnny Sharp and the Wart arrive on the scene; and it is in such sequences as this that what Bakhtin (1981: 261) calls the 'doubly-voiced speech' of fiction is most evident.

> I'd better try to describe this pair of blisters. Personally, speaking for myself, I always skip the bits in novels where they describe people: you know – 'He had a strong, sensitive face and finely-chiselled nostrils,' or 'Her eyes were like pools of dewy radiance, her lips were redder than pomegranates' – that sort of thing doesn't get one anywhere, I mean it doesn't help you to see the person, does it? But descriptions of Johnny Sharp and the Wart are important, as I shall relate in due course. I'll start at the top and work downwards.
>
> (pp. 15–16)

In fact, George describes his own function towards the end of the opening chapter as that of 'impartial historian' (p. 25). Ducking the questions of whether or not we believe him and the inherent tautology of the phrase, we can safely say that George is a very different narrator from the proselytizer of *Tom Brown's Schooldays*. I hope it will become clear that he is somewhere between the ostentatiously rhetorical contrivance of Hughes and the impersonality of Alan Garner who sits, with conscious Joycean artistry, behind *Red Shift* quietly paring his fingernails.

Red Shift, *by Alan Garner*

On the publication of *Red Shift*, I was asked to write a review article about it for *Children's Literature in Education* (Benton 1974). Towards the end I stumbled across a phrase which gave me my title: '. . . the author requires the co-operation of the detective imagination in his reader to puzzle out everything from the original cosmic mystery to the intricacies of Lewis Carroll's code which Tom and Jan use in their letters to each other' (Benton 1974: 11). 'Detective imagination' is still the best précis I can find to describe the author–reader relationship. Alan Garner gives his readers a many-sided puzzle and expects them to find their own key. Gone is the friendly, bluff patronage of Thomas Hughes's man jogging along at our elbow, anxious to get readers. Gone, too, is the earnest, fair-minded George, keen to 'tell' us his story. Instead, we are left to engage with the text unaided. We have to listen to the voices; watch for clues about mood, relationships and settings; reflect upon the significance of things said and done in ways that have not been demanded of us before. Here are the opening two pages. There are no chapter headings or divisions in the novel. I have added the line numbers for ease of reference.

> 'Shall I tell you?'
> 'What?'
> 'Shall I?'
> 'Tell me what?' said Jan.
> 'What do you want to know?' 5
> Jan picked up a fistful of earth and trickled it down the neck
> of his shirt.
> 'Hey!'
> 'Stop fooling, then.'
> Tom shook his trouser legs. 'That's rotten. I'm all gritty.' 10
> Jan hung her arms over the motorway fence. Cars
> went by like brush marks. 'Where are they going? They
> look so serious.'
> 'Well,' said Tom. 'Let's work it out. That one there is
> travelling south at, say, one hundred and twenty kilometres 15
> per hour, on a continental shelf drifting east at about
> five centimetres per year –'
> 'I might've guessed –'
> '– on a planet rotating at about nine hundred and
> ninety kilometres per hour at this degree of latitude, at 20
> a mean orbital velocity of thirty kilometres per second –'
> 'Really?'
> '– in a solar system travelling at a mean galactic velocity

of two hundred and twenty kilometres per second, in
a galaxy that probably has a random motion –' 25
'Knickers.'
' – random knickers of about one hundred kilometres per second,
in a universe that appears to be expanding at about one
hundred and sixteen kilometres per second per
megaparsec.' 30
Jan scooped up more earth.
'The short answer's Birmingham,' he said and ducked.
Jan looked across the flooded sand quarry behind them
towards the Rudheath caravan site among the birch trees.
'Come on.' The earth was still in her hand. 35
'Where?'
'What were you going to tell me?'
'Oh, that.' He took his shoe off and turned it upside
down. 'It really is grotty being gritty. I was going to tell
you when I first saw you.' 40
'When was it?'
'When you came back from Germany.'
'Germany? The earth ran through her fingers. 'Germany?'
We've known each other longer than that.'
'But I didn't see you until you got out of the car: and 45
then I – saw you.'
'I wasn't away more than a fortnight.'
'What was it like?'
'Anywhere.'
'The people you stayed with?' 50
'Ordinary.'
'So why go?'
'To see what it was like.'
'And she found that the ground was as hard, that a
yard was as long – No. She found that a metre was 55
neater –'
'Tom –'
'Yes?'
'Lay off.'
He put his head on her shoulder. 'I couldn't stand it 60
if you went now,' he said. They walked from the
motorway fence along a spit of sand between the lakes.
'"Grotty" is excessively ugly,' said Tom. 'A corruption of
"grotesque". It won't last.'
'I love you.' 65
'I'm not sure about the mean galactic velocity. We're
with M31, M32, M33 and a couple of dozen other galaxies.
They're the nearest. What did you say?'
'I love you.'
'Yes.' He stopped walking. 'That's all we can be sure of. 70
We are, at this moment, somewhere between the M6 going

> to Birmingham and M33 going nowhere. Don't leave me.'
> 'Hush,' said Jan. 'It's all right.'
> 'It's not. How did we meet? How could we? Between
> the M6 and M33. Think of the odds. In all space and 75
> time. I'm scared.'
>
> (pp. 7–8)

To engage in the dialogic of fiction with a text like this clearly requires considerable mental alertness. What is happening when we read?

In my slow-motion replay, several features stand out in sharp focus against the blurred background of the secondary world that I try to piece together as the text unfolds. The first five lines: five questions. Already the story seems to be turning back on itself with the elliptical pattern of a Fool's wit. Tom is 'fooling' in both the literary and colloquial senses, as Jan's remark (line 9) suggests. Echoes of *Lear* reverberate from the outset. The first five lines are also intriguing through their allowing us to eavesdrop upon two characters whose existence and talk are unmediated by a narrator. As with the start of *The Otterbury Incident*, we begin with the word-game. Here it consists of adolescent verbal sparring and banter to catch the awkwardness felt at 'telling about' emotions but, none the less, it is a word-game of the same order as George's.

Then, without warning, as if the *Lear* echoes had provoked a sudden cosmic dimension to the text, the universe is sent spinning like a top. Tom's 'astronomical posturing' (lines 14–30) carries the message of an expanding universe in a terrifying image of countless planets and galaxies hurtling round their concentric courses, while, at the centre of this vortex, the two characters 'fool' around with handfuls of earth. The nervous energy and volubility with which Tom speaks represent simultaneously an intellectual showing-off about their cosmic insignificance and an emotional defensiveness about their local significance to each other. Macrocosm and microcosm are words which carry their Elizabethan echoes over into this text. More pertinent to our purpose, however, is that they indicate the two narrative perspectives upon which the meaning of this passage rests. As I read, the text signals to me that the important thing about, say, 'trickling earth', 'hanging arms', 'cars on the M6' is not simply their descriptive function but the fact that these things are all existing somewhere, sometime, in the uncertainty of space. It is only through the text signalling *uncertainty* in this way that I can fully appreciate certainty when it appears. It does so as the conversation develops over these opening seventy-five lines. Certainty appears in the form of Tom's and Jan's love for each other: '"That's all we can be sure of"' (line 70). Yet '"How did we meet? How could we? Between the M6 and M33. Think of the odds. In all space and time. I'm scared"' (lines 74–6). What sort of certainty is it that relies on universal accidents? Who would not be fearful? Such has been the lover's cry of panic down the centuries.

Already we have to read in a different way. The text insists upon this. These signs on these pages make meanings in the reader's imagination which break out of the bonds of linear narration. We are forced to accept a different contract with different rules. There is no overt relationship between implied reader and implied author: instead, we are faced with the existential nature of a made story. The covert author is showing, not telling; and what he shows us is two eighteen-year-olds on a fragment of rock hurtling through space and time, trying to find stillness and permanence; trying in fact, to find their own *once*, upon a time.

Three short examples must suffice to indicate 'the ways of telling' with which the reader has to engage in order to create the secondary world of this novel. They derive their nature from a text that has been pared to the bone. With the disappearance of the dramatized narrator, and with the implied author hidden from immediate view, the text exists 'of itself', a separate entity, a made object unintroduced by its maker. The reader has to make the introductions. Reading becomes interpretation, for immediately the reader is made aware that apparently straightforward statements are signifying more than surface narration. This is readily apparent in my first example:

> Jan picked up a fistful of earth and trickled it down the neck
> of his shirt. [lines 6–7]
>
> Jan scooped up more earth. [line 31]
>
> The earth was still in her hand. [line 35]
>
> The earth ran through her fingers. [line 43]

These four separate statements punctuate the opening page and a bit. In the context of Tom's and Jan's exchanges it is impossible to read them without a mounting sense that these crumbs of earth are signalling the precariousness of human existence as a dumb echo of Tom's ostentatious talk about time and space. Holding earth in the fist betokens a deceptive stability; letting earth run through the fingers, like sand through an hourglass, is the true instability of things.

My second example occurs immediately after these opening pages, when Tom climbs to the top of the tower of the sand-washer, thirty feet up. The text (1973/75: 10) reads:

> 'If you drop,' he called to Jan, 'it doesn't half rattle your teeth. But if you jump out as far as you can, it's flying, and you hit the sand at the same angle right at the bottom, no trouble. It's the first time that grips. You have to trust.'
> He leapt through the air clear of everything and ploughed the sand with his heels.
> 'Coming?' He looked up at her.
> 'No thanks.'
> 'It's not what it seems . . .'

Again, as one reads, there is this sense of 'more going on' in and around the text than is actually stated. In the context of Tom's and Jan's declared love for each other on the previous page, sentences like 'It's the first time that grips. You have to trust' just cannot exist with innocent poker-faces claiming to be mere description of Tom's thoughts about jumping into the sand-pit. Moreover, if you accept this reading, what prophetic irony lies in the last three lines? The sand-washer incident both symbolizes Tom's falling in love and hints at the disillusion that is to come.

Thirdly, at the point where Tom forces himself to ask Jan when she is to leave for London, the text (1973/75: 9) reads:

> The motorway roared silently. Birds skittered the water in flight to more distant reeds, and the iron water lay again, flat light reflecting no sky. The caravans and the birches. Tom.

Who, the reader is entitled to ask, is speaking to me? In the first example, clearly it was an undramatized narrator telling me that 'Jan did this' or 'The earth was that.' In the second, the characters were speaking – mainly Tom. Here, though, as a reader, I am engaging with the text in a different way. I am experiencing the situation through the consciousness of Jan. No narrator is telling me about the M6, the lake, the birds and so on. Instead, I am allowed to experience the awareness that Jan has in these moments. Hence the words of the text show the details of the scene through the filter of Jan's consciousness. This is why we get not the 'novelist-historian' depicting reality but the reality that is perceived by a character, as it is registered on her senses. This explains both the apparent illogicality of 'the motorway roared silently' and the severe impressionistic phrasing of the last six words.

Although the reader's engagement with the text is different in style in each example and, in Bakhtin's sense, there is this evident medley of voices, none the less there is a narrative consistency to the discourse throughout, as indeed there must be if we as readers are to submit to the story illusion. From these examples, as in all three books I have discussed, we can see at work the two complementary features of narrative experience that this chapter has argued are essential to the process of reading fiction: the dialogic imagination giving impetus to the creation of a secondary world. Thus the reader's 'responsive understanding' (in Bakhtin's phrase, 1981: 280–1) entails being aware, firstly, of the way a text orchestrates a range of discourses into a common score such that their individual expressive voices can still be heard and, secondly, of the richly sensuous experience of the secondary world that this dialogism makes available.

The implications of the foregoing argument for the literature classroom are, I hope, self-evident. The central point is quite straightforward: the secondary world that each child makes when reading or listening to a story is *the* basic subject-matter of literature lessons. These individual experiences are what we have to work with: releasing them into the texture of classroom talk and coaxing them into the language of children's writing about literature are the main challenges to methodology. The following chapter takes up these matters.

4 The implied classroom dialogue: fiction in school

The public dialogue: resources and approaches

The house of fiction has a cosmopolitan population. With the vast increases in book production, translations and the international exchanges in the publishing world during the past two decades, there are now far more authors and titles available to the English teacher than ever before. Aidan Chambers's (1983) recommendation for inclusiveness, that pupils should be encouraged into 'wide, voracious, indiscriminate reading' as the first step to becoming habitual readers, is now easier to fulfil with such variety on offer. Yet this profusion is not without its problems, chief among which is knowing how to discriminate amid the diversity and sheer numbers of available fictions.

One recent study (Roberts 1990) bravely offers a ground-plan to account for all types of fictional texts. It recognizes four divisions – two types of learned fiction and two types of popular fiction. Learned fiction is either *canonical* (the classics of the past) or serious (the intellectually-oriented fiction of the present). Dickens might stand as the symbol of the former; Golding or Greene are representatives of the latter, writers whose books clearly aspire to achieve canonical status given time. Popular fiction is either *plain* (contemporary best-sellers), or *junk* (vernacular or, in Roberts' preferred gloss, genre stories). The books of James Herbert, or best-sellers riding on the back of film versions such as *The Godfather*, are examples of plain fictions; whereas 'junk' is the uncompromising catch-all term used to describe the science fiction, crime stories, romances, westerns and the like that are lumped together to form the bulk of fiction publishing. The description is, of course, implicitly hierarchical; yet what fascinates Roberts is the enduring appeal of the books in this last category, a puzzle that leads him to give his study the endearing title *An Aesthetics of Junk Fiction*. In fact, the title is rather a misnomer, for this is more of a descriptive and analytical review than an aesthetic study. It is stronger on texts than on reading, stronger on criticism than on theory; yet, for all that, it offers English teachers some useful insights into the satisfactions readers gain from their reading habits.

In particular, Roberts argues the importance of a familiar concept in contemporary literary theory – though he declines to name it – that of intertexuality, which, as was claimed in Chapter 1, is an asset to be cultivated as a source of personal growth in literary competence and a quality to be shared and enjoyed as the mark of being part of the community of readers. A central notion is that when readers engage with junk fiction they are entering a 'bookscape' in which they must learn to read a system rather than individual texts. Junk is 'a literature without texts' in which the reader is 'reading not the text but the genre by means of the text', and 'the ultimate justification' for the activity lies in 'the interplay of its stories'.

This intertextual satisfaction is familiar enough in children's reading and goes some way towards explaining the evergreen appeal of the series writers. Yet, it leaves a trail of questions about readers and texts in its wake. What are the pressures and influences that mark literary progress? Have the young disciples of, say, Enid Blyton that Whitehead (1977) identified become the adult junk-readers that Roberts (1990) now discusses? What might we deduce from a study of individual literary histories? Just when and how is it helpful for teenagers to be made self-conscious of these personal histories? About texts, one wants to know what it is about the morphology and conventions of different sorts of fictions which is the source of their appeal. How much of the attraction of story lies in its linguistic patterning? How much in what we called in Chapter 3 'the ways of telling'? The questions are not new, and those to do with the reader's literary progress and with issues of quality have been discussed elsewhere (Benton and Fox 1985). The question that remains central, particularly in the current climate of English teaching, is not so much the quality of what is available but the quality of the work undertaken by pupils. Literature teachers need to demonstrate a discriminating inclusiveness towards both the texts and the classroom activities they devise. Given the variety and number of books available and the plethora of advice and classroom aids, it is vital for literature teachers to build their work upon principled activities and to avoid what Roger Knight (1989) tellingly labelled 'trivial pursuits'.

Knight helpfully discriminates between those approaches to literature which are genuinely supportive, assisting young readers in unfolding the fictional experiences they share, and showing a respect for the books with which they deal, and those, by contrast, which are meretricious gimmickry, less concerned with the literature than with what can be done to it or with it. He singles out Little *et al.*'s *GCSE Contexts* (Heinemann 1989) for particular opprobrium:

> *GCSE Contexts* is full of ACTION – a key-word in the complex plans for 'tackling' texts and bringing them to heel. There are secrets to wrest from the chosen books, among them *Great Expectations*, *Animal Farm*, *Brighton Rock*, *The Crucible*. The means are to hand, a variety of instruments smacking of the laboratory rather than the study: time charts, line graphs, bar graphs, spider diagrams, target charts, ripple charts, pie charts and stepping charts. Those books – disturbing, refractory, exhilarating creatures, sprung from highly individual imaginations, can thus all be, literally, brought into line . . .

> The individual books hardly seem to matter; they become the arbitrary occasion for the games and the gimmickry.
>
> (Knight 1989: B11)

Yet, while one can accede to the criticism and enjoy the journalistic fun, the alternative image of the English teacher which Knight offers of one 'with book in hand, carefully reading and discussing with his [sic] pupils what they together understand and respond to on the page' (1989: B12) seems quaintly anachronistic. There is a middle way, one which bases its classroom activities upon a knowledge of reading and response and whose concern is always to take readers back inside the world of fiction in order to explore it and illuminate it more fully. The best example is the *Cascades Coursework Folder 14–16* (Barnard and Fox 1990).

The *Cascades* folder takes as its starting-point the four elements of response discussed at the end of Chapter 2 and works these through their unique expression in respect of particular novels – eleven of them in all. In doing so, the authors convey that sense of honouring both the texts and the readers that, in the Introduction, we found in the theoretical stances of Iser and Rosenblatt. Individual readers will feel their responses are valued; pupils of all abilities will find that ways-in to the novels are opened up for them. There are three units of work for each novel, varying in their orientation according to the special qualities of the particular text. Moreover, there is a development from one unit to the next which shifts the focus from a necessary understanding of the situation of the fictional characters, to an awareness of how the story has been constructed, to an appreciation of the principal issues imaginatively embedded in the text.

An example is the suggested programme of study for Ouida Sebestyen's *Words by Heart* (1987). The three linked units concentrate respectively upon what Lena learns about herself in chapters 1–3 while introducing us to the main characters; the organization of events in the two-week time-span of the novel; and, in the final unit on people and prejudice, upon how the novel treats issues relating to racism. The first unit involves individual rereading, note-making, and some role-play and 'hot-seat' interviewing as a lead-in to written assignments.

The second unit enables young readers to discover how the novel is made. This is narratology in action, introducing students practically to the task of sorting out the events of the '*histoire*' from those presented in the '*récit*', and of distinguishing the landscape of external incident from the landscape of the internal consciousness of Lena through whom the story is told. The focused attention, in the form of diary 'Notesheets', upon selected extracts from the novel is a particularly helpful feature of this unit, coaxing readers to explore their individual 'readings' in detail. Students are encouraged to work through the text, individually or with a partner, and to log the events in columns:

> The *first column* shows events as they occur. They have been selected for their importance in moving the story along – this is the 'surface plot'.
>
> The *second column* is for a different kind of plot. If you have already worked on unit 1 about what Lena learns, you'll remember looking closely at the lessons she

> learned through the first three chapters. The second column develops the idea of what happens inside Lena's head throughout the two weeks – thus it is headed, 'Lena's thoughts/feelings'.
>
> The *third column* is intended to help you see how events are either anticipated or looked-back-to in the novel.

The assignments at the end of this unit again require students to draw together their ideas about the structure and development of the narrative in an individual piece of writing.

The final unit on *Words By Heart* is potentially the most difficult to handle in the classroom and, certainly, in print. The approach here is to explore the issues of racial prejudice as they are presented in the words and actions of the fictional characters. The purpose of this element is explicitly given at the start:

> *People and Prejudice*
> The arrival of the Sills family in Bethel Springs – the only black people in the town – brings closer and closer to the surface of the community's life the racist attitudes which the residents had previously been able to ignore.
>
> This unit is about the ways in which issues relating to racism are presented through characters, their words and their actions. It looks at:
> - Claudie and Ben Sills
> - some of the white people who live in Bethel Springs.

By building up what are, in effect, character dossiers on these characters through close attention to the textual information, readers are in a position not only to describe what is made manifest in the plot but also to delve into what is implied below the surface, often ironically hidden beyond the boundaries of even a character's own self-awareness. As before, the assignments offer a variety of ways in which readers can explore these issues.

Students are invited to write about Claudie and Ben Sills and their different influences on Lena; a study of Mrs Chism and the part she plays in the novel; what the preacher says about Ben at the funeral; and a chapter from the autobiography of Winslow Starnes. The assignments are framed in such a way as to be supportive yet challenging. For instance, if students choose to write the third option, they should think about the following:

> The preacher does not say or do much in the story – he seems unable to cope with events (see, for example, pages 156 and 161). He would have to say something about Ben Sills at the funeral service, however. Try to write his address to the congregation about Ben and add some comments of your own on the way you have written the funeral address. For example, it may be interesting to see what your preacher chooses not to say; what he does or does not say directly to Ben's widow, Claudie; and to Lena, who was with Ben when he died.

The methodology and the detailed classroom strategies here are anything but trivial pursuits. The activities are purposeful and geared to the sort of reflective reading that is at the heart of good English teaching.

The private dialogue: eavesdropping upon readers

So far we have adopted a broad view of the implied classroom dialogue in looking at the variety of texts available and commenting upon contemporary approaches to fiction with mixed-ability classes. Learning through literary experience is, of course, a public and shared business; but it is also an intensely personal and private one too. It is appropriate, therefore, to listen in to that other dialogue which readers experience during reading – the one they conduct with themselves – in order to gain a sense of how young readers shift from that early phase of 'getting into a story' to the point where they are 'lost' in the secondary world of the fiction. It is a crucial move, arguably the most significant one in a developing reader's growing sense of story, and likely to determine whether or not he or she will become a habitual reader.

There are a number of studies of individual readers coming to terms with particular books, one of the most insightful being a volume in this series (Fry 1985). My present purpose is more modest and narrowly focused. It aims to provide an example of how two readers, Kim and Rebecca, responded to the opening phases of reading Russell Hoban's, *The Mouse and His Child* (1969). The data, collected and analysed by their teacher, Maggie Miller (1989), took the form of reading-journals. The pupils were asked to log their reading experience with details of the date, time of day, physical context and any other relevant conditions, and to write their journals along the lines of the principles mentioned at the end of Chapter 2.

The particular point of interest, in addition to the students' initial reactions to the story, is to try to locate the transitional stage between 'getting into the story' and 'being lost' in it. Here is the first page of Kim's Journal:

The Mouse and his Child by Russell Hoban

8.35 p.m.	I am sitting in bed.
p. 11	The toy shop sounds warm and inviting. The toys are bright and there are a great many. If I went near that shop I would go straight in without thinking what I was doing, as it looks cosy. I think it's really sweet, heart-touching the way the tramp turned, unwanted, from the window and did the dance the father mouse did. The little mouse is so innocent especially when he asked the elephant if she was his mother. It was unkind of the elephant to scoff at the little mouse and be unkind when he wanted affection. At first I thought the elephant was friendly but now I think she's a bit too stuck up. The mouse and his child were sold. I hope they were given to nice people. I think that they were given to someone unkind and they run away. I think I will enjoy this book.
8.50 p.m.	p. 18
6.00 a.m.	Curled up in bed.
p. 19	I feel sorry for the mechanical animals because they keep having to do their dancing etc. It's sad the way the little mouse crys when he sees the dolls house. I am glad the tramp found the mice. I was not surprised that they did not . . .

Table 4.1 Summary of Kim's reading

Text	*Summary of responses*	*Element of response*
p. 11	Response to writer's description of toyshop in terms of:	
	1 How it sounds and 2 How it looks.	Aural/pictorial
	3 Reader enters the toyshop.	
13	4 Tramp imitates Mouse father's role in the dance.	Interacting (with character and scene)
18	5 Innocence of Mouse child. 6 Unkindness of elephant. 7 Character of elephant reviewed.	Interacting (with character)
18	8 Mouse and his child sold: 9 To nice people? 10 They will run away.	Anticipation and Prediction
18	11 'I think I will enjoy this book.'	Evaluation/prediction

The journal responses are presented in terms of the pages of text to which the individual comments relate and the specific element of response displayed by the reader. In order to chart the stages of a growing involvement with various aspects of the text, each response has been numbered in Table 4.1 and then analysed sequentially.

Initially, Kim hovers at the edge of the reading experience listening to the narrative voice, and comments:

1 '*The toy shop sounds warm and inviting.*'
The transition from an aural to a visual medium comes in the next sentence:
2 '*The toys are bright and there are a great many.*'
In the third sentence the reader speculates about the possibility of making an entry:
3 '*If I went near the shop I would go straight in without thinking.*'
Between the third and fourth sentences of the journal it is clear that the reader has finally entered the toyshop, and the secondary world of story. She has chosen her point of entry, not by means of the character with whom the story opens – the tramp – but has gone in by herself, as it were, in response to the invitation implicit in the narrative voice.

The note of speculation present in Kim's first three responses disappears when she ventures into the narrative and becomes more closely engaged with the reading.

From her position both inside the shop and the narrative, she looks out of the window and mentions the tramp for the first time, finding:

4 '*. . . heart-touching the way the tramp turned, unwanted, and did the dance the father mouse did.*'

She lifts this striking image of the human imitating the clockwork toy's movements cleanly out of the text and puts it intact into her journal, recalling it in conversation after reading.

During the next four pages of text the reader is engaged at an interactive level with the specific toys grouped around the doll's house. Through his conversation with the elephant, she establishes one of the Mouse child's main qualities:

5 '*The little mouse is so innocent especially when he asked the elephant if she was his mother.*'

And, in the knowledge gained by further acquaintance and insight, she is already reconsidering an initial implied assessment of the elephant's character:

6 '*It was unkind of the elephant to scoff at the little mouse and be unkind when he wanted affection.*'

7 '*At first I thought the elephant was friendly but now I think she's a bit too stuck up.*'

The simple statement of fact in response 8 records the new line of development taken by the narrative:

8 '*The mouse and his child were sold.*'

Sentences 9 and 10 make an interesting pair of responses. Firstly, the reader anticipates an ideal solution for the future of the Mouse father and son:

9 '*I hope they are given to nice people.*'

Secondly, she predicts the more likely outcome:

10 '*I think that they were given to someone unkind and they run away.*'

The first is indicative of the reader throwing in her lot with the fortunes of the main character in terms of where her sympathies lie. The second comment shows that she is beginning to engage with the narrative form, in terms of an expectation of the story-line's development. These two anticipatory comments – hoping for the best but expecting the worst – are based partly on the reader's previous literary experience of story patterning. She knows that at the onset of the story, with the text before her, the chances are that all will not run smoothly. Such expectation, however, serves to strengthen the lines of communication leading further into the novel.

Thus the comment that closes the first session is both evaluative and predictive and sets the seal on reading:

11 '*I think I will enjoy this book.*'

Prediction is made outside as well as inside the narrative, as it were, as the reader steps back thoughtfully from the events of the plot in order to review the extent of her engagement. The invitation to 'play a game devised by the author' that characterizes the phase of 'getting into the story' has been accepted.

Table 4.2 Rebecca's reading

Time	*Comment*	*Condition*
1.10.88 5.15–5.45 p.m. pages 11–19	I can remember a similar tramp I once saw in London almost the same I felt so sorry for him, he must be so lonely and cold. But what could I do? Everyone seems to pretend he does not exist or are frightened of him. Already the elephant seems to be the sort of person I don't like ie. dominating and pompous. Paragraph on the bottom of page 16 represent the harsh, cruel outside in comparison to the protected easy atmosphere in the house, or so the child thinks. How could the elephant reject the child who asks for his support? He is really confused and objects that he has to follow a set course to life, he wants independence! All of the clock-work animals want to be individual.	Bored and quite tired after homework. In a chair.
2.10.88 8.55–9.05 a.m.	It is really strange when the . . .	Registration

Table 4.3 Summary of Rebecca's reading

Text	*Summary of responses*	*Element of response*
p. 11	1–3 Tramp: 'real' world/story world.	Picturing (text-free/ text-bound)
13	4 Reactions of others to tramp.	
14	5 Evaluates elephant.	Interacting (with character)
16	6 Explicit allusion to the meaning of the final paragraph, contrasting the world inside and outside the dolls' house.	Interacting (with language)
18	7 Rejection of elephant because she rebuffs Mouse child.	Interacting (with character)
19	8 Sees Mouse child as confused.	
19	9 Clockwork toys' ambition to be independent noted.	

Rebecca presented her journal in tabular form (Table 4.2). This is summarized in Table 4.3 and analysed below.

Rebecca's account of Chapter 1 begins (and ends) with the tramp, who has a strong association for her in terms of a tramp that she once saw in London. Her first response recalls a specific occasion or encounter with this 'real-world' tramp. A comparison between her remembered tramp and the tramp in Hoban's narrative is hinted at in the first phrase:

1 '*I can remember a similar tramp I once saw in London almost the same.*'
It is debatable how fully this connection between the text-free and text-associated tramps served to bring the reader into the story. The mixture of tenses in the following response makes it difficult to know which tramp Rebecca is referring to:

2 '*I felt so sorry for him, he must be so lonely and cold.*'
When asked, Rebecca could not remember. The two had fused in her mind and were interchangeable at the beginning, though not by the end, of her reading of the first chapter.
The third response reflects a fairly powerful sense of guilt and helplessness which relates to the London tramp. Rebecca remembered reliving uncomfortable feelings of inadequacy at this point and the tramp in her mind was the one she had encountered outside the text:

3 '*But what could I do?*
Her own feelings are reflected in her view of the crowd's reactions to the tramp in the story:

4 '*Everyone seems to pretend he does not exist or are frightened of him.*'
The fifth response results from having moved into the toyshop. Here the reader quickly identifies in the character of the elephant, personality traits she dislikes:

5 '*Already the elephant seems to be the sort of person I don't like ie. dominating and pompous.*'
The sixth response refers specifically to a paragraph in which the Mouse child perceives a difference between life outside and inside the dolls' house and shrinks from the inevitability of going out into the world:

6 '*Paragraph on the bottom of page 16 represents the harsh, cruel outside in comparison to the protected, easy atmosphere in the house, or so the child thinks.*'
The reader is aware that the Mouse child is mistaken in making such a simple assumption. He does not yet possess the experience which would enable him to judge the worth of either environment, but Rebecca is aware that the child's view of the situation is different from hers (and, by implication, from the narrator's). She has made an assessment along the lines that the dolls'-house society is a sham and the Mouse child is fearful of his destiny. This was confirmed in her post-reading discussion.
The rhetorical question in response 7 criticizes the elephant's treatment of the Mouse child for the same reason as Kim:

7 '*How could the elephant reject the child who asks for his support?*'
Responses 8 and 9 note the characters' wish for independence and individuality and mark the reader's first awareness of this as a narrative theme:

8 *'He [the Mouse child] is really confused and objects that he has to follow a set course to life, he wants independence!'*
9 *'All of the clockwork animals want to be individual.'*

Rebecca's entry into the novel is dominated by the text-free association of her London tramp. The slight mismatch between this 'real-world' figure and the description of the author's creation in the story world suggests that the reader was not initially open to the tramp's role in the narrative. She began her reading by superimposing her own tramp construct on to that of the author, expecting him to behave in a way that corresponded with the one she had seen. Both are social outcasts but, whereas Rebecca tends to portray her tramp as a victim of society, the author's character may well have 'dropped-out' by choice. He may be 'cold' but he may not necessarily be 'lonely'. Although Rebecca observes that he is shunned by the shoppers and saleslady, the tramp appears impervious to this treatment. As she is drawn further into the text, however, her image comes closer to the tramp portrayed by the author and she senses how Hoban uses this figure to ease the reader into the story.

This chapter has discussed two complementary dialogues about fiction in school. The implied dialogue in which the reader participates with the narrator and the characters is seen in Kim's and Rebecca's accounts, which are essentially examples of the private pleasure reading affords. Its complement is the public pleasure of sharing these personal 'readings' with others through the actual classroom dialogue outlined in the *Cascades* material. Together these 'twin pleasures of reading' (Kermode 1975) form the basis of a secure methodology for the teaching of fiction.

PART TWO

Poetry

5 Thirteen ways of looking at a poem

'Thirteen Ways of Looking at a Blackbird' by Wallace Stevens (1953/63).

'Thirteen Ways of Looking at a Blackboard' by Peter Redgrove (1960).

Wallace Stevens wrote the poem, Peter Redgrove the pastiche. The first is imagistic and elusive, yet leaves a string of strong pictures lodged in the mind like a series of mental 'stills'. Stevens shares some literary bird-watching with us: the blackbird is spotted from the hide of his imagination and observed in different ways as a means of exploring the nature of the real. The poem begins:

I
Among twenty snowy mountains,
The only moving thing
Was the eye of the blackbird.

II
I was of three minds,
Like a tree
In which there are three blackbirds.

III
The blackbird whirled in the autumn winds.
It was a small part of the pantomime.

When the poem strays from these Magritte-like word-pictures into an occasional discursive section it verges on the portentous, if not the pretentious; ideas in such poems, it seems, need anchoring in pictures of reality if they are to tell us anything about the nature of reality.

The second poem smacks of a literary exercise. It includes some sly digs at its original without resorting to parody. It is a word-game which, because it does not take itself too seriously, avoids both the pitfalls and the high intent of the earlier poem. As such, it attains the limited and functional success of self-consciously wrought 'creative writing'. Redgrove shares some educational observations with us: in (on?) the blackboard he spots a playful way of symbolizing them. The poem begins:

> I
> The blackboard is clean.
> The master must be coming.
>
> II
> The vigilant mosquito bites on a rising pitch.
> The chalk whistles over the blackboard.
>
> III
> Among twenty silent children
> The only moving thing
> Is the chalk's white finger.

Stevens's poem is predominantly in the past tense – a measure of its tone of considered experience; Redgrove's is nearly all in the present – an indication of the immediacy of its appeal, its awareness of saying things for effect.

Two *related* poems such as these throw into sharp relief the limitations of some of the ancient and modern questions about reading poetry. What can we guess about authorial intention? In what respects are poems related to life and/or to other poems? How does the reader produce an interpretation of a poem? How does his or her interpretation relate to questions of value judgement? Such issues keep the literary critics and theorists in business. The concern of this chapter is with a different but none the less central matter – the phenomenon of reading itself.

If we take our cue from Stevens and Redgrove we must come at the act of reading a poem obliquely and attempt to characterize it through a series of statements – many of which may be paradoxical – which exist, as it were, in apposition to each other rather than develop as an argument. Collectively, they may amount to a description of the process of reading a poem which is 'open' enough to allow for the uniqueness of every poem and every reader, yet focused enough to identify features that are peculiar to this sort of literary experience. Louise Rosenblatt (1978) discriminates between the *reader*, who brings his or her accumulated literary and life experience to bear upon the act; the *text*, which is simply the words on the page; and the *poem*, which is created only when reader and text interact. With definitions thus delimited, texts and readers are plentiful but a poem is a rare happening. The present purpose is to examine this rarity and to ask what it is that distinguishes the reading of a poem from any other type of reading. Many of the statements could be cast in terms that relate to any of the three aspects of the interaction; they may be grouped, for clarity, as five statements pertaining to the reader, four to the text and four to the poem. There are (at least) thirteen ways of looking at a poem.

The reader

1 *The reader is invited to 'look at' a poem yet to 'dwell within' it*

Poem texts are ostentatious; they are also obstinately miscellaneous. When considering the act of reading, Rosenblatt is surely wrong to extend the term 'poem' to include fiction and plays (1978: 12), for, even though novels invite a circling back and round, the infinite variety displayed by poem texts signals that the initial responses, when compared with those provoked by the predictable, linear ways in which stories are presented, are likely to be more diverse. Instead of the eye tracking back and forth along regular lines of print to engage with a fiction, it is invited to a more varied exercise where the disposition of the words on the page is of greater significance than in the rectangular blocks of story text. The sense of artifice is more immediate. Readers are aware of looking at something which is drawing attention to itself by the way in which it is deployed. The conscious effort of construction that this sort of 'onlooking' (to use D. W. Harding's word (1962: 145)) entails accounts for the heightened spatial awareness we experience when reading most poems. The spaces around the words on the page are ones we inhabit mentally as readers to 'look at' the text, as it were, from various viewpoints; rather as, when looking at a piece of sculpture, we feel impelled to move around the object or, when looking at a painting, we may be made aware of what lies outside the canvas. Edgar Allan Poe makes the point when he says, 'it has always appeared to me that a close *circumscription of space* is absolutely necessary to the effect of insulated incident: it has the force of a frame to a picture' (Poe 1846/1963: 165). Granted we initially have to read a poem text forwards; none the less, our ways-in to its meaning will be many and varied and will depend in part upon the vantage points we adopt and the sort of approaches we make during the reading.

Yet, the poem yields a meaning only if we also 'dwell within' it imaginatively. We may look at a Henry Moore or a Picasso and not be able to interact with the work; similarly, a poem text may remain just a collection of words. The indwelling value of the poem becomes available to its reader only if the act of reading includes those features that are integral to the nature of the art form. Typically, this requires readers to be alert to sound and rhythm, to hear the tune on the page as a tune within their own consciousness as they read. It is this mental performance of the text that allows access to the poem and to the possibility of dwelling within an imaginative experience: to become an 'insider' rather than an 'outsider'. It is harder to achieve this status with poetry than with story. The fact that most poems draw attention to themselves makes it more difficult for readers to become immersed. We may become easily lost in the secondary world of a story; it is harder to get lost in a poem text since its surface features are continually reminding us of how it should be read. When the reader is charmed on first encountering a new poem, he or she experiences an 'ambivalent magnetism' that lies in the paradox that these surface features both attract and keep at bay.

2 *The reader's stance is both 'efferent and 'aesthetic'*
The stance the reader adopts in respect of the text dictates whether the poem will be created. The journey metaphor – invoked to describe reading by writers from Coleridge (1817/1949) to Calvino (1982) – implies that, at the point of embarkation, what the reader brings is as important as what the text offers; and part of the emotional and mental luggage the reader carries is a sense of the sort of journey that is anticipated. With a poem, the reader starts with an expectation that this reading experience is to be different from that of a typical novel.

In the last two decades, studies in the development of literacy have focused, among other things, upon function. Knowing what writing is for and, in particular, developing the growing sophistication of the skill from 'expressive' beginnings into 'transactional' or 'poetic' purposes (in the terms of Britton *et al.* 1975) have been identified as significant elements in learning to write. The complementary processes lie in coming to know how a text demands to be read. Rosenblatt (1978) provides a corresponding schema to Britton's: the initial development from decoding to fluency in reading is accompanied by a growing differentiation of the 'efferent' or 'aesthetic' purposes to be served. In 'efferent' reading the reader's concern is with what will be carried away from the act; the orientation is utilitarian, the focus is directed towards the information that lies *beyond* the reading event. By contrast, in 'aesthetic' reading the reader's concern is with the feelings and ideas being produced by the act of deciphering; the orientation is to savour what is being lived through at the time, the focus is on the experience itself *during* the reading event.

Both schemas smack of caricature, and both Britton and Rosenblatt put up the notion of a continuum to shield their concepts from this charge. To categorize an act of reading with one of two labels is clearly facile. What actually happens as we move around a poem (to extend our earlier metaphor) is that we have to adopt a 'shifting stance', shuffling to and fro along the continuum between the 'efferent' and the 'aesthetic'. For, even when we are free from critical or pedagogic pressure to show a definite 'yield' from our reading of a poem (in the form of notes or essays), the linguistically condensed nature of poetry is such that the reading process has to be 'efferent' enough for us to carry away a meaning as well as 'aesthetic' enough to give us pleasure.

3 *The reader both produces the poem from the text and reacts to what he or she produces*
Reading is active and reactive together. With a poem, readers experience this 'double-take' with peculiar power. We may look at Blake's lines

> Tyger! Tyger! burning bright,
> In the forests of the night;
> What immortal hand or eye,
> Could frame the fearful symmetry?

and as we construct a provisional meaning from the words this meaning echoes against a background of literary and life experience, words knock against each other in unfamiliar ways and we begin to discover what Lawrence (1961: 255) called the true power of poetry – a 'new effort of attention' that breaks fresh perceptions of the familiar and the routine.

The first stage of a 'double-take' is a glance, the second a long, sustained look. The reading of a poem is a series of literary 'double-takes', where readers engage both in the swift interpreting of the words and in the reflective interpreting of their responses to the words. The way words are deployed in poems demands this effort to 'attend twice at once' (Ryle 1949: 158), which, because of its impossibility, typically leaves the reader in limbo, somewhere between the deconstruction of verbal artifice and the development of personal response. It is an uncomfortable position for the inexperienced reader. There is none of the sustained invitation into the secondary world of fiction. The reader is put on the spot. A double demand is being made – to read the words and to read one's own sensibilities. The next statement adds a gloss upon this phenomenon.

4 *The reader's social relation is less with an implied author and more with the real poet*
Far from joining in a ghostly dialogue with an implied author, a narrator and a cast of characters in a story, the reader of a poem knows the demand is being made directly and uncompromisingly by the single voice of the poet. True, in some long narrative poems and dramatic monologues, the reader may feel in the company of angels and devils, mariners and spirits, dukes and duchesses, saints and clergy; likewise, he or she may feel privy to a host of conversations among ordinary folk that, for example, characterize ballad poetry from medieval times to the present day. None the less, the social contract between reader and author is different from that of the novel. Typically, the novel presents characters to explore the development of motives and feelings in a series of situations; even long narrative poems do not aspire to such detailed exploration. In poetry, characters stand for certain qualities the poet wants to symbolize: they are metaphorical – versions of a single voice, not the voices of carefully developed people. Poets may choose to play the ventriloquist in some of their poems, but, if they go *beyond* throwing their own voices, the very form of poetry becomes transmuted into poetic drama. In fact, in most poetry, Wordsworth's description of this social relationship as 'a man speaking to men' can be taken at face value. For readers, this means being alert to the way thinking and feeling are expressed in the voice that addresses them.

5 *The reader exercises both an intelligence of thinking and an intelligence of feeling*
Poems are places where thinking and feeling remain unified. Thought may subdue feeling, feeling may overwhelm thought; but, simultaneously as it sustains the artifice of every poem, the same 'cool web of language winds us in . . .' (Graves 1961). Working with words takes the heat out of experience for both poet and reader. The act of reading a poem lies between the turmoil of the individual consciousness and the immediacy of the workaday world. And as readers take time out for this experience they bring their whole selves to bear

upon it. They cannot do otherwise if the text demands it powerfully enough. Thoughts are imbued with feelings – uncompromising, ambivalent, contradictory, elusive; feelings are constrained by thinking – directed and rational, autistic and free-ranging. The meaning constructed from the words on the page will be an amalgam from such sources. Moreover, unlike other types of reading, unless the reader receives intelligences from both antennae – allowing thought and feeling to operate upon each other – then the poem will not be evoked.

The text

As with reading a poem, so now in writing about the experience, a fresh perspective helps to capture the phenomenon. Accordingly, the next four statements bring language into the foreground.

6 *The language of poetry is both 'true' and 'false'*

> A sentence uttered makes a world appear
> Where all things happen as it says they do;
> We doubt the speaker, not the tongue we hear:
> Words have no words for words that are not true.

W. H. Auden's sonnet 'Words' (1969: 320), of which this is the first quatrain, dwells on the relationship between language and truth. It is concerned particularly with the sort of truth that literature carries. With great subtlety, it contrives simultaneously to exemplify what it argues.

The argument revolves around the ambiguous relationship between words and truth: ambiguous because on the one hand language is 'true' in itself, an enclosed system, as the fourth line indicates. On the other hand, language is 'true' in the sense that words are the natural form that truth takes, as evidenced in our need to gossip and make up poems and stories.

The exemplification lies in the fact that this sonnet itself embodies the notion that a poem is a verbal model through which we construe some sense about existence. It asks:

> But should we want to gossip all the time,
> Were fact not fiction for us at its best,
> Or find a charm in syllables that rhyme,
>
> Were not our fate by verbal chance expressed?

Language, by its metaphorical nature, fictionalizes the world of 'fact' in which we exist; fiction's 'charm' lies in the chance that we may find, captured in poem or story, glimpses of the reality that lies beyond words.

But what does this argument-cum-example tell us about the status of the language of poetry? Simply, it suggests that, while words carry their usual lexical definitions and familiar meanings with them into a poem, their appearance in this verbal form lends them unusual definition and unfamiliar meanings. The language of poetry is not that of ordinary discourse, even though the individual words may be the same. Ordinary words undergo a sea change within the design of a poem. From the standpoint of everyday usage, words are thus both 'true' and 'false'; or better, perhaps, words carry two sorts of truth, one that owes allegiance to the primary world we all inhabit, the other owing allegiance to the secondary world of imaginative artifice.

7 *The language of poetry may both puzzle and clarify*

On first encounter, a poem may be just a blur of words. The special use of language, the reader's sense that these words are the chosen few – no others will do – and the condensation of meaning implied lend an element of word-puzzle to many poems. The riddling quality of expression, the delight in pun and word-play, the often complicated syntax, the elliptical patterning of the language – all these familiar qualities may puzzle, delight or frustrate the reader of a poem.

Yet the words are also a medium for 'making clear'. The sculptural analogy is helpful again. The feeling that the artistic shape already exists, whether a sculpture locked in stone or a poem or story imprisoned in formless words and images, is commonly remarked upon by artists in different media. The aesthetic task becomes not so much invention as discovery and clarification – the effort is to render that which is invisible (because of the inchoate medium in which it exists) clear and plain to the naked 'mind's eye'. Poet and reader both wrestle with words and, in their complementary ways, experience this sense of hidden form awaiting expressive release. The notion is caught in one of Michelangelo's sonnets (1961):

> The marble not yet carved can hold the form
> Of every thought the greatest artist has,
> And no conception ever comes to pass
> Unless the hand obeys the intellect.

For the reader, attentive before a Michelangelo sonnet or sculpture, just as for the artist who fashioned it, one aspect of the making of meaning comes through the process of taking away superfluous material. In order to solve the puzzle the poem presents, we mentally chip away at the mass of impressions the words evoke, striving to create a poem that stands free and clear. Our spatial awareness is brought into play and, through it, we experience poetic form. As the form of a sculpture is released from the rock that holds it, so the form of a poem is released from the jumble of words and images in which it originates – a process reflected in the notebooks and early drafts of many poets. And just as the writer reworks and prunes the raw material, so the reader edits and re-edits the host of impressions, memories, images, feelings and ideas that a poem sets going in an effort to fashion something that will exist in consciousness like a piece of verbal sculpture. The invitation of poetic form, as writers from Michelangelo to Alan Garner have acknowledged, is to read a stone book.

8 *The words of a poem are to be read by both ear and eye*
The distinction here is not simply the functional one between speaking a poem aloud or reading it silently. Rather it is to stress that, whenever we read a poem, our performance has aural and visual dimensions simultaneously. If we read well, we cannot stop ourselves sounding the words in the head; there is, as we have said above, a tune on the page to be played and a design in the mind to be explicated. The voice of the 'inner speech' that we hear as we are reading a poem comes to us through both ear and eye. Frye (1957: 263) makes the point: 'In every poem we can hear at least two distinct rhythms. One is the recurring rhythm . . . a complex of accent, metre and sound-pattern. The other is the semantic rhythm of sense . . .' And in developing this notion in respect of lyric poetry he uses the terms 'babble' and 'doodle' to indicate 'the two elements of subconscious association' which operate during reading.

'In babble,' he tells us, 'rhyme, assonance, alliteration and puns develop out of sound associations.' The sound-patterns that Ruth Weir (1962) recorded of her two-and-half-year-old son Anthony's pre-sleep monologues illustrate the fundamental quality of language and meaning which poetry exploits – namely, that sounds, and the shaping we give them through rhythm, precede 'sense'.

By contrast, 'doodle' describes 'the first rough sketches of verbal design in the creative process' and indicates the increasing tendency, after Caxton, to address the ear through the eye. The impulse to put words into patterns as seen in the proliferation of verse forms is a symptom of the visual dimension of poetry. Frye (1957: 263) sees riddles as the primitive signposts to 'the whole process of reducing language to visible form'.

The language of poetry speaks to both ear and eye; it combines the abstract art of the aural and the concrete presence of the visual. Reading with the ear, words are performed and celebrated in pursuit of the *experience* of meaning; reading with the eye, words become windows through which we see *extractable* meanings. Poetry thus holds its reader in a double spell: we find both 'a charm in syllables that rhyme' (in Auden's words above) and a riddle in the verbal patterns on the page.

9 *The text of a poem is the result of playing with words within the discipline of form*
The central paradox of all creative activity is that it grows from both freedom and constraint, the play of the imagination operating, in this case, in the rule-governed medium of language. Out of this mix comes the 'AHA' reaction (Koestler 1967/75), the 'effective surprise' (Bruner 1962/65), the verbal 'topsy-turvies' of young children (Chukovsky 1963) and the claim that the affinity between poetry and play is 'apparent in the structure of creative imagination itself' (Huizinga 1949/70).

All anatomies of inspiration, by Rosamond Harding (1948) and her successors (Ghiselin 1952; Vernon 1970), point to the combinatorial activity of the artist – the creation of 'the new' achieved through seeking the link between elements of 'the known'. There is nothing we can imagine, Stephen Spender (1946/52) reminds us, that we do not already know. Poets break fresh perceptions by the way they operate on things already familiar. And the way such insights occur is intimately related to the way words work as they come into being to form the text of a poem. The creative process involves verbal play – combining words in unusual patterns, exploiting ambiguities, delighting in 'topsy-turvies' – enjoying all the potentialities for playing around with the medium of language. But, as well as enjoying the medium for itself (which, if left to itself, would produce only the randomness of a writer's notebook), there is the complementary pressure towards form – a shaping which, with the novel, is signified by the desire for 'closure'; given the spatial qualities of poem texts, their shaping is more a matter of 'enclosure'. The poets' art lies in their skill at capture; it is a delicate skill, as their images show, exercised through a 'net of words' or in the 'cool web of language'. Yet it is only when the poem has been thus caught and enclosed within the formal discipline of the text on the page that the verbal play can achieve any artistic significance.

The poem

So far the reader and the text, in turn, have been given a high profile in this collection of statements about reading poetry. Finally, we come to 'the poem' itself. These last four 'ways of looking' inevitably subsume elements of reading that have gone before. They focus upon the virtual nature of the poem and upon the peculiar mode of interacting that produces the aesthetic experience.

10 *A poem is an event in time yet an artefact in space*

For a poem to be evoked through the interaction of the reader and the text, it must come into existence in two dimensions. 'A poem should not mean/But be' concludes McLeish (1963: 50–1), insisting that a poem is not a record of experience but the experience *itself*. Its infinitive is to be, not merely to communicate. Of course, a poem *does* communicate but it achieves a 'double discourse'. It speaks in words laid out in linear sequence, it comes into being through time; we read a poem forwards. Yet it speaks also in words laid out in patterns, it comes into being through its spatial relationships; we read a poem as a design.

This two-dimensional existence gives a poem a peculiar status – not that, as we have seen, of the secondary world of fiction, but rather that of a separate, self-contained image: as clear and telling as the reflection in a mirror but equally as inviolable and apart. A poem relates intimately to the actual world, catching facets of its substance in this looking-glass image, tantalizing us with the boundary line between the real and the reflected, yet by its nature keeping to its own plane of existence. So, whether we read of Blake's tiger 'burning bright' or of Burns's love as a 'red, red rose', of Hughes's 'hawk roosting' or of Larkin's 'Whitsun weddings' – or, for that matter, of Stevens's blackbird or Redgrove's blackboard – the tiger, the lover, the hawk and the rest remain as looking-glass pictures. They reflect aspects of the actual world and they may well appear to be the more 'real', but they exist only within the medium of the poem. This peculiar status of poetry experience is what Ted Hughes celebrates in 'The Thought-Fox' (1957), where the imagined fox 'enters the dark hole of the head', its vivid presence remains in suspended animation in the reader's mind and the separateness of its existence is established as Hughes concludes 'The page is printed.' Hughes himself has commented upon the capturing of this animal that is 'both a fox and not a fox'. The virtual existence is attained because 'the words have made a body for it and given it somewhere to walk' (1967: 20).

11 *A poem exists simultaneously as a pattern of words and a pattern of experience*
A poem offers a unique mode of knowing. In order to make sense of all experiences, we look for patterns: the ability to shape our lives into some sort of comprehensible order is fundamental to our sense of identity and to our sanity. What we know, therefore, is delineated in more or less formed patterns of feeling and thinking, some of which may be clearly defined, habitual and understood, whereas others will be elusive, occasional and only dimly sensed. The uniqueness of reading a poem is that it embodies, in miniature, a way of coming to terms with experience that, in itself, reflects the patterned way in which we perceive all our experience. Robin Skelton (1978: 76) develops the point:

> The poem not only presents a pattern of experience but also an experience of pattern itself. It is also, I think, true that the poem, because it communicates in intuitive, emotional, sensual, and intellectual ways, and because it involves its reader in sharing as well as recognising an experience, presents a kind of 'total' perception which is not available elsewhere. The reader undergoes and observes an experience at the same time . . . The poem is a pattern which presents us with the speech of a personality caught in the very act of perception, and we, as readers, both become and understand that personality and that act, thus achieving a sense of 'wholeness' in our response to, and apprehension of, experience . . .

The interaction between reader and text that produces the poem thus operates with a sense of pattern at several levels. Not only is a poem a made pattern of words on a page and a pattern of sounds in time (as statement 10 claimed), but it also reflects, in the '"wholeness" in our response' to which Skelton refers, the pattern-making facility that we exercise willy-nilly in coming to terms with all experience.

12 *Creating a poem involves reading both the parts and the whole together*
In his discussion of how poetry, fiction, and scientific and historical prose communicate both truth and pleasure, Coleridge (1817/1949) concludes that a poem is 'a species of composition' which proposes 'for its *immediate* object pleasure, not truth'; and further, that it is unique in 'proposing to itself such delight from the *whole*, as is compatible with a distinct gratification from each component *part*'. Coleridge thus points to a phenomenon integral to the

evocation of a poem: the reader's pleasure in a poem derives from an awareness of a qualitative and necessary unity. It is qualitative because the reader's valuing of the poem will depend upon how well its constituent parts cohere; and it is necessary because an acceptance of this 'species of composition' as a poem at all is conditional upon the sense that all elements (metre, rhyme, diction, imagery, . . .) are interdependently related.

The process of reading a poem in itself reflects the gratification Coleridge describes. We read through and then reread; we shuffle to and fro about the poem, savouring some lines, asking questions about others; we look for development in feeling, idea or image; but, above all (or, better, unifying all), we read with the assumption that the composition has been well wrought. Because poetry is such a condensed and precise form of language, any blemish – an inappropriate word, a jarring rhythm – undermines the integrity of the whole. In reading a poem we anticipate an inevitable sense of the appropriate.

13 *A poem operates both centrifugally and centripetally*

If we pause to monitor our own or other's responses either during or immediately after reading a poem, it quickly becomes clear that such responses can be considered in two broad groups: those that refer to readers and their idiosyncratic associations and those that refer to the text and its singular construction of experience. Two kinds of pleasure are thus available in aesthetic reading, as Frank Kermode (1975) has pointed out: one pleasure that is 'a private delight', undetermined by the text, where the reader fills out from his or her own free-ranging imagination, and another pleasure that is public, determined by the text and 'consists in knowing what it is that "holds a book together"'. Frye (1957: 73) makes a similar distinction in more strictly verbal terms when he says that during reading our attention moves in two directions at once:

> One direction is outward or centrifugal, in which we keep going outside our reading, from the individual words to the things they mean, or, in practice, to our memory of the conventional association between them. The other direction is inward or centripetal, in which we try to develop from the words a sense of the larger verbal pattern they make.

Of course, this two-way process occurs to some extent with any sort of reading, but in the reader's creation of a poem it is an essential feature.

Given what we have said about the existential nature of a poem (statement 10), the way it reflects in miniature the pattern of our perceiving (statement 11), and the interdependence of the parts and the whole (statement 12), the interplay between the reader and the text can only be sustained (and the poem can thus only be evoked) by exploiting the central paradox of language; that is, that meanings and experiences, and our thoughts and feelings about them, are both *produced by* and *expressed in* language. The magical relationship between words and their referents is nowhere more apparent than in poetry where, as soon as they are uttered, words move inwards and act centripetally – they name, fix and isolate particular experiences; but they also move outwards and act centrifugally – they evoke, generate and associate these experiences with others retained in memory or conceivable in imagination. The unique ways in which a poem speaks to its reader, and which these last four statements in particular have tried to capture, are all hinted at in Louise Rosenblatt's words (1978: 14):

> 'The poem' comes into being in the live circuit set up between the reader and 'the text'. As with the elements of an electric circuit, each component of the reading process functions by virtue of the presence of the others. A specific reader and a specific text at a specific time and place: change any of these, and there occurs a different circuit, a different event – a different poem.

Ideas *in* poems, as we noted at the outset, need anchoring in word-pictures of reality; ideas *about* reading poems needs the same treatment. As we have seen, a poem does not mean what it says, it says what it means. Similarly, an essay about the process of reading a poem must reflect the virtual nature of a phenomenon that can only be approached obliquely and from various angles.

6 The importance of poetry in children's learning

There is a twofold problem in realizing the power of poetry in children's learning: firstly, we must understand where that power lies and what poetry does better than any other form of language use; and, secondly, we must reappraise our methods of working with poems in school and, in particular, align them with what we have come to know about the nature of literary response and the relationship between literature and learning. Accordingly, the first part of this chapter is about the uniqueness of poetry and the second about classroom methodology. Children's experiences of hearing, enacting, discussing and making poems permeate both.

What poetry offers

A few years ago the East Anglian poet Edward Storey took a class of primary-school children to the local church to see what stories they could find, to implant a story by Charles Causley about other children and another church and, as it turned out, to make a narrative poem of his own to mark the occasion. Causley's well-known poem 'Mary, Mary Magdalene' (1979) derives from the custom that the local children of Launceston in Cornwall have of throwing a pebble for luck on to the back of the granite figure of the saint which lies recumbent on the east wall of the church which bears her name. The ballad proceeds through a dialogue between a girl and the saint and describes six phases of a woman's life through its main turning-points and ceremonies – from baby, to schoolgirl, to lover, to bride, to widow and finally to mother – cleverly reversing the last two so that the poem ends where it began and the cycle can start again.

When Edward Storey's class returned from exploring a wet and windy graveyard, they came with news of robbers' graves, a headstone about an Indian princess and the tiny graves of unknown children whose names had been partially obscured by moss. Back inside the church they talked of the stained-glass windows and the eagle-winged lectern, and listened to Causley's poem. Someone must have noticed how the wish-bone vaulting in the church roof looked like the timbers of an upturned boat, and this became the image for a transformation as vivid as that at the start of Sendak's *Where The Wild Things Are* (1967). Here is Edward Storey's poem (1982).

A Song of a Church Visit with Children

(for Class 4J Doddinghurst C.E. School)

We sat in an upturned boat
beached on the shores of Spring,
with flowers bright as Angel-fish
and light on the polished wing
of a bird in a cage of colour
where winds made the rain-bells ring.

We sat where the timbers arched
their wish-bone shapes above,
a wooden spire for our keel
and the eagle for the dove
in search of a singing rainbow
with words as warm as love.

We listened to a story
older than ship or crown
of Mary, Mary Magdalene*
who threw a pebble down
to grant each lucky child a wish
in that distant, salty town.

We listened to the weather
outside our stranded ark
and heard a thousand voices
speaking from the dark
and fading stones of history
where the living seldom talk.

There were robbers' graves around us
on which grass never grows
and a lost princess who slumbers
where no noisy ocean flows
tugging at sea-weed bell-ropes
when the March-wind blows.

There were graves of unknown children,
names nibbled away by moss,
and a tree the shape of an anchor
and a man on the mast of a Cross
who was killed one stormy Easter,
stretched out like an albatross.

* Mary Mary Magdalene is a reference to Charles Causley's poem of that title, which was read in the church.

We sat while the day turned over
and the words spilt from each hand
and the fish went back to flowers
and the water turned to sand
  and our upturned boat became a church
  as we sailed back to land.

But when these creaking timbers
crack and fall to dust,
when the coloured port-holes crumble
and the cabin hinges rust,
  who will come here, I wonder
  to listen and think of us?

Poems matter because they are a prime source of stories; and stories in verse, as we have seen, hold listeners in the double spell of both the fiction and the form. Narrative, as we have learned from those who have developed the concept in literature and learning, notably Hardy (1975), Meek *et al.* (1977) and H. Rosen (1982), is a primary act of mind. The narrative imagination is our common human property; it is the way we make sense of experience – including the experience of going to the local church with your classmates and a visiting poet and becoming part of the process that blends the anecdotes, the chance comments and the histories inscribed in the stone book of the building into this well-wrought poem. This school visit on a wet day has evoked a very still poem: the children are sitting surrounded by stories – ones coloured in the church windows, implied in the icons and embedded in the architecture. They listen to Charles Causley's poem, to the voices of the past and the stories some of them have discovered on the gravestones – and, of course, to the Christian story reflected all around them – until, in the last two verses, the transformation is reversed, the boat becomes church, and the poem shifts from the secondary world back to the primary one. It leaves us with a question which both indicates the significance of such Wordsworthian 'spots of time' and also hints at more pervasive issues of how we continue to interpret our history and traditions. Poetry is uniquely able to embody the general within the particular, to diagnose the indwelling value within the external features. Class 4J and any other children listening to this poem are hearing the narrative imagination at work in ways that connect their own stories and experiences with our common human impulse to create secondary worlds of our own and to enjoy those made by others – a point Auden made for us at the beginning of Chapter 2. Poetry educates the imagination by making us look afresh at the primary world through the power and vision of its secondary creations.

A second source of the power of poetry is more explicitly cultural. Every society has its storyteller, whether it is the elder in the tribe, the poet in the medieval court, the ballad-monger in nineteenth-century London streets or a rabbit called Dandelion in *Watership Down*. Poems and stories establish and confirm the identity of a culture. This body of literature constantly renews itself; it is inclusive, invitational, organically growing from the city streets as well as the country churchyard, permeated with its own literary history and influenced by television and other media. What matters is the continuity and our sense of being a part of it. What poetry offers – and what Storey's poem exemplifies – is just this experience of belonging to a changing yet permanent culture. Thus, the customs and children's games from Launceston are shaped into a poem which is read to children in another church at the other side of the country and in turn becomes merged with the stories in Doddinghurst, which eventually lead to 'A Song of a Church Visit with Children', a poem to be shared with children everywhere. Many, no doubt, will hear the poem as part of similar visits in their own towns and villages; some already have. In such ways poems are the cells of our living culture.

The power of poetry lies, too, in the realization that for writers and readers it is both fun to make things with words and that, in doing so, language is in action in its most potent form. Auden (1973b), again, reminds us that 'there is only one trait that is common to all poets without exception, a passionate love for their native tongue.' This innate love of language is there in children too, seen nowhere more clearly than in the accounts we have of how very young children gain mastery over words, playing with the sounds and rhythms of snatches of language, as Ruth Weir's *Language in the Crib* (1962) shows. It is evident, too, in the work of the Opies and in the delight young children take in comic and nonsense verse where language draws attention to itself and the rhyming sounds and metrical patterns have the power to conjure the experience seemingly 'out of the air' rather than, as here, acting as agents to give shape to the event in the poet's mind. Paradoxically, a love of language for its own sake becomes a love of language for the sake of what it can do for us in helping us to represent and understand our experiences. For 4J to see their images, comments and anecdotes of this church visit fashioned into the pattern of a poem is to offer them, implicitly, knowledge of both the playfulness of language and its discipline.

So far I have argued that the power of poetry lies in our recognition of the importance of the narrative imagination, the need for cultural continuity and the development of linguistic mastery. These are features that poetry shares with many aspects of literary experience. We need to ask, therefore, what qualities are unique to poetry, what it can offer that other genres cannot. Again I want to focus the argument by reference to Edward Storey's 'Song' and acknowledge that, although every poem is unique, all poems have some attributes in common.

The first of these features is the peculiar use of language. 'Song' has an almost Keatsian richness. The poem's extended church/boat metaphor is sustained by a collection of smaller images which seem to grow out of each other as the poem proceeds. Auditory and visual images predominate: we are invited to sit and listen to the sounds of the wind, the stories, the voices of history, the 'noisy ocean' and the 'creaking timbers' and to mark the vivid colours of the windows, the structure of the roof, the shapes of the Christian symbols and the age of the stones. Storey evokes the interior of the church through these surreal effects in words that are sensory, precise and concrete yet which are simultaneously looking outside themselves, creating the sense of significant memory, a fondly recalled event, and that atmosphere of being in the presence of the living past that 'church-going' can bring. This contraplex, two-way movement, which we identified in the final statement in the previous chapter, operates everywhere in poems, most obviously as we read verse 6:

> There were graves of unknown children,
> names nibbled away by moss,
> and a tree the shape of an anchor
> and a man on the mast of a Cross
> who was killed one stormy Easter,
> stretched out like an albatross.

As soon as they are uttered, the words move inwards and act centripetally – they name, fix and bring into focus the images of children's graves partly covered in moss, the Easter story and the central icon of the Cross. But they also move outwards and act centrifugally – they evoke, generate, and associate these images with our own experiences of children and churches, and with the biblical story and, perhaps, that of 'The Ancient Mariner'. Words working in this way are clearly offering a reading experience different from any other. They are not delimited to lexical definitions and referential meanings. These are words that are alive with a plurality of meanings from their contexts, their associations and their sensory qualities; they are alive with what Ted Hughes (1967: 18) calls 'the goblin in a word'.

A further quality that poetry offers is that of form. All art involves the shaping of experience in a chosen medium. In language, this formal ordering is at both its most subtle and its most overt in poetry. In Storey's 'Song', the forward movement is strongly felt through the optimistic, song-like, three-beat line, the 'continuo-effect' of rhyming every other line, and the running-on of lines within a verse as each one is built up to make a single sentence. Yet, offsetting this momentum are the constant reminders of stillness at the start of each verse – 'We sat . . .', 'We listened . . .', 'There were . . .' – each time followed by a particular word-picture which, while it catches the same sense of romance and wonder, is none the less enclosed as a separate painting in its stanza-frame. The tautness of this structure, the way words appear to drop into place with an inevitable appropriateness and the heightening of experience that such patterning produces, all combine to give that sense of contained energy that any well-crafted poem possesses.

Thirdly, each new poem is a fresh look. Its focus is sharp, and the clear eye of the poet makes us aware of some insight or idea, the ghost of some lost emotion or the significance of some detail – how the church becomes a 'stranded ark', maybe, or the implications of the question with which the poem ends. The details of the church and churchyard give an intricate texture to the poem and lend it its particular character. It is this skill of close observation that again is peculiar to poetry. 'The essential quality of poetry', claimed D. H. Lawrence, 'is that it makes a new effort of attention and "discovers" a new world within the known world.' By attending to the stories that lie between people, the church/boat metaphor emerges, a new way of looking is created and no church visit is quite the same again for those who read and reflect upon the poem.

Above all, perhaps, good poems are places where writers and readers exercise both an intelligence of thinking and an intelligence of feeling (see Chapter 5, statement 5). 'Song' is not a direct recital of the poet's feeling, yet there is no doubting the interplay of thought and emotion that permeates the poem. The mounting fascination as the church yields up its stories, the excitement of the histories in the stones all around and the feeling of closeness in the shared experience finally give way to the question in the last verse with its speculations about Time and the individual's place within history. There is a sadness certainly in the images of change and decay, but also the hint of that all-but-unconscious sense of the continuity of the species, of belonging with the living and the dead forever in Time. Poetry matters because feeling and thinking remain in close touch with each other. Thought may subdue feeling, feeling may overwhelm thought; but, because of the concentration of language and the discipline of expression, feelings become *embodied* in verbal form, not merely indicated by verbal reference.

'The art of literature, vocal or written,' as A. N. Whitehead says, 'is to adjust the language so that it embodies what it indicates' (quoted in Auden 1973b). Together, the qualities outlined above, uniquely blended in poems, are the reason why the child's awareness of what language is and does can potentially become deeper and more subtle through poetry than through any other form of language use.

Poems in the classroom

Writing a few years before I. A. Richards's celebrated work (1924; 1929), George Sampson (1921) reminds the English teacher that:

> If literature in schools is not a delight, if it is not in all senses, a 'recreation', an experience in creative reception, it is a failure.

Sadly, in subsequent years, the combined forces of the criticism industry and the examination system effectively snuffed out much of this delight. 'Practical criticism' became the method with sixth-formers and undergraduates; comprehension exercises became the lot of schoolchildren. In the past decade, however, we have begun to learn how to honour George Sampson's principle and to give poetry back to its readers. Reader-response theory and the particular influence of Louise Rosenblatt's (1978) transactional theory have altered the climate of poetry teaching. The development of a methodology that is based upon informed concepts of *reading* and *response* rather than upon conventional, narrowly conceived ideas of *comprehension* and *criticism* is now the priority. At the heart of contemporary thinking about classroom method is the uniqueness of the reading event. Comprehension can only develop and criticism can only be well founded if they are rooted in the processes of reading and responding.

Certain operational principles follow from this premise.

(a) Reading a poem is different from reading a story or any other text. Most poems children encounter are short; the words can be taken in within seconds. Rereadings of lines or verses, changes in pace or tone, sorting out complex syntax, savouring an image or a rhyme – all happen within a small compass and dictate a reading process that is more varied and unpredictable than any other. The meanings lie, as it were, in the spaces around the verses and between the words as well as within the words themselves. These spaces are ones we inhabit mentally as we 'look at' the text from various viewpoints (Chapter 5, statement 1). Granted we initially have to read a poem forwards; none the less, our ways-in to its meaning will be many and varied. Exposing children to a lot of poetry so that they hear, read, write, speak, dramatize and illustrate poems as a regular part of their English lessons is the essential means to give children a sense of themselves as readers of poems; it is the best way, too, to build reading confidence and create the taste for poetry which many young people seem to lack as they go through secondary school.

(b) As has been argued in the previous chapter (statement 8), poems are read with both ear and eye. The distinction here is not simply the functional one between speaking a poem aloud or reading it silently. There are aural and visual dimensions in all poetry reading. If we read well, we cannot stop ourselves sounding the words in the head. With younger children the fun of rhyming sounds and strongly marked rhythms is easy enough to encourage and there are many excellent ideas, for example, in *Exploring Poetry: 5–8* by Jan Balaam and Brian Merrick (1987). As children get older there is a danger that the visual dominates, that the poems stay print-bound on the page. Performances that lift the words off the page – shared readings, choral speaking, taped radio programmes etc. – are both exacting disciplines in themselves and ways of keeping children alert to the 'auditory imagination' from which poems are created. Again there are many sources of classroom activities to serve these ends (Benton and Fox 1985; M. and P. Benton 1988), and the more international character of poetry in recent years, especially the spread of Afro-Caribbean poetry, has helped to remind us that the language of poetry combines the abstract art of the aural with the solid presence of the visual.

(c) Giving children access to a wide variety of poetry experiences is essential. It has long been accepted practice that children's own writing should be interleaved with their reading of poetry. There are dangers of falling into habitual teaching patterns here (Benton 1986: 20), and 'creative writing' is both an uncomfortable phrase and an easy victim. Yet in recent years there have been many publications (Hughes 1967; Koch 1970, 1973; Brownjohn 1980; Rosen 1981; Pirrie 1987) which have shown how the disciplined, imaginative play of creative writing can produce remarkable results and develop children's command of language. Encouraging pupils to respond to poems in a variety of ways – live readings, tape-recordings, displays and so on – helps to demystify the experience; pupils should be offered the chance to experiment, to play with the words, sounds and shapes of poems in the same way that they play with paints and materials in an art lesson.

As well as variety in activities, there should be a variety of voices. The resources are rich, and it is relatively easy to give children a feel for the varieties of English in which poetry is expressed and a sense of the heritage of earlier centuries. Both the Bullock Report (1975: 129) and the Kingman Report (1988: 11) stress these points. The best work on poetry will look for opportunities to have poems by, say, Blake and Coleridge rubbing shoulders with ones by Roger McGough and Charles Causley. The best anthologies provide this. It is equally important that pupils experience oral and folk poetry, songs and poems from around the world. In the past decade publishers have provided many more books by women poets: Fleur Adcock, U. A. Fanthorpe, Phoebe Hesketh, Elizabeth Jennings and others are now widely known. There has been a similar expansion in Afro-Caribbean poetry, with the work of James Berry, John Agard and Grace Nichols being especially prominent. Together with the appearance of many poets writing especially for children in an accessible, humorous, often idiomatic way – Michael Rosen, Roger McGough, Kit Wright, Gareth Owen and others – the variety of voices available to the poetry teacher is seemingly infinite. Through poetry, children have access to a society of clear, single voices and a range of feelings for which there is no substitute.

(d) When it is appropriate to dwell on a poem for discussion or study, the key is to provide time and opportunity for individual reflection. Articulating and reflecting upon personal responses are fundamental to the reader's early apprehension of a poem. Jotting around a text or in a journal helps the reader in attending to his or her own responses. Many poems invite these procedures. Chapter 8 discusses these matters in detail; for the moment, an example is given below.

Phoebe Hesketh runs a writers' group in Lancashire which includes several teachers. Recently the group read and enjoyed the poem in Figure 6.1 (Hesketh 1988). The secondary-school pupils who have seen it enjoyed it too. It is printed with the annotations of fourteen-year-old Marian as she took her 'mental walk' around the poem. Read the poem aloud first and then follow Marian's thought-track.

All the pupils made their jottings before sharing their impressions in groups. It is in this private talking to oneself and in the spaces behind public talk that poems are evoked. Discussion helps to test views, modify ideas and prepare for a more

Paint Box

He tried to tell them what he felt
could say it only in colours –
Sunday's white page shading to grey
of evening clocks and bells-in-the-rain.
Monday morning, bright yellow brass
of a cock crowing.
Story-time, purple.
Scarlet is shouting in the playground.

His world's a cocoon
round as an egg, an acorn
sprouting green.
The schoolroom square and hard;
his desk hard and square
facing the enemy blackboard.

'You must learn to read,' they said
and gave him a painting-book alphabet.
Apple swelled beautifully red. Balloon
expanded in blue.
C was a cage for a bird;
his brush wavered through
painting himself
a small brown smudge inside.

Phoebe Hesketh

1st thought
during poem - goes through colours in his paintbox, explaining them. 1st + 2nd lines 'talking with colours' suggest an artist

2nd thought
2nd verse - shapes curved and straight-edged. Like 'square + hard' - very abrupt. I think we're talking about children.

3rd thought
3rd verse A for apple B for Balloon C for cage etc. Methodical, confusing? 'painting himself as a small brown smudge'. Is this suggesting that he is doing self-portrait or is he painting a smudge for himself?

4th thought (re-read)
This is definitely a poem for children, or maybe it's about children? I don't like how it rhymes, uncanny. White Sunday page to start, gradually filling in.

5th thought
re - 1st verse. colours mentioned - white yellow purple scarlet 2nd verse green 3rd red blue brown

6th thought (re-read)
a slow child, trying to express himself going on journey to school. He's inside himself - can't get at 'an egg, acorn' scared of teacher, enemy blackboard can't cope

Figure 6.1 'Paint Box' by Phoebe Hesketh, and a reader's annotations

considered statement if one is required. Marian wrote about the poem at some length. Near the beginning she said:

> I must admit the first time I read the poem I was confused. Things didn't quite fall into place and I wasn't even certain I knew what it was about, other than observing lots of colours being mentioned, and linking that to the title. I decided it was the first verse which was throwing me, so I read it again.

Then she went on to talk about the details of the poem and ended with two accounts of the final lines: a literal-minded one and, as an afterthought, a reading that gives an insight into the whole poem.

> The 3rd verse quotes the teacher dictating 'You must!', which I do not feel is a very understanding attitude. The painting-book alphabet is very methodical. The apple

> and balloon when coloured, expand and swell, lovely words explaining them getting larger and almost coming alive; for C, the author used cage. I would have preferred to see a cow or a cat, something far simpler for a young child to understand. The closing sentence, 'a small brown smudge inside'. My first thoughts on this were that it was a sentence with two meanings. I opted for, in my opinion the correct one after re-reading the line, what Hesketh was trying to conclude was that, although the child was able to develop his ideas in his head, even using colours all he could establish on paper was a brown smudge. I can imagine the frustration of knowing what balloons, apples and cages look like, but being unable to produce a portrait. An after-thought about the 3rd verse, after commenting on the use of cage for the letter C being inappropriate, is that Hesketh used a cage as another way of portraying the feeling of being enclosed and the boy being unable to show his feelings. The boy being like a bird in a cage like the child in his classroom – there is no way out, no escape.

Poems need time. At first, they may be just a blur of words, as Marian indicated. Given careful phasing along the lines suggested above, so that readers take on responsibility for exploring and developing their responses, pupils have a much better chance of coming to own a poem. In doing so, of course, they are not only learning about poems: they are also learning about learning.

To sum up, the starting-point is that poems must be experienced before they can be analysed (Fox and Merrick 1981). Properly handled, literary understanding and critical evaluation develop *as a result of* reflective reading and responding: the two 2Cs are part of the 2Rs and are stronger for being so. If they cease to be part of the whole reading/responding experience, then comprehension degenerates into inquisition, criticism into mechanical analysis, and a gap opens up between the reader and the poem which reduces the latter to fodder for just another sort of textbook exercise. Poetry, as was said earlier, needs to be given back to readers. It is the job of our methodology to see that this happens. Only then can the importance of poetry in children's learning outlined in this chapter be more fully realized.

7 Poetry for children: a neglected art

The problem of poetry

Poetry has had bad luck. It has suffered a double misfortune: neglect where it most needs attention and concern where it is best left alone. The neglect can be sensed in various ways. A few poker-faced questions turned in upon oneself will help. Try these:

- When did I last buy a slim volume of poetry to read for my own enjoyment?
- How often do I read poems to children? talk about them? dramatize them? chorally speak them? What are my very good reasons for not doing these things as often as I would like?
- Who are my top ten pre-war poets for children? Which ten poets who have published verse for children since, say, 1980 would I recommend for other teachers and librarians?

And, since I am an avid reader of children's literature,

- Does my use of the phrase 'children's literature' usually imply *any* poetry?

Handling poetry is the area of the primary/middle-school curriculum and the secondary English curriculum where teachers feel most uncertain of their knowledge, most uncomfortable about their methods and most guilty about both. Nor is the neglect of poetry confined to the individual's reading and teaching habits: in the 1970s it became institutionalized. There are over 600 pages in the Bullock Report: three and a half pages are given to poetry. How was it possible to entitle this monolith *A Language for Life* and to all but ignore the art in which language is at its most alive? Sadly, the neglect comes closer to home. A skim through the ten or a dozen books on children's literature that have formed a mini-publishing boom in this area during the past two decades demonstrates the scant attention that has been paid to poetry for children. It is significant that in one of the very few pieces on the subject, Ian Serraillier (1975) should begin by expressing his surprise that the 471 pages of *Only Connect* (Egoff 1969) contain nothing about verse for children. Fifteen years on, and Peter Hunt (1990) produces his admirable *Children's Literature* yet without a mention of poetry. The record of the professional journals, with the notable exception of *Signal*, is little better. Why is it that, when we speak of children's literature, we mean fiction and exclude poetry?

The neglect shows in both our knowledge and our pedagogy: the body of this and the next chapter focuses attention on these areas. Yet it would be foolish to proceed without acknowledging the misplaced concern that commonly fills the vacuum left by our lack of interest in and enthusiasm for poems. The concern I mean is that which leads to 'doing' poetry as a duty, feeling that it should form part of the English curriculum and finding a place for it in utilitarian terms. Having found the time for work on poetry, it is all too easy for the conscientious teacher to approach it with strategies more appropriate to the cognitive areas of the curriculum. Concern as a feeling of disquiet thus has the effect of elevating a series of pragmatic concerns into a teaching method: the anxiety to pin the meaning down, to explain words, to take the class on a guided tour through a poem, enlivening it with metaphor hunts and simile chases, inexorably takes over. Worry about rightness, both of a poem's meaning and of our teaching methods, predominates, and the worry is conveyed to the children so that the classroom ambience of poetry becomes one of anxiety at a difficult problem with hidden rules rather than one of enjoyment of a well-wrought object. 'Poetry begins in delight . . .' With young children, above all, our rightful concern is with this delight. Concern over understanding in the narrow literal sense that requires explanation, annotation and analysis is misplaced.

Why is it that poetry is such a problem? Where do the difficulties lie? In crude terms, there are four factors: the poetry, the children, the pedagogy and the teacher. Taking them in turn, it is hard to believe that fault lies with the poetry. After all, the great poets of our literature offer much that is accessible to children, and there is a substantial bibliography of writers who have written poetry specifically for a young audience. Moreover, there are many signs that the current golden age of children's literature is being sustained by poets as well as novelists, and since 1970 more new poetry for children has been published than perhaps ever before. The raw material is available.

Equally, it is hard to find fault with the children. Few teachers need the fascinating and exhaustive work of the Opies to authenticate what they know from personal observation and experience: children have a natural affinity with verse, song, puns, riddles, jokes, word-sounds, rhymes, chants and so on. Playing with words, inventing rules, enjoying patterns and repetitions; imagining monsters, fairies, witches, talking animals, magical lands: the child's 'inward eye' and the poet's are more alike than we commonly realize. George Sampson (1946) asserted this over forty years ago. Children are creative (and destructive) by natural impulse, not through any form of reasoning. So it is by a kind of creative instinct that they like poetry. 'They are still living in that mysterious world to which music belongs. In their world, the writs of reason do not run. Children, like the lunatic, the lover and the poet, are of imagination all compact.' The 'imaginative conditions' within the child, then, are right for the enjoyment of poetry.

Perhaps the fault lies in what we do with poetry in school. In those classrooms where poetry is a duty, not a delight, this is no doubt the case. Yet we are also living in a golden age of the teaching aid. Resources and pedagogical advice wink at us from the pages of every educational publisher. The variety is infinite and tempting: there are textbooks, source books, anthologies, poetry cards, poetry tapes, spoken-word records, poetry secretariats, 'rent-a-poet' schemes and creative-writing courses. In practical terms, poetry is better served now than it has ever been, if only we have the time and the wit to take advantage.

We are left pointing a self-accusing finger. Poetry is a problem area in school mainly because many teachers either dislike it or feel ill at ease with it. The free speech that a poem both embodies and invites is risky in the same way that educational drama is risky, which is why both these activities are often Cinderellas in the English curriculum. There are many reasons for our comparative lack of interest in poetry. Two obvious ones are worth underlining. The Bullock Report (1975) expresses the first in terms calculated to perpetuate the malaise:

> It has to be acknowledged that poetry starts at a disadvantage. In the public view it is something rather odd, certainly outside the current of normal life; it is either numinous, and therefore rarely to be invoked, or an object of comic derision.

Keep telling the public that, and they will soon believe it. The cultural commonplace that poetry is a minority art is a useful cover phrase when we wish to avoid the question of who makes up this minority. I suspect that only a small proportion of English teachers are paid-up members. Along with the rest of society, most English teachers find reading fiction, watching film and television or going to the theatre more entertaining pursuits than reading verse. Poetry survives in the gaps, if at all. (When *did* you last buy a book of poems?) The other truism about poetry is that generally it requires more effort from the reader. It is harder work to remake a poem in the imagination simply because poetry is the most condensed form of language that we have. By the same token, a child's knowledge of what language is and does will become deeper and more subtle through poetry than through any other form of literature. To deprive children of poems is to deny them the society of clear, single voices and an irreplaceable range of feeling. We neglect poetry at our peril. We need to know more about what is available and what to do with it.

Poetry for children

Having pointed to past neglect, it is only fair to say that poetry is now much better served than it was even ten years ago. Perhaps the single most useful source book is *Poetry 0–16* (1988) by Morag Styles and Pat Triggs: an essential guide, attractively presented, to the rich bibliography of writers for a young audience. *Signal*, too, has championed the cause of poetry and, among other things, has produced one of its excellent bookguides, *Poetry for Children* (1986) by Jill Bennett and Aidan Chambers. The best historical perspective is that given by the Opies in *The Oxford Book of Children's Verse* (1973), which plots the course of verse for children with copious examples from the minor roads of English literature. This anthology starts with Chaucer and finishes with Ogden Nash, on the curious principle that death is *the* criterion for inclusion. None the less, amid the plethora of minor names, those whose work has lasted down the generations still stand out: Blake, Lear, Carroll, Rossetti, Stevenson, de la Mare, Farjeon emerge as major figures.

Elsewhere (Benton and Fox 1985) I have discussed the principal strands of verse for children, and there is no need to rehearse these in any detail here, except to underline that it is our professional responsibility to be aware of this developing literary history. Didactic verse, nonsense poetry and lyrical poetry all have a strong tradition in the evolving literature for the young, and each is represented in tones and conventions that reflect different periods of development. In recent years, the mainstream tradition of children's poetry, maintained by Charles Causley, Ted Hughes and others, has been joined by new voices speaking in quite different idioms. As noted in Chapter 6, Roger McGough and Brian Patten have continued the Mersey sound throughout the 1980s with several anthologies each; Michael Rosen, Kit Wright, Gareth Owen, Allan Ahlberg have each published several volumes for children, their subjects tending to stay close to the homes, schools, families and friends of their young audience and to enliven such matters with wry humour and sharp attention to detail. Afro-Caribbean poets, too, have published specifically for children: John Agard's and Grace Nichols' work enriches the literature for children with new rhythms and fresh vocabulary with all the brightness of the oral tradition from which their writings originally spring. In short, poetry for children is arguably now stronger and more varied in its appeal than it has ever been. It offers a rich resource to the literature teacher: armed with the guidance of the annotated guides and bibliographies mentioned above, and through implementing some of the classroom activities I have urged elsewhere (M. Benton *et al.* 1988: 210–12), there is no need for poetry to remain a neglected art in future.

8 Poetry in the classroom

A methodology for reading and teaching

Young readers know about the differences between story-reading and reading poetry: you can hear them any day in the classroom. Their most common cliché about reading a *story* is to talk about 'getting into it'; they tend to prefer books that are easy to get into, rather as though they are putting on a comfortable jumper. In fact, they are describing that easy transition that a good novel-opening provides from the primary world of fact into the 'secondary world' of fiction that Tolkien (1938/64) writes about. Yet children do not use this phrase about encounters with new poems. They say something similar but significantly different. They talk of 'getting it' or 'not getting it' – suggesting their awareness that most poems are cast in the medium of riddling word-play where ambiguity, association, sound and rhythm all contribute to meaning. They know that there is an element of puzzle and that their reading is one in which they will 'by indirections find direction out'.

The questions for the literature teacher that this awareness poses are, firstly,

- What is the difference between reading for information and reading literature?

And more precisely,

- What is the difference between *how* we read fiction and *how* we read poetry?

In view of what was argued in Chapter 5, the riders to such questions, in Rosenblatt's terms, might be:

- How do we avoid doing 'efferent' things to 'aesthetic' objects? How do we keep the aesthetic experience alive?

Given the constraints of the classroom, there are no easy answers but they must lie in the creation of a receptive ethos, in the shared enjoyment of reading and performances and in encouraging individual commitment to particular poems.

A methodology that entails a phased procedure for individual work as a lead-in to group activity is fundamental. The sequence is, by now, familiar enough: *monitoring* one's own responses via jottings or journal-writing; *reflecting upon* responses via some second-phase activity – tape-recording or free writing to develop one's ideas, for example; and *expressing* one's responses via individual, pair or group work. If the procedure is straightforward, it remains all too easy to neglect one more of these steps in coming to know a poem when the demands of school press us towards eliciting value judgements in oral work and markable essays in written work. Such pressures need to be resisted in the early stages with a new poem; instead, we need to facilitate pupils in this procedure which, through self-monitoring, enables readers to represent to themselves what they think, through reflecting enables them to hold and refine their ideas, and through expressing these ideas enables them to assess their own reactions against those of their peers.

Recent studies (M. Benton *et al.* 1988) of young readers responding to poems have indicated how the details of a reader-response-centred methodology for working with poems might look. Figure 8.1 gives a diagrammatic picture of the phases of such work; if the symbols and straight lines seem programmatic, it is important to realize the flexibility built into this model and also that successive phases may well only take a few minutes of a lesson, or that one phase may blend into the next quite naturally.

The exit arrows on the right of the diagram indicate the flexibility that poetry-teaching needs: sometimes the first encounter with a poem may be the last; at other times a series of lessons can be given over to all the phases. Frequently, we will not know the extent of the activities that the poem(s) will bear until we are actually busy doing the work with the class. The multiple exit points allow for a due sense of praxis – our self-awareness, during the course of teaching, to know when to make further demands, when to cut our losses, when to change direction and when to bring work to a close.

The continuum down the left side of the diagram signals the shift from individual apprehension of the poem through successive activities towards a fuller comprehension. At its most explicit, this entails a movement from evocation to critical evaluation. The distinction between apprehending and comprehending is crucial. They both form part of a continuous process. Would we want to talk, even to ourselves, if we were permitted to do so only when comprehension was complete?

The central spine of the diagram shows the successive phases in a response-centred methodology.

The diagram attempts to honour the principles that a poem is 'an event in time' (Rosenblatt 1978: 12) and that the individual evocation needs room to develop before the sharing of responses. Approaches to poems are governed by a range of factors, not least by the attitude of the class and their familiarity with poetry. *Browsing* and *reading out* poems, *finding out* about particular poems or poets, *enabling tasks* such as sequencing and cloze may all have a part to play at different times to prepare pupils for the particular poem(s) a teacher wants to introduce.

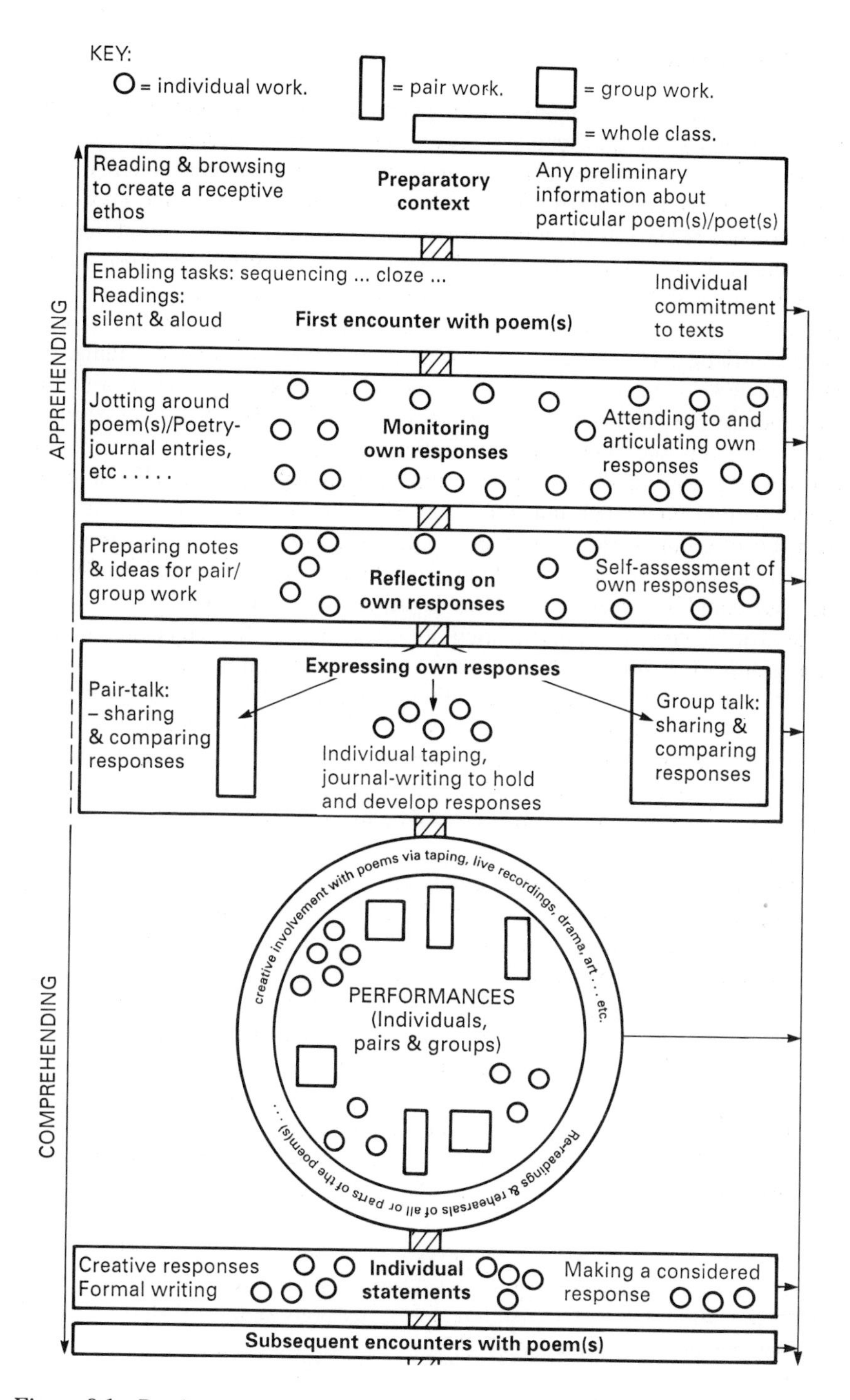

Figure 8.1 Reading and responding to poems – a flexible methodology (Benton *et al.* 1988: 205)

After any preparatory lead-in to the poem(s) and the initial readings, the framework allows for the fact that there are certain activities pupils can and must undertake by themselves. *Articulating* and *reflecting* upon personal responses are fundamental to readers' early apprehensions of a poem. Jotting around a text or in a journal aids readers in attending to their own responses. At first, pupils may be reluctant to believe that their contributions are as important as those of the teacher, but it is foolish to underestimate how powerfully many areas of the curriculum appear to value memorization and the passive reception of second-hand knowledge. There is a need to convey the fact that, in aesthetic reading, the pleasure lies in the richness of the personal responses that occur, and the challenge in the idiosyncrasy of the process of responding. Similarly, readers must be given the opportunity to reflect on their own responses before participating in group discussion. It is in the private talking to oneself and in the spaces behind public talk that the poem will be evoked, and at this stage the demands of group work may well push aside what the reader is trying to grasp. Reflecting on tape, for example, about a text the pupil has chosen to introduce to the class would be a useful and enjoyable task to be carried out at home.

Reading poetry is especially rich in opportunities for independent and peer-group work and for the teacher to develop strategies which will enable readers and texts to work on each other. Hence, the phase when pupils are *expressing their responses* might include a whole-class discussion controlled by the teacher, but it is here that pairs and groups can most usefully share and develop their initial responses with each other. There will always be occasions when it is appropriate for some individuals to continue to work independently, and this is allowed for.

The central part of the diagram emphasizes *performance*. Learning by doing is particularly apt with poems since, as we have already seen, much of their appeal and meaning derives from sound and rhythm. Activities which lift the words off the page are not only enjoyable in themselves but valuable aids to understanding. A special attraction of presentation is that the English teacher can turn for resources to other areas of the curriculum. Music, drama and art are areas from which poetry lessons have become unnecessarily distanced, either through an institutional tendency to separate subjects off or in a misguided attempt to safeguard the supposed 'academic respectability' that education rarely grants to the arts (see Part Three). Preparing a performance takes the pupils back inside the poem(s). Rereadings and rehearsals involve discussion about pace, intonation, thought and feeling which, at its best, can engage pupils in the closest form of textual analysis without them really realizing it. There is no shortage of ideas for this phase: the ubiquitous 'Thirty six things to do with a poem' (Fox and Merrick 1981) and *Teaching Literature 9–14* (M. Benton and Fox 1985) are useful starting-points.

The *individual pieces of writing* that might follow the performances are likely to be more sensitive and detailed for having been preceded by such activities. The importance of this phase is that the whole attention of the pupil is brought to bear upon the whole text from which each pupil is evoking, or has evoked, his or her own poem. A creative response demanding cognitive and affective skills can be as revealing of the nature of the pupil's engagement with the text as any critical statement.

One significant change of emphasis that is highlighted by this methodology lies within the conventional three-part guidelines often given to pupils in studying and writing about a particular poem. As an aid to thinking and writing, pupils are commonly urged to ask themselves three questions and to frame their written work upon the basis of their answers: What sort of poem is it? How does it work? What do I feel about it? These are text-oriented questions, with a concern for efficient evaluation. Once the reader's responses are let in on the act of critical writing then the emphasis alters. The three-part guidelines become:

- an opening statement of the reader's experience of the poem 'as an event'; what the reader thinks the writer is looking at;
- a discussion of the text blueprint; how the poem works for the reader – that is, which cues guided the evocation of the poem;
- an evaluation of the two worlds brought to life during the event, those of the reader and of the text.

At the heart of this methodology is the uniqueness of the reading event. Comprehension and criticism are thus rooted in the processes of reading and responding.

Coming to terms with a poem

How does this methodology operate in practice? Figure 8.2 shows one example of a GCSE student mapping her responses to a poem by Robert Frost before comparing her 'reading' with those of her classmates. Sara carried out a three-phase activity:

- She read the poem in the normal way and noted down how many times she read it before making her first jotting.
- She jotted down her own responses to the poem, numbering them in sequence as she went along.
- Finally, on a separate sheet of paper, she made a simple diagram of her 'reading' by ruling five horizontal lines (one for each of the five verses) and plotted the numbers on her diagram in the appropriate places. Solid lines represent continuous reading, broken lines where she jumped from one part of the poem to another. The vertical lines at the side show how many times Sara read the poem before making her first jotting. As the diagram indicates, she read the poem twice and then made her notes:

  Sara was reading carefully but still finding the poem a puzzle. She commented:

> Read it through a couple of times. I noticed that the last line was important. The last verse was very strong and hard to understand. My mind created an image almost at

> once. A dirty flat with a solid wooden door with paint peeling off it. The window was small and open. The place was bare, shadowy and musty, the window didn't let in much light.
>
> I'm not sure that the image really helped me to understand the poem, as now I don't think the poem has anything to do with people knocking on a door. The poem created an eerie, sensitive feeling, the person involved seemed to be frightened and scared of something, maybe the World. I felt really sorry for him or her.
>
> The picture of a prison cell then came to me, but climbing out of the window contradicts this. I kept reading the poem over and over, but I still can't understand it.

The elements of response here, and those of Sara's peers, were, as might be expected, a mixture of mental images, questions, personal memories and associations, and an attempt to fit all these disparate reactions into a sense of the overall theme of the poem. Fitting the parts into a whole is fundamental to achieving coherence and meaning in reading. Yet, Sara's reading strategy, as evidenced in her diagram, was highly idiosyncratic – a phenomenon which, again, is to be expected but which is at odds with so much conventional classroom practice where the teacher takes the class on a guided tour through a poem, pointing out the main attractions of such sight-seeing and inevitably imposing his or her own 'reading' on the whole experience. The lesson for the teacher here is the need to take a less dominant role, to commit the students to the poem to be studied by providing them with the mental space and time to reflect upon their own individual 'readings'. It is only in this way that readers come to take possession of a poem, to make it their own. Poems, of course, need live readings, performance, celebration; but they also need silent readings, reflection and reading with the eye as well as ear. With the fashionable pressure for group work, for 'talking to learn', there is a danger that we neglect the equally crucial learning activity, 'silence to think'.

Sara's work shows her coming to terms with Frost's poem through the first three or four phases on the diagram. She is now ready to compare notes with others and to develop her understanding of the poem more fully. Her notes and writing so far may form part of an ongoing poetry journal, a parallel document to the reading-log for fiction (Chapter 4). The journal requires the provision of several dozen poetry books – anthologies and slim volumes by single authors – which, after all, are *the* basic resource if we intend to take poetry teaching seriously. The journal is the poetry-reader's commonplace-book. Figure 8.3 shows the guidelines for the one that Sara and the class were keeping.

Principles of practice

The journal puts into practice certain principles which together give direction and purpose to the work while at the same time encouraging choice and commitment. Point 9 is an obvious lead-in to drafting a more formal piece of writing, probably in essay form. Point 10 invites reflection upon the reader's

The Lockless Door

It went many years,
But at last came a knock,
And I thought of the door
With no lock to lock.

I blew out the light,
I tiptoed the floor,
And raised both hands
In prayer to the door.

But the knock came again.
My window was wide;
I climbed on the sill
And descended outside.

Back over the sill
I bade a 'Come in'
To whatever the knock
At the door may have been.

So at a knock
I emptied my cage
To hide in the world
And alter with age.

Robert Frost

1 Image of a flat, dirty and old. A battered door, closed tightly, open window with roof falling away steeply below. No person.

2 Why?

3 eerie feeling

4 The person involved seems to be scared and frightened of the outside world.

5 Another image is of a prison cell. A prisoner being freed but not wanting to face the world after being shut away for so long.

6 Locked in somewhere nowhere to go

7 waiting helplessly for a knock to come

8 the mind?

9 praying for what? The person to go away. Why?

10 maybe frightened of seeing someone

11 importance of last line

12 not a person knocking, something, a memory.

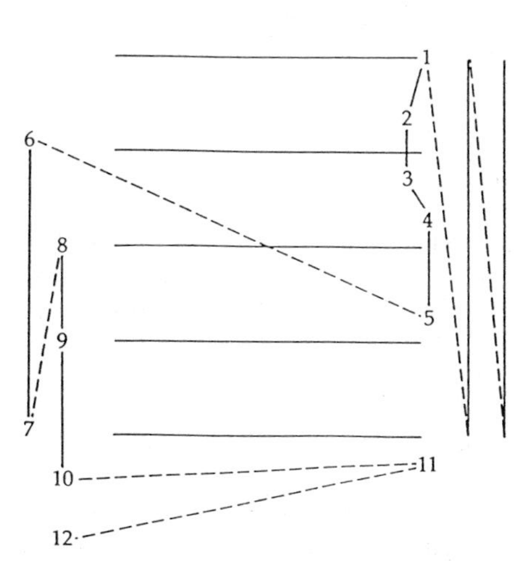

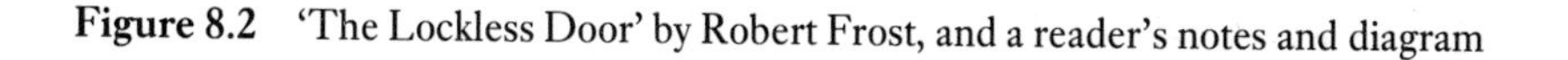

Figure 8.2 'The Lockless Door' by Robert Frost, and a reader's notes and diagram

Keeping a Poetry Journal

You'll be spending two or three hours on your own, in the company of a large number of poetry books. At the end of this time we'll be sharing what has happened. Here are some ways to make use of your journal.

1 Sometimes a poem strikes you on first meeting. Jot down your thoughts and feelings as you read. Try to capture all that you experience.
2 Perhaps you've read a poem several times. Now, give yourself, say, five minutes, and write. Let your hand follow your pen – see where it takes you.
3 Copy out words or phrases or lines that you like, and try to explain why you like them.
4 If you like the whole poem, copy it out in the back of your book.
5 Make a list of the questions you have about a poem you like.
6 Sometimes we're very moved by a poem that reminds us of a personal experience. If you like, describe that personal association.
7 Sometimes words make pictures in our heads. Make a sketch of such a picture, and add words which created the picture.
8 Perhaps a title or a line or a feeling gives you an idea for a short story or a scene in a play or a poem of your own. Write it.
9 If there's a poem you get to know really well, try to answer these questions:
   - What interests you about the poem? What does it 'say' to you?
   - As you reread it, how does your sense of the poem develop?
   - Does the whole poem work for you? Say what you like (and perhaps dislike) about it.
10 Look back through your entries. 'I like poems which . . .' Can you see any connections between the poems you've chosen to write about?

Figure 8.3 Guidelines for keeping a poetry journal

personal style: when pupils can say what their preferences are, then there is every chance that, given some continuity with this activity through school, they will become poetry-readers in future from time to time from choice rather than compulsion.

These principles might be summarized as follows:

(a) Children's appreciation of poetry will be enhanced if they are also writers of poetry.
(b) Exposure to a wide variety of poems – different styles, 'voices', verse forms, periods – is the seed-bed from which a love of poetry is most likely to grow.
(c) Critical analysis has no place in poetry lessons with children up to the age of about fourteen; and even with older secondary-school pupils it is often inappropriate.

(d) Because their meaning derives in part from their sound and rhythm, poems need to be read aloud. The key to classroom activities is *performance* – providing opportunities for children to speak and listen to poetry.
(e) The younger the children, the more poems should be allowed to speak for themselves. Explanations and annotations do not matter. With older middle-school and secondary-school pupils occasions will increasingly arise when it is right to dwell on a particular poem. The key here is *reflection* – providing opportunities for children to reread, make notes and share impressions in an informal atmosphere.
(f) There can be no *one* method of teaching poetry, since poems are obstinately miscellaneous creations. The trick is to derive the method according to the qualities of the particular poem to be taught.

PART THREE

Literature, painting and picture-books

9 Looking at paintings: representation and response

Representation and response

Writing about the art of making images, Gombrich (1960: 98) quotes a celebrated remark by Matisse: 'When a lady visiting his studio said, "But surely, the arm of this woman is much too long," the artist replied politely, "Madam, you are mistaken. This is not a woman, this is a picture."' This exchange focuses upon my purposes in this chapter, which concern two fundamental concepts we need to keep in mind when working with pictures: representation and response. Perhaps the most important contribution to visual theory since E. H. Gombrich's *Art and Illusion* – the significance of which has been likened by one recent commentator as comparable to that of Reynolds's *Discourses* (1789) nearly two centuries earlier (Bryson 1991: 62) – is Richard Wollheim's *Art and Its Objects* (1980) and his *Painting as an Art* (1987). His second chapter in the latter book, 'What The Spectator Sees', concentrates on issues of visual experience which Gombrich had earlier addressed in the corresponding section, 'The Beholder's Share', of his classic study. Both write in the mainstream perceptualist tradition as distinct, for example, from semiological approaches to visual representation (Bryson 1991), or from approaches which resist the idea that representation is grounded in perception or in our phenomenological experience of the world, in favour of defining it according to the historical conditions of its origin and reception (Nochlin 1991).

According to Michael Podro (1991: 165), the two main theoretical questions posed by mainstream theory that have been paramount since *Art and Illusion*, are, firstly, 'How is it that we can convincingly show the look of the three-dimensional moving world on what we are still aware of as a still two-dimensional surface?' and, secondly, 'How does the presence of the surface and the facture of the paint enter our awareness of the subject depicted upon it?' Wollheim's answer (to which Podro's own seems remarkably similar) lies in his concept of 'seeing-in'.

Seeing-in is an experience familiar to any visitor to an art gallery who has spent time gazing at a particular painting, occasionally moving in close or adjusting the angle of viewing. It is to have a dual-aspect yet unitary experience in response to a painting. It is unitary in that the viewer's absorption in the image is inclusive of two features: the viewer sees both the depicted objects or figures and yet also sees the marked surface as evidenced in, say, the brush strokes, the density of the texture, the cracks in the paint, the glare and so on. Wollheim argues that the connection between representation and seeing-in is essential. Writing about how painters achieve naturalistic effects, he says, 'Specifically, we need to invoke the phenomenology of seeing-in: two-foldness' (Wollheim 1987: 72). He calls the two complementary aspects of seeing-in the *recognitional aspect*, where the spectator discerns something *in* the marked surface, and the *configurational aspect*, which indicates the spectator's awareness *of* the marked surface *per se*. Both aspects of this two-foldness operate in the spectator together, and it is this simultaneous awareness of 'a depicted subject' and 'the marked surface' which ensures that the framed scene registers both in depth and as flat.

Literature teachers may register both a recognition and a cause for unease at this point. We feel on familiar territory when seeing-in appears to be a similar process to the one young readers undergo during the initial stages of learning to read. Constructing a meaning and decoding print are analogous in their two-fold nature to the recognitional and configurational aspects of Wollheim's concept. The likeness, is unsurprising, since contemporary reading theory is based on a largely psychological account of how we make textual meaning, and Wollheim's visual theory is similarly one that is 'committed to a psychological account of pictorial meaning' (Wollheim 1987: 306). Reading – whether of a painted image or a written text – seemingly involves a dual engagement with the substance and the medium. The unease arises when we then ask whether this dual engagement of Wollheim's 'two-foldness' is, in fact, simultaneous. For what actually happens when we look at a painting and become aware of both the depicted subject-matter and the marked surface is that the mind shuttles rapidly back and forth between the two. As we noted earlier (Chapter 1), Gilbert Ryle has pointed out that 'we cannot attend twice at once' (1949: 158) but what the mind can do is to switch perspective with remarkable speed and facility. Is not Wollheim's 'twofoldness' more accurately described as 'bi-focalism'?

There is a lively debate among visual theorists on this question of simultaneity (Gombrich 1960: 4–5; Wollheim 1987: 104–5 and 360; Podro 1991: 184), which, given what has been argued in earlier chapters of this book about the reader's role in engaging with literature, assumes a greater importance than that of an academic footnote. For what is again at issue is the nature of the reader's response, only this time the focus of attention is a painting. What I wish to argue is that it is plausible to describe the reader's/viewer's response to the represented image in terms of the 'bisociated mind' (Koestler 1964/1975: 303; see Chapter 1) of the spectator, operating on the continuum of detachment and involvement as outlined in the discussion of the secondary world in Chapter 2. In effect, this is a middle position between that of Gombrich and Wollheim. The former denies the possibility of simultaneity, arguing on the basis of the well-known figure–ground reversals (duck/rabbit; vase/faces; young woman with a plumed hat/old woman with a shawl) that the viewer's attention alternates and that it is literally inconceivable to focus on both elements together. Where paintings are concerned this leads him to assume, in Michael Podro's words, that 'there's a psychological incompatibility between seeing the actual surface and seeing the scene depicted on it' (Podro 1991: 184). Wollheim, on the other hand, insists upon the unitary nature of 'twofoldness' as fundamental to visual competence: surface and scene are essentially part of the same phenomenon of aesthetic viewing. Yet, while it is easy to counter Gombrich's reliance upon figure–ground reversals because they comprise two homogeneous images, rather than the heterogeneity of surface and scene, it is unconvincing in the light of common experience to wrap up both aspects in a single enclosing concept which denies the mobility of imaginative participation and the variability of attention that the viewer customarily exhibits before a work of art.

Wollheim's twofoldness is that of the 'ideal viewer', rather similar to the 'ideal reader' who has appeared in literary theory from time to time (Culler 1975). By contrast, what real readers/viewers do is adopt a rather more pragmatic, maybe cavalier, role. Diané Collinson (1985: pp. 271–4) puts herself engagingly into the shoes of 'the ordinary spectator' strolling through an art gallery and invents a typical thought-track as a way of disentangling the elements that go to make up the aesthetic experience of viewing paintings. In a passage that recalls Iser's 'indeterminacy gaps' (1978: 170–9), Rosenblatt's concept of 'evocation' (1978; 1985: 39) and my methodological notion of 'introspective recall' (M. Benton *et al.* 1988: 26), Collinson says:

> Perhaps aesthetic experience is even better typified by the gaps between 'the ordinary spectator's' phrases; by the wordless moments when the spectator is poised in the act simply of apprehending the painting rather than when remarking on it. Indeed, if we think back to the remark 'Ah, that sunlit field', it is the 'Ah' more than 'that sunlit field' that reveals the sensuous immediacy of the aesthetic moment. For it is not an experience in which we formulate an intellectual judgement to the effect *that* a vision of a sunlit field has been wondrously depicted. Rather, we experience the vision for ourselves; we are admitted to the painter's point of view. It is a distinguishing mark of aesthetic experience that it is one of participating in, or inhabiting, the world of the picture. Most of the comments or remarks indicative of the experience are retrospective in that they are *about* it rather than a part *of* it.

This account seems to be consistent both with the responses that the students display in this and subsequent chapters of this book and also with the analysis of aesthetic response to literature that has been offered in earlier chapters. It invites us to consider aesthetic experience as 'participating in . . . the world of the picture' and, in so doing, adopts a stance for the viewer which is comparable to that of the reader who chooses to enter the secondary world of fiction. We can become 'lost' in a painting as we can in a poem or story, in the sense that we become absorbed *for a time* in the 'world' that is to be explored; but, as was argued in Chapter 2, absorption is a variable quality, not a stable state, and sooner or later

Figure 9.1 *Coming from Evening Church* (1830), by Samuel Palmer

the mind becomes more alert to the linguistic character of a text or the marked surface of a painting and, consequently, less alert to the invented world that is portrayed through these verbal and visual media. Moments later, the reader/viewer may become reabsorbed, and so continue to shuttle to and fro in what was termed earlier 'the dimension of psychic distance' (Chapter 2), experiencing varying degrees of involvement in and detachment from the world depicted in the work of art and varying degrees of critical or analytical insight into the ways in which the work is constituted.

Talking about a painting: *Coming from Evening Church*, by Samuel Palmer

Let us now eavesdrop upon these characteristics of representation and response in practice. Two sixteen-year-old GCSE students, Sarah and Susie, were looking at a colour slide of Samuel Palmer's painting *Coming from Evening Church* (1830) (Figure 9.1). They had been told nothing about Palmer nor seen any of his paintings before. The picture dates from his Shoreham years and is described by Raymond Lister (1985: plate 20) as '. . . one of Palmer's most numinous works, a vesper hymn in paint'.

The students spent a few minutes looking and silently formulating their own first impressions in note form. Then they decided to discuss their responses, adding to their notes where appropriate. The following sequence of extracts from this collaborative activity shows them moving in and out of the world of the painting, interpreting both details and overall theme and, in these first exchanges, orientating themselves in relation to what we can call 'the implied viewer'.

Extract 1

Susie: (*Writing*) We decided the sun was setting in the viewer's position.
Sarah: Behind the painter.
Susie: In the audience's . . . yeah, behind the painter . . . even though he's dead . . .
Sarah: To project the red colour.
Susie: Whereas the moon was rising.
Sarah: I said the overall painting is reddish and the moon is full and low in the sky.
Susie: I said it was earthy colours like really sort of rich red, yellow, green and brown. It's a real sort of harmony of earthy colours, isn't it?
Sarah: Yeah, it's very natural.
Susie: But you're sort of like misled by the naturalness of it, the colouring because it looks unnatural when you look at the detail of, like, the hills . . . they look very unnatural don't they? Sort of humpety bumpety, humpety bumpety.
Sarah: Yeah.

Susie: Like bubbles and the houses . . . see that house there – it looks sort of fat doesn't it? Fat and round and homely and you'd never, sort of, see houses like that around would you? It's quite an old painting isn't it? . . . looking at their dress . . . isn't it?

The first three utterances suggest the position of the implied viewer in complementary ways: Susie is conscious of her spectator role and talks in terms of the 'viewer' and the 'audience' and seems to have some difficulty in detaching herself from this immediacy to concede Sarah's description that the sunlight must be assumed to come from 'behind the painter' – 'even', as Susie says, 'though he's dead'! As they quickly realize, the light is a mixture of the dying sun and the rising moon, and this creates both an unearthly atmosphere and an ambiguous feeling when you inspect the details; as the girls put it, they are both 'natural' and 'unnatural'. It is this strange luminosity together with the arching trees that lead them a few moments later to identify the overall theme of the painting:

Extract 2

Susie: It's got to be a sort of mega religious intentions, hasn't it? . . . the way it's sort of a harmony of earthy colours and the way it's framed by those two trees up in the corner . . . They have them in the church so that, like, as you're walking into the church and saying how holy and earthy people we are . . . sort of thing . . . What are you going to say now?

Sarah: I was going to say the impression projected is religious and homely.

The light, the 'harmony of earthy colours', the tall Blakean trees that act as a frame within a frame all point to the 'religious and homely' atmosphere that Sarah jots down in her notes. There is an interesting shift of perspective, too, in the middle of Susie's remarks: when she first mentions the two framing trees she is clearly referring to the composition of the painting; her later comments indicate that in her mind's eye she has transferred the schematic outline of the framing arch into the conventional doorway arch of the traditional church. The metaphoric power of Palmer's painting is clearly evident here in her response – encouraged, no doubt, by the effect of the intricate leaf patterns where the trees meet to form the rough, cusped arch.

During the next few minutes they are note-making and discussing details of the 'ivy creeping everywhere' and the appearance of the hills, until they come to focus on the portrayal of the people. They agree about the sense of community but disagree about the technique of painting the faces of the individual figures.

Extract 3

Susie: (*Writing*) The painting is . . . portraying people as harmonious . . . by walking in procession together and symbolizing community.

Sarah: Yeah.

Susie: And it's really effective in that way, isn't it? And then, because they symbolize community life, it's framed by the woodlands, by the elements, by the sky, the wood, by nature . . . nature . . . I think the background for these people represents nature because it's so sort of naturally coloured and naturally textured and convincing.

Sarah: Yeah.

Susie: So idyllic . . . idyllic?

Sarah: Idealistic.

Susie: Idealistic . . . and they're sort of framed at the end by these lovely trees. There's not much detail in their faces is there?

Sarah: No, that's because the paint is so thick; [you] can't see the details in thick paint.

Susie: I know, but, like, perhaps it's significant that they don't have any sort of fine features in their faces because everyone's got . . . you know, when you're painting people you always want to put the eyes and the nose and the mouth to sort of like pick out the individuals, but because they don't want to pick out individuals they want to represent . . . anybody rather than somebody.
(*Pause*) I'm going to put something down about the faces because I think that's significant.

Sarah: What? About . . . they've haven't really got any . . .

Susie: H'mm.

Sarah: I don't think it is . . . because I just think it's the technique of the painter . . .

Susie: Look, you know when you're painting a picture . . . you start thinking of what everything you do represents and what you're trying to tell your audience . . . you're trying to prove to your audience . . .

Sarah: Yeah, I know, but the paint he's chosen means that the . . . his faces aren't very big. I mean, he's got eyes and mouth but he's not trying to make them look like anyone.

Susie: No, he's just got the sort of, like, fundamental things about people.

Sarah: Yeah, but he's not trying to make them look like anybody so it doesn't matter. He doesn't want them to look like people because they're not specific people – it's just a community of faces.

In commenting upon the serpentine procession of figures that takes the eye into the picture and leads it to the central icon of the church, the students focus not upon this formal element *per se* but upon its symbolic significance. Susie's first two utterances extend her line of thinking in the previous extract and suggest that she has sensed the way the composition situates the actual church within 'the church of nature'. There is a two-stage shift in the spectator's viewpoint: as we look at the leading couple in the procession pausing, as it were, under the arched doorway of the church of nature, the eye is then led along the processional aisle of the path they tread and up to the doorway of the actual church, situated in the elevated position of a natural altar, behind which the illuminated hills, the sky and the rising moon provide a dramatic backdrop like a stained-glass window. The symbolism and composition are perfectly harmonized: each of the girls' adjectives, 'idyllic' and 'idealistic', seems appropriate.

The discussion then turns to the absence of detail in the way the faces of the people have been painted. Representation and response are intimately related in these interchanges. Susie's concern is with the significance and intention of this aspect of representation; Sarah's approach is more painterly and alert to the constraints of technique and materials that the artist is using. Together they show an awareness of both the depicted scene and the marked surface as parts of a unified response to the painting, as their final remarks make clear. This is Wollheim's 'seeing-in' in action; 'twofoldness' is evident in Sarah's comments about 'the paint he's chosen' and 'a community of faces' in her final two utterances.

Near the end of their discussion the students concentrate upon the buildings, particularly the church.

Extract 4

Susie: Hey . . . that church being in the centre of the painting is very significant, isn't it? . . . Which . . . and like, there's a white light . . .
Sarah: Yeah, but it's very hidden by that house . . .
Susie: Yeah, I mean the spire . . . it's very white and it's very late in the evening isn't it?
Sarah: That's because it's the highest, isn't it?
Susie: Yes, but it's very significant-looking because, if you look at it, it's very dead in the centre isn't it?
Sarah: The lines of the construction are very . . .
(*Looking at the slide close up.*)
Susie: What's this building here?
Sarah: That's the rest of the church.
Susie: No, it isn't.
Sarah: Yes, it is.
Susie: Can you see this? There's a roof . . . I'll show you . . . it's like this . . .
Sarah: Is that a tree?
Susie: Another church? A sort of dome on the top . . . like the . . .
Sarah: Could just be a tree.
Susie: That? A tree?
Sarah: Yeah, yeah . . . look, that's a tree.
Susie: No it isn't – that's a building, isn't it? Or another tree . . . yeah. That's not a tree at all.
Sarah: It's not green, it's a brown tree . . . it's a round tree.

Again, the personal style of each student is apparent as, characteristically, Susie begins to interpret the significance of the central position of the spire, while

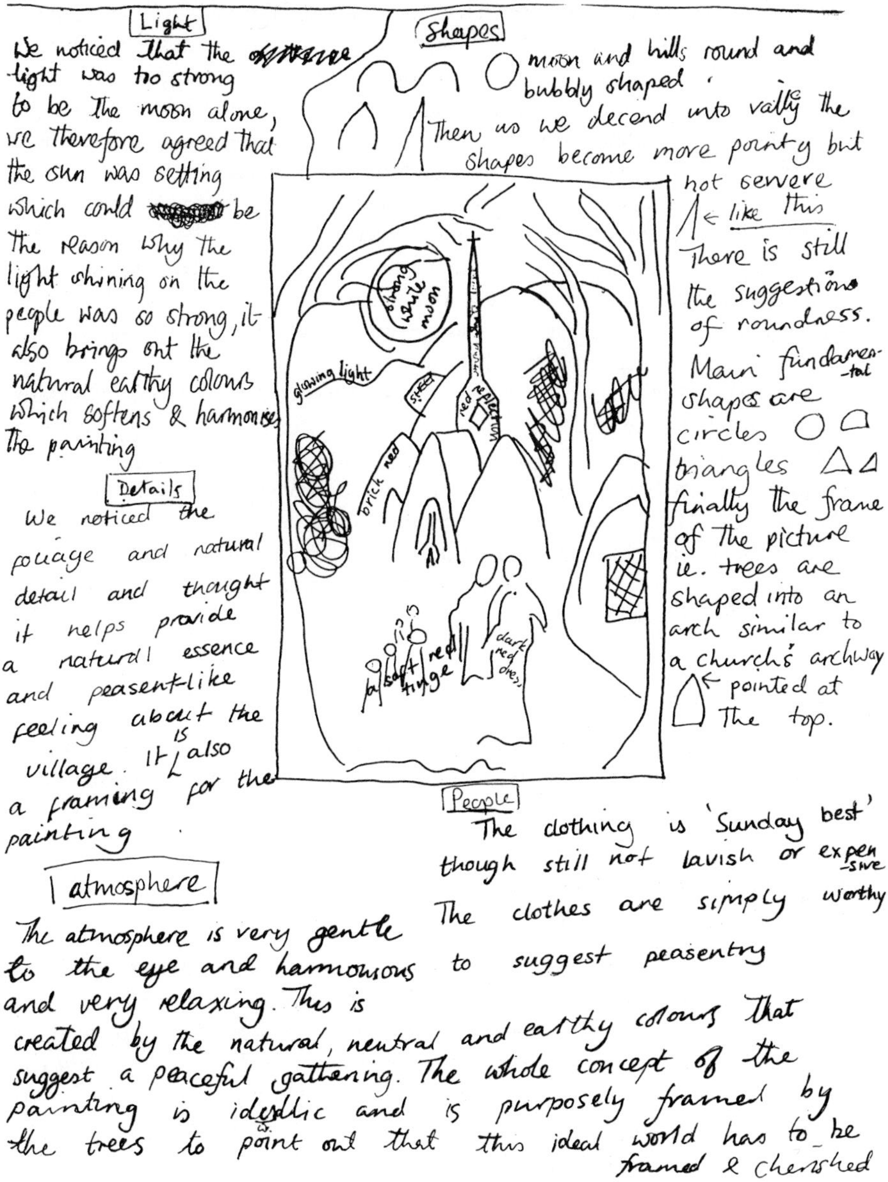

Light

We noticed that the light was too strong to be the moon alone, we therefore agreed that the sun was setting which could be the reason why the light shining on the people was so strong, it also brings out the natural earthy colours which softens & harmonises the painting

Shapes

moon and hills round and bubbly shaped.
Then as we decend into valley the shapes become more pointy but not severe like this
There is still the suggestions of roundness.
Main fundamental shapes are circles triangles
finally the frame of the picture ie. trees are shaped into an arch similar to a church's archway pointed at the top.

strong white moon
glowing light
steep
red reflection
brick red
pale soft red tinge
dark red dress

Details

We noticed the foliage and natural detail and thought it helps provide a natural essence and peasent-like feeling about the village. It is also a framing for the painting.

People

The clothing is 'Sunday best' though still not lavish or expensive
The clothes are simply worthy to suggest peasentry

atmosphere

The atmosphere is very gentle to the eye and harmonious and very relaxing. This is created by the natural, neutral and earthy colours that suggest a peaceful gathering. The whole concept of the painting is idyllic and is purposely framed by the trees to point out that this ideal world has to be framed & cherished

Figure 9.2 *Coming from Evening Church* (1830), by Samuel Palmer – students' annotated sketch

Sarah comments upon the technical construction of the image. They become understandably puzzled about just which of the depicted buildings are parts of the church. The group of steeply-gabled roofs, one with a sort of domed top as Susies remarks, contrasts markedly with the elongated spire which breaks the soft lines of the similarly domed hills behind. Palmer's overriding concern here with the composition of shapes rather than precise detail has the effect of drawing the viewers into a close scrutiny of this aspect of the image: is it a village building, a tree, the rest of the church or another church altogether? The issue remains inconclusive, just as the painting is indefinite; yet, there is no sense of frustration in the girls' remarks, rather a tacit understanding of the conventions of this sort of painting where the achievement of compositional harmony to express Palmer's pastoral vision is more important than fine detail.

As a means of making a final statement after this collaborative looking, talking and note-making, the students were invited to sketch an outline of the picture in the centre of the page and to arrange their comments on the light, the natural detail, colours, people and shapes around their sketch (Figure 9.2, from M. and P. Benton, 1990a: 53). This task enabled them to summarize their main ideas, an activity which learners do not often do naturally for themselves. It was not only useful by enjoyable and provided a satisfying closure to their experience of Samuel Palmer's painting.

Three phases of looking

In exploring some theoretical approaches to representation and response and observing how they work out in practice, we have essentially been asking three questions:

- What happens *to* your eye?
- What happens *behind* your eye?
- What happens *beyond* your eye?

The first concerns the viewer's *perception* of a painting, the means by which this object of contemplation is taken in. The second concerns the viewer's *conception* of a painting, the means by which it becomes lodged within the mind when the individual has taken possession of it. The third concerns the viewer's *construction* of meaning, the way in which an interpretation is formulated. Each takes us progressively further into the experience of looking at a painting. The process, as was suggested earlier (Chapter 8), is not unlike that of coming to terms with a poem. Indeed, not only are there many historical links between these 'sister arts' (Hagstrum 1958), but there are also many correspondences in contemporary literary and visual theory. A few of these connections will both conclude this chapter appropriately and, at the same time, relate it to Chapters 1 and 5 in the sections on fiction and poetry which share the common function of establishing the principles of aesthetic response upon which the subsequent discussions are based.

Central to the idea of representation is the ubiquitous 'conceptual image'. Gombrich (1962: 76) points out that all art originates in the human mind; it is conceptual, not something 'out there' in the visible world. This phenomenon is most easily seen in children's drawings, which are typically remote from representation, because children draw what they *know* and not what they *see*. He develops the notion of the conceptual image in terms that complement those of Iser and Rosenblatt:

> . . . the painter relies on our readiness to take hints, to read contexts, and to call up our conceptual image under his guidance. The blob in the painting by Manet which stands for a horse . . . [is] so cleverly construed that it evokes the image in us – provided, of course, we collaborate.
>
> (Gombrich 1962: 10)

There are three particular features of this collaboration between the reader/viewer and the poem/painting that are worth stressing, each of which relates, respectively, to one of the three key questions discussed above. The first, illuminating the viewer's perception, is what Gombrich calls '*guided projection*' and it finds its complement in Louise Rosenblatt's insistence that 'aesthetic reading' must honour the uniqueness of both the reader and the text. Speaking of impressionist painting, Gombrich (1962: 169) says that

> . . . the beholder must mobilize his memory of the visible world and project it into the mosaic of stokes and dabs on the canvas before him. It is here, therefore, that the principle of guided projection reaches its climax. The image, it might be said, has no firm anchorage left on the canvas . . . it is only 'conjured up' in our minds. The willing beholder responds to the artist's suggestion because he enjoys the transformation that occurs in front of his eyes . . . The artist gives the beholder increasingly 'more to do', he draws him into the magic circle of creation and allows him to experience something of the thrill of 'making' . . .

Rosenblatt (1938/70: 113), similarly, says that 'every time a reader experiences a work of art, it is in a sense created anew.' Sarah and Susie, too, show us, particularly in extracts 1 and 2 where they discuss the houses and the church, that re-creative reading involves making a synthesis of those elements within the reader's/viewer's own nature and those aspects of experience to which the text/painting actually refers.

Secondly, as in painting so in literature, the work of art contains 'indeterminacy gaps' (Iser) or 'incomplete images' (Gombrich 1962: 119) which, for readers/viewers, become spaces which we are required to fill. We feel the presence even of features we cannot see. The incompleteness of Palmer's depiction of one of the shapes leads to some lively exchanges between the two students about what they are looking at, as we have seen in extract 4. What we observe here is the two viewers' struggle with the second phase of looking outlined above – their efforts towards a conception of this detail. The pressure to complete their conception of that area of the painting is dictated by the degree of indeterminacy in the image. There are similar structured gaps in literary texts that, as Iser shows, draw the readers in and call upon them, in Barthes's sense, to become writers' – composers of their own virtual texts in response to the actual one.

Thirdly, crucial to the process of synthesizing all the diverse details and perspectives we experience when coming to terms with a text or painting is the operation of what Iser (1978: 119) calls '*the wandering viewpoint*', which is seen not only as a means of describing the way in which the reader is present in the text but also as fundamental to the third phase of reading paintings and poems – the construction of meaning. Moreover, Gombrich's influence in theorizing this aspect of aesthetic experience is acknowledged by Iser and invites us to extend its application into how we interpret visual as well as verbal art. Iser (1978: 119) writes:

> Here we have one of the basic elements of the reading process: the wandering viewpoint divides the text up with interacting structures, and these give rise to a grouping activity that is fundamental to the grasping of a text.
>
> The nature of this process is shown clearly by a remark of Gombrich's: 'In the reading of images, as in the hearing of speech, . . . it is the guess of the beholder that tests the medley of forms and colours for coherent meaning, crystallizing it into shape when a consistent interpretation has been found.

The 'grouping activity' which Iser mentions is supported by references to Frank Smith's *Understanding Reading* (1971), thus further aligning the ways in which readers and viewers make meaning. We have seen something of this procedure in the 'wandering viewpoint' of the two students as, for example, they move from colours, to the shape of hills, to the house, to the dress of the people, all within a few utterances (extract 1).

When we try to tease out the components that go to make up a unified process in order to understand that process better, there is always the danger that the parts do not add up to whole. Particularly in this area of aesthetic response to represented images, the three phases of perception, conception and construction of meaning may not cover that elusive but none the less real sense of delight that expresses and confirms the viewers' feeling of aesthetic pleasure. Diané Collinson's remarks quoted earlier suggest the same idea; so do Susie's comments, at the end of the taped discussion, when the students are reviewing their responses to Samuel Palmer's painting:

> It seems to be in a valley because of these huge hills and these hills make me laugh, they're like bubbles . . . so sort of unrealistic. And the way it's sort of framed . . .

Her enjoyment of the whole experience of looking at the painting is evident. Visual pleasure clearly derives from the interplay of exploring a recognizable scene and appreciating the artifice with which that scene is represented.

10 Reading paintings . . . reading poems

My general aims in this chapter are to explore the reading process in relation to the arts of painting and poetry and to argue the need for their greater integration in the classroom. I have four particular purposes:

- to show how, in practical classroom terms, some of the issues raised in the previous chapter can be developed;
- to give a sense of the range of available material and to indicate the engaging variety of teaching approaches that this rich and diverse resource opens up;
- to present, through a sequence of examples, the subtlety and complexity of the students' responses and, in doing so, to suggest how a programme of study might be developed which takes students into increasingly sophisticated readings of pairs of paintings and poems; and
- to summarize the elements of response that viewers/readers customarily display to paintings and poems and to indicate the implications for teaching.

Since an earlier part of this book has been devoted exclusively to poetry, the emphasis here will be upon paintings. All of these are examples of representational art, not only because these appear to have a more ready acceptance with school students, but also because such paintings are overwhelmingly the ones about which poets choose to write.

Getting started: paintings and poems in the classroom

Nothing reminds us more painfully that reproductions are not art than to compare the richness of Samuel Palmer's *Coming from Evening Church* as it hangs in The Tate Gallery with the indistinct, lifeless, black-and-white version in Chapter 9. Curiously, a better colour reproduction may be even more misleading simply because it is so persuasive and because reproduced images are now so much a part of our culture that we take them for granted. It is worth reminding ourselves and our classes of the uniqueness of original paintings compared with their ubiquitous appearances in books, slides and postcards and, with the more famous images, their uses as advertisements, T-shirt motifs or carrier-bag designs. The commercialization of art, of course, operates at every level, from the saleroom auctions of originals for huge prices, to the art-gallery shop selling lapel buttons proclaiming 'Van Gogh lives!' In itself, the status and value we place upon originals and reproductions can provide an interesting source of debate with older classes, maybe as part of Media Studies; the opening chapter of Berger (1972) remains an excellent starting-point. The particular point that needs to be clear when beginning work with painting, however, is the nature of the image the class is viewing. Berger identifies the issue sharply (1972: 31):

> Original paintings are silent and still in a sense that information never is. Even a reproduction hung on a wall is not comparable in this respect for in the original the silence and stillness permeate the actual material, the paint, in which one follows the traces of the painter's immediate gestures. This has the effect of closing the distance in time between the painting of the picture and one's own act of looking at it. In this special sense all paintings are contemporary.

The point can be brought home in various ways:

- Ask the class to examine a good colour reproduction of a painting carefully, and to note what they see of the 'marked surface'. Can they see any paint, any brush-strokes, any cracks – or just coloured dots? It should become clear that reproductions can only show a flat pattern of colours and not the texture of an original.
- As part of the gallery visit, ask students to make a close comparison of, say, a postcard of a painting with the actual painting, perhaps listing some of their findings on the back of the card.
- Ask students to write down the sizes of the original paintings as they look at a varied selection of reproductions in, say, book or poster form. Then get them to visualize these actual sizes, maybe by discussing the best place in the school for these originals to hang.

Apart from helping to make the class more visually alert, such activities signal that looking at pictures needs time. Paintings reveal themselves through a sort of dialogue, one that as viewers we initiate. It is important to help students realize that, just as we can browse through a book or magazine, so we can browse in an art gallery; but that to get beyond the glazed, supermarket looking that often characterizes gallery visits requires the effort of getting used to talking about paintings. As the two students showed us in the previous chapter, finding words to describe and analyse pictures is the best way to progress from the passive looking, usually fleeting and often frustrating, to the active role of the viewer who is seeing-in to a painting and beginning to interpret what is found there.

Working with paintings in the classroom is not difficult, provided you have suitable resources to hand. Slides can be a mixed blessing: apart from the practical problems over the availability of machinery and blinds which still prevail in many classrooms, what slides gain by their immediacy of impact can be offset by the distance between the image and the viewer. The procedures and classroom layout that so often accompany the use of slides usually imply a teacher-directed lesson where controlled attention on the single image is the aim. This is appropriate in some circumstances, and clearly, as with students able to work on their own like the two quoted in the previous chapter, slides have their place in pair/group work; but, in many cases, it is both a more feasible and a more flexible arrangement to work with a selection of posters, mounted cut-outs from magazines or brochures, and postcards. These reproductions seem to generate a more ready rapport with students – partly, no doubt, because the viewers are often choosing from a selection, but also because there is a greater sense of ownership when you can handle the picture in front of you. Books of paintings are obviously useful but have limited flexibility; however, there are three books of paired paintings and poems which are especially suitable in the present context: *With a Poet's Eye*, ed. Pat Adams (1986); *Voices in the Gallery*, ed. Dannie and Joan Abse (1986); and *Double Vision*, ed. Michael and Peter Benton (1990a).

Every teacher will have his or her own enthusiasms for particular paintings, and it is right to develop these. Two paintings that I have found especially engaging as 'starters' are:

- Manet's *Bar at the Folies-Bergère* – see Farr *et al.* (1987) for information and ideas;
- Arcimboldo's *Fantastic Heads* – see *Arcimboldo Poster Book* (1987) for information and background.

Pairings of paintings and poems, such as are found in the three books mentioned earlier, can be introduced in a variety of ways. Handling these visual and verbal materials needs care, since clearly the relationship between student, painting and poem is not a neat triangular one. In most instances the painting has not been constrained by the poem, but the poem has by the painting; and much depends upon the method and order via which the student approaches the two works of art. Generally, in order to accommodate this asymmetrical relationship between the reader, painting and poem, it is best to start with the painting, so that the viewer's responses are not closed down by those of the poet.

Some pairings that work well in the early stages of exploring the two arts are:

- Henry Wallis's *Chatterton*, 1856, (The Tate Gallery) with John Ash's poem 'Poor Boy: Portrait of a Painting' (in *Double Vision*, pp. 76–81).
- Van Gogh's *Cornfield with Crows*, 1890 (The Rijksmuseum, Amsterdam) and the group of poems by B. C. Leale and three school students in *Double Vision*, pp. 39–41.
- Uccello's *St George and the Dragon*, late fifteenth century, (The National Gallery), coupled with U. A. Fanthorpe's 'Not My Best Side' (in *Double Vision*, pp. 30–3).
- John Everett Millais's *The Boyhood of Raleigh*, 1870, (The Tate Gallery) and Roger McGough's accompanying poem in *Double Vision*, pp. 19–20.

Developing responses: a sense of time and space

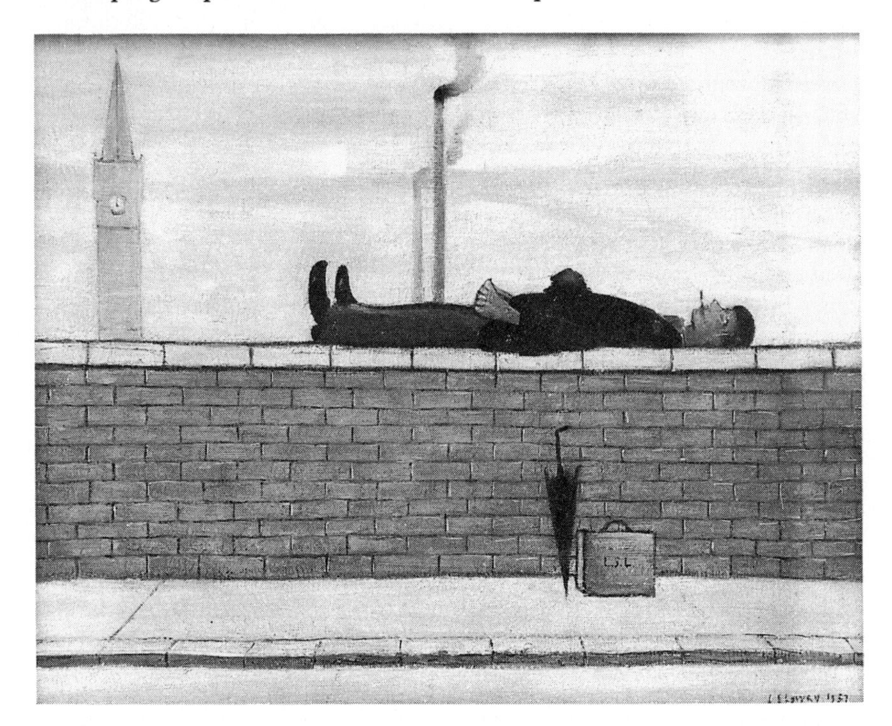

Figure 10.1 *Man Lying on a Wall* (1957), by L. S. Lowry

Man Lying on a Wall

Homage to L. S. Lowry

You could draw a straight line from the heels,
Through calves, buttocks and shoulder blades
To the back of the head: pressure points
That bear the enormous weight of the sky.
Should you take away the supporting structure
The result would be a miracle or
An extremely clever conjuring trick.
As it is, the man lying on the wall
Is wearing the serious expression
Of popes and kings in their final slumber,
His deportment not dissimilar to
Their stiff, reluctant exits from this world
Above the shoulders of the multitude.

It is difficult to judge whether or not
He is sleeping or merely disinclined
To arrive punctually at the office
Or to return home in time for his tea.
He is wearing a pinstripe suit, black shoes
And a bowler hat: on the pavement
Below him, like a relic or something
He is trying to forget, his briefcase
With everybody's initials on it.

Michael Longley

L. S. Lowry's *Man Lying on a Wall* (Figure 10.1) (Salford Art Gallery) and Michael Longley's accompanying poem (Abse 1986) make bigger demands on secondary-school students. Lowry's painting originated from an incident when he was travelling by train and saw a tired business man lie down on a wall in this unconventional manner. It might be 'read' of course in many ways: as a jokey bit of phallic symbolism; as an old-fashioned theatre backdrop. Or, as Julian Spalding (1979) comments, having noted Lowry's initials on the briefcase,

> The man's hat lies on his chest. Could it be his last rites? The spire points up, the black umbrella points down. Has Lowry in fact laid himself to rest . . . in his own industrial landscape?

Or, we might speculate, could it be simply that Lowry is acknowledging his own description of himself as 'one of the laziest men I know'? Or, again, with Michael Longley, we might translate the visual image into verbal ones, seeing in the man's position and expression the conjuror's art of illusion, an effigy on a tomb in church or a body borne in a funeral procession; or be tempted, as the poet is, into guessing who this man is and what is he doing there. Both painting and poem are inscribed with a sense of time and space. It is interesting to discover how students operate within these perspectives.

How does the eye move round the painting? Where do we focus? Which details do we notice and in what order do we notice them? How do the parts build up into a sense of the whole picture? A Year-10 GCSE class followed the approach to this pairing outlined in *Double Vision*, pp. 10–13, which invites viewers/readers to map their responses to the visual/verbal texts and to make a diagram of them as Sara did with Robert Frost's 'The Lockless Door' (see Chapter 8). Clearly, I can give only the briefest indication of some rich and provocative responses. First Sasha (Figure 10.2).

Setting, viewpoint, story, mood, style – these are the sorts of things that most of the students commented on. Initial reactions were often puzzled. As Jane put it, 'At first the picture seemed bare and meaningless, the objects appeared as if they had been scattered across the scene and nothing made any sense to me.' The invitation to map their route through the details and to reflect on their first and subsequent responses opened up the painting, and the majority of students moved through such early puzzlement to record some telling observations.

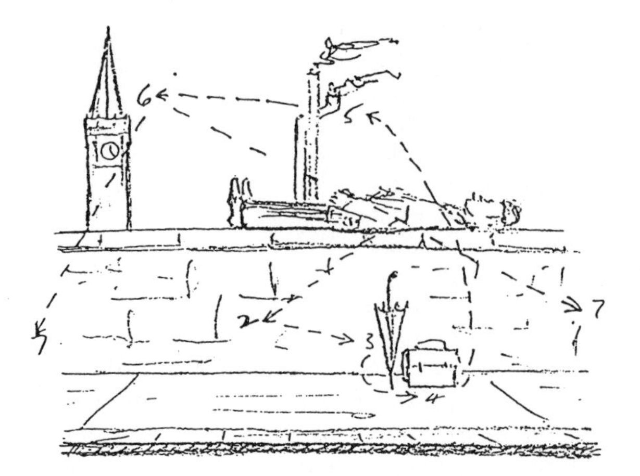

1. I thought maybe he was drunk. I wondered why he was lying down. Who is he?
2. Maybe it's the wall of a bridge.
3/ It looks like he is a business man by the
4. black Umbrella and the brief case.
5. Are they chimmneys of a factory? Maybe the scene is in a factory
6 Big Ben? Perhaps this is in london or a big city
7. How long does the pavement and wall go on for each way

Is the man tired, dead, drunk, bored, meditating, waiting for something, resting. Where has he just come from? Where is he going to? What is the signicance of the church tower and chimneys? Maybe to show the man is high up, level with the roof tops so I think prehaps it is a bridge. Or are they also to show the setting of the picture (an industrial city?) Is the man smoking - this would mean he is not asleep or dead. Does he wear a hat?
Clock says 4 pm.
The man is himself (the artist)

Figure 10.2 *Man Lying on a Wall* (1957), by L. S. Lowry – a student's diagram and notes

Not so with the poem! Although jotting round a poem before discussion was a more familiar activity, the students generally reacted in a critical or dismissive way towards Michael Longley's poem. Perhaps this was simply a result of it coming second: the poem had deliberately been held back for fear that it might 'close down' the painting for the students. The reverse appeared to have happened. Ian's assessment in his final piece of writing captures this widespread feeling, as well as raising a more general issue of image-reading. Here is the first page of his essay.

> *Comparison Between Michael Longley (Author of 'Man Lying on a Wall') and My Opinion on the painting 'Man Lying on a Wall' by L. S. Lowry.*
>
> My immediate reaction to the painting was to the whole simplicity of the painting, or you may even call it a sketch. Unfortunately I feel that the author has made more of the picture than necessary. Michael Longley has tried to complicate and see more into the drawing than there is there. By doing this he has spoiled the best aspect of the picture that makes it special. We all know that L. S. Lowry is famous for his simple paintings. I feel Lowry was trying to show how unimportant and simple man is to the well being of this world. The poem has complicated this thought and I think ruined the whole image of the painting that a reader of the poem should have. The poem should have been written in short simple lines with verses of three lines each a maximum, this structure would immediately give the reader an idea of the simplicity.
>
> Leaving the structure of the poem and moving to the content I at last see some of the simplicity being passed through the words. The words are easy to understand almost in a childish way which is the way I think of the picture. The picture has definitely got a childish feel about it. The larger than life hands as he tried to cram all the fingers in a small space, the smoke has a harsh mark of the pencil not sensitive as the great masters would do. There is hardly any perspective, the spire could be built on top of the wall, it is only our knowledge that leads us to believe that the spire is in the background.

Ian's perceptive remark in this last sentence suggests that he would be quite comfortable with Herbert Read's (1943) reminder:

> We do not always realize that the theory of perspective, developed in the fifteenth century, is a specific convention; it is merely one way of describing space and has no absolute validity.

What can we say so far about this asymmetrical relationship between painting, poem and student, particularly in respect of the ways time and space are represented? Clearly, the students are alert to the entwined narratives of the painting, the poem and their own interpretive response, and to the different vantage points from which these stories are constructed. They are aware, too, of the deliberate placing of objects in space and, whether, as Ian shows, they feel the poet has read the painter's use of space correctly. How do these temporal and spatial elements interrelate?

In representational art, the notion of a painting as a 'frozen moment' is a commonplace. The viewer, therefore, not only perceives the spatial qualities presented, but is tempted into interpreting the temporal significances implied *around* this 'moment'. Conversely, a poem exists, as Rosenblatt (1978: 12) tells us, 'as an event in time': however short the duration might be, our initial perceptions extend in time, even if only for a few seconds. The reader, therefore, not only perceives the temporal development of the verbal string during reading, but is also moved to interpret the spatial significances *around* the words laid on the page.

Put another way, by giving ourselves 'real' time (by 'taking our time') before a painting, an inevitable 'narrative' time asserts itself as we use fictional forms to describe what we see. And, by giving ourselves 'real' time with a poem, the spaces around the words on the page become ones we inhabit mentally as readers, to 'look at' the text, as it were, from various viewpoints.

Two other pairings of paintings and poems which invite exploration of this theme are Bonnard's *The Bowl of Milk* (The Tate Gallery) with John Loveday's accompanying poem in *With a Poet's Eye*, pp. 74–5, and Paul Nash's *Totes Meer (Dead Sea)* (The Tate Gallery) with Anna Adams's two-part poem in *Voices in the Gallery*, pp. 132–3.

By working with students on paintings and poems that themselves handle their subject-matter with an overt concern for questions of time and space in how they represent their themes, we are achieving a double benefit. Firstly, in practical terms, we are enabling students to learn to look longer at paintings and dwell longer on words. It is the desire of every gallery curator to make us pause and then stay for a time before a painting, to give it more than a casual glance; first encounters with new poems, too, however engaging the initial impact, can often seem like reading in some opaque new language. Using writing to think with in the form of jottings helps extend the time we give, it helps to keep the aesthetic experience central and enables meanings to be evoked, and it helps us to take possession of the works of art and make them our own. Secondly, in the development of students' responses, we are involving them with the fundamental issues of representation in the ways in which these abstractions of space and time are located in particular images and words. Through such means, abstract ideas become more manageable; they can be explored in a specific context in two complementary media. The effect is to increase the potential for students' understanding of how the two arts operate and thus to build confidence and deepen their abilities in reading paintings and poems.

Integrating responses: a poem reading a painting

With the following pairing we start from issues of picture-space and picture-time, but the main concern here is to illustrate not only how student responses can achieve a high degree of sophistication, but also how students' readings of painting and poem become so finely integrated that it is clear that their responses to both art forms here mutually illuminate each other in ways that could not happen if studying paintings and poems remain separate activities. The painting

Figure 10.3 *The Siesta* (1876), by J. F. Lewis

(Figure 10.3) is John Frederick Lewis's *The Siesta*, 1876, (The Tate Gallery); the poem is by Gareth Owen (in *Double Vision*, pp. 27–9).

The Siesta, by J. F. Lewis: a feminist critique

Lewis lived for over a decade in the Middle East and his paintings became popular in Victorian England, earning him the nickname 'the harem painter', due to his predilection for painting flimsily clad women set in luxurious, exotic interiors. In terms of the previous discussion this is an interesting painting to use to explore viewers' responses, since the subject-matter is finely balanced in its space–time relationships. There is no depiction of movement: the repose of the siesta is pervasive. No breeze disturbs the curtains; no petals litter the table: all is stillness, heat, lassitude. Lewis has organized his canvas space to enable us to feel the warm air, the shaded light of the interior, the mildly heady atmosphere of this 'secondary world' made of colour, line and mass. Yet it *is* a siesta, not an 'empty' room. What is shown is but a momentary state, but the question of time is also *painted into the composition* – the time of day, of year, of the age of the woman, of the life of the flowers, . . . Even with a picture such as this, without an obvious narrative, reading the painting involves us in an act of translation – rendering its spatial relationships into temporal ones. Yet Lewis was not known as 'the harem painter' for nothing, and, plainly, the picture demands to be read in another light.

Feminist criticism, which approaches painting as a 'discourse of gender difference' in Nochlin's (1991: 13) phrase, urges an uncompromising view of *The Siesta*. Nochlin goes on, 'representations of women in art are founded upon and serve to reinforce indisputably accepted assumptions held by society in general . . . about men's power over, superiority to, difference from, and necessary control of women'. From this ideological standpoint it is hard to regard *The Siesta* as anything but visual rape by Lewis and, by extension, by the male art establishment of mid-Victorian England. There is no doubt that the image of woman as the transcendent object of art (and, by implication, of the male gaze) became a dominant feature of nineteenth-century painting. Painting the female nude became increasingly popular with Lewis and his contemporary male artists, and female figures, even when clothed as here, were often portrayed 'asleep, unconscious or unconcerned with mortal things', devices calculated to allow 'undisturbed and voyeuristic enjoyment of the female form'. The phrases are those of Parker and Pollock (1981: 116) who, speaking in general terms about the 'painted ladies' of nineteenth-century art, say:

> Woman is present as an image, but with the specific connotations of body and nature, that is passive, available, possessable, powerless. Man is absent from the image but it is his speech, his view, his position of dominance which the images signify.
>
> (p. 116)

As they go on to mention, the woman's status as the object of the male viewer outside the painting is sometimes reinforced by the gaze of a subordinate male onlooker inside the painting. There is no such figure in *The Siesta*, but the point is worth recording in view of the narrative stance that, as we shall see presently, Gareth Owen adopts in his poem.

Given a general sense of the atmosphere of the painting and the cultural assumptions that invest it, what catches the eye about the composition? The feeling of enclosure is strong, created both by the visible right angles of the carpet and of the sofa on which the woman reclines and by the implicit corner of the room behind her. The folds of the curtains are suggested partly by vertical lines but also by the distortion of the right angles and outlines of the screen behind these hangings. The brown sofa is scrappily sketched, having the effect of merely surrounding the figure rather than bringing her forward, as if holding the woman in represented space to save her from fading into the local background. This tendency to merge the figure and the furniture reflects the subject of the painting and is also seen in the way the lower folds of the green dress on the woman's left side melt indistinctly into the sofa and, on her right side, fall like liquid over the edge of the low dais to the floor. The image above the waist, particularly her face, is more clearly defined as she reclines before us, supposedly oblivious of the world, actually on display. She is the passive, vulnerable image about which Parker and Pollock write, here given a suggestive colouring by the red folds of the underskirt and the red lips against the paleness of her bare arm and bosom.

This contrast carries over into the three objects Lewis chooses to place in the room – the flowers, the fan and the bowl of fruit. The erotic symbolism of the fan, its red-tipped handle enclosed in an amorphous white shape, is unmistakable. Clearly this object is not for immediate practical use since it is out of reach, its handle towards the viewer not the viewed, and depicted non-naturalistically in space against a dark background, maybe of a cushion. The fruit, four peaches behind which are some black grapes, is similarly out of the woman's reach and highlighted to suggest sensuous luxury not food. The flowers are perhaps the most extraordinary feature of the whole composition: three decorated vases, the tallest with a mixture of roses, poppies and lilies; the nearest with a small posy of roses; and the vase in the rear with a single spray of lilies. Together they make a dishevelled collection, but it is their dominance that is so striking: the main vase of flowers is roughly two and half times the size of the table on which it stands. Even allowing for the foreshortened perspective, this exaggerated presentation invites the viewer to interpret their symbolism in the language of flowers: roses are for love, poppies for sleep and dreams, lilies for purity; while collectively they signify transience. These details, like the rest of the composition, conspire to produce an image whose fantasy potential is deliberate and obvious.

Students' initial responses to the painting

What do secondary-school students make of *The Siesta*? Four GCSE students – Sarah and Susie (whom we have met before), Ben and Rachel – followed the procedure below. The students knew nothing of Lewis, nor had they seen Gareth Owen's poem before. The procedure was as follows:

About 25 minutes

- Students looked at a slide of the painting in silence and recorded their initial responses without discussion.
- They read through the poem twice, discussed in pairs and made notes on poem-sheets while talking.
- Then they made lists of the eight individuals or groups mentioned in the poem, and what is made *explicit* about them.

About 45 minutes

- The pairs were rearranged and the students compared lists and discussed what was *implicit* in poem/painting.
- The pairs joined up to become a group discussion.

What did the four students notice about the painting according to their initial jottings? There appear to be five interrelated concerns which, to a greater or lesser degree, they all comment upon: colours, symbolic details, the setting, the woman's pose and, finally, the implied story.

Ben is the most explicit about the importance of *colour*: 'Colouring is a major factor in the painting, used to pronounce [sic] various items the artist wants to.' He, like the others, notes how the eye is caught by the reds and oranges of the flowers, the dress and the woman's mouth; others, too, comment on the peaceful browns and greens creating a 'shadowy and rich' atmosphere (Sarah), or 'bright and carefully applied colours . . . [that] suggest richness and style' (Susie).

Details, too, are 'purposely arranged and the patterns are quite feminine to perhaps complement the woman i.e. flowers, vases, rich materials etc.' (Susie). Rachel comments on the 'mega detail' and notices the latticework patterns on 'the green drapes, sofa and floor'. The fan, the food and other details are also mentioned; but the ones that assume an emblematic significance are the flowers and the dress. The poppies and roses, with their overtones of sleep and love, are mentioned by both Ben and Sarah as an 'important part of the painting', suggestive of qualities with which the painter wishes to invest the central figure. The dress is 'long and loose' (Susie) and 'heavy not summery' (Sarah); 'she's overdressed' (Rachel), and three of the four comment on the implications of the bright red underskirt and 'why the artist has shown so much of it' (Ben).

Understandably, the *setting* is a puzzle. There are sufficient clues in the details, the nature of the light and the title to suggest a hot climate, but where? Ben opts for Spain, even though, he notes, the woman does not look Spanish; Rachel suggests France rather than England; Sarah is unspecific, content with the peaceful siesta atmosphere. Susie's remarks show insight both into the picture and into the processes of image-reading. She notices 'the architecture is very Islamic, a sort of Eastern promise; the window frames are arched and curved and look very similar to a mosque's windows.' Yet, while she holds in mind a literal sense of place, 'perhaps somewhere where there is Arabic architecture', she also feels the theatricality of the setting, implying her sense of the picture as a stage or film set. This dualism – the search for a literal analogue and the awareness of a staged illusion – indicates how responses to settings have both painterly and narrative dimensions. For where the comments on colour and details are predominantly painterly, those on the position and person of the woman move in a narrative direction.

The woman's *pose* evokes comment from all four students. 'The way she is lying portrays heat and extreme fatigue – from what?' (Ben). 'Her pose is ladylike but dramatic' (Sarah). Rachel sees the figure as a 'voluptuous sleeping beauty'. Susie gives a more detailed impression: 'the woman sleeping looks and feels theatrical. With her hand placed beside her face and the whole of her face looking towards the painter, almost presenting herself to her audience like a film star.' The students' language here shows them edging towards narrative. Ben's question implies a story, and, in different ways, the girls' comments suggest that they interpret the figure as part of a dramatic tableau.

The further move towards *storying* is apparent in three of the four students' initial responses. Sarah simply comments that the woman is 'the only character' and maintains a more painterly view of the composition, noting that the 'woman does not stand out, she blends with the furniture.' By contrast, Ben and Susie speculate about whether the woman is promiscuous; and Ben goes on to suggest a possible 'broken relationship', adding 'the way she lies is as if she is in a pose waiting for someone.' Rachel expresses the 'frozen moment' of a narrative succinctly: 'Is everyone else just out of the picture . . . looks like there should be other people in the garden? . . . Has something just happened?'

The range of comments shows the students reading the painting as a composition where colour, line, mass and the arrangement of details cohere to form an image in space which, in turn, evokes an interpretation cast in narrative terms. While there is no explicit criticism of the way the artist has presented the image of the woman, there are plenty of indications that they have felt the underlying sexuality of the picture and have sensed that this woman is 'on show'. The stance that Gareth Owen adopts compounds these views of the painting as, in the guise of his narrator, he takes on the role of the fantasizing onlooker.

*'**Siesta**', by Gareth Owen: an approach through narratology*

First, let us concentrate on how the poem 'reads' the picture, before proceeding to hear how the students responded to both works of art.

Siesta

Each day at this same hour
He comes to her
His lady of the afternoons.
Behind closed lids she hears the whispering brush strokes
Gathering in the light, the windows and her sleeping form. 5
Her countenance is often in his dreams
But these are things not spoken of.
Outside the room where all this happens
In a splash of sunlight by the kitchen door
A maid trades amorous gossip with the gardener's boy 10
While shelling peas into her widespread lap:
A petal falls, someone puts out washing
And in the orchard among the oranges
Her husband, whose idea it was,
Tends to his bees, his face inside a net. 15
'I'm working on your mouth,' the painter tells her.
She does not know his christian name.
Her shut lids tremble. Just so
She used to close her eyes in childhood
Feigning sleep or death 20
Then open them in sudden laughter

To see her father's great moon face
Filling the everywhere:
Then later he was further off
And later still an absence 25
Like a place she took her heart to ache in.
Remembering this, she feels herself
Absorbed into the room
And in the darkness there
Beyond the limits of herself 30
Senses the painter with his canvas gone away
And lines of curious, reverential strangers
Filing past the open door
To gaze on her
Like one already dead. 35

Jerome Bruner (1986: 12) has argued that story must construct two landscapes simultaneously: the landscape of action and the landscape of consciousness. In order to explore how the poem reads the painting and to show how these two landscapes are related in the text, we need to draw some narratological distinctions. Genette's (1980: 27) formulation is the classic one. He 'unpacks' the concept of narrative into three meanings, distinguishing them as *story*, *narrative* and *narrating*. The story ('*histoire*') is the signified or narrative content; the narrative ('*récit*') is the signifier or discourse, the narrative text itself; narrating is the action of producing the narrative. Crudely, the story is 'the what', the narrative is 'the how' and the narrating is 'the telling'.

So here, a narrator tells us a story surrounding the painting of a woman (narrating); he presents a discourse (narrative); and his discourse represents events some of which take place before and after the narrative (story). Both the double time-structuring ('story-time' and 'discourse-time') and the two landscapes (of 'action' and of 'consciousness') can be displayed diagrammatically (Figure 10.4).

Time is represented by the woman's life-line, the solid part between the arrows showing 'discourse-time' – the period depicted in the poem – within the overall 'story-time', the chronological series of events in her life. Part of the beauty of the poem is the impression it gives of the way the landscape of consciousness, and the tenses we use to express it, are apprehended in moments of tranquillity. The woman shifts from present to past to future events in a series of superimposed images that is appropriate to a person in repose. The events in the woman's history are as follows:

1 As a child the woman enjoys playing a game with her father in which she feigned sleep or death; her antics were a source of intimate pleasure for father and daughter.
2 'Later' (adolescence?) their early intimacy changes to become a more adult separation; this is symbolized by a shifting perspective from a 'close-up' image

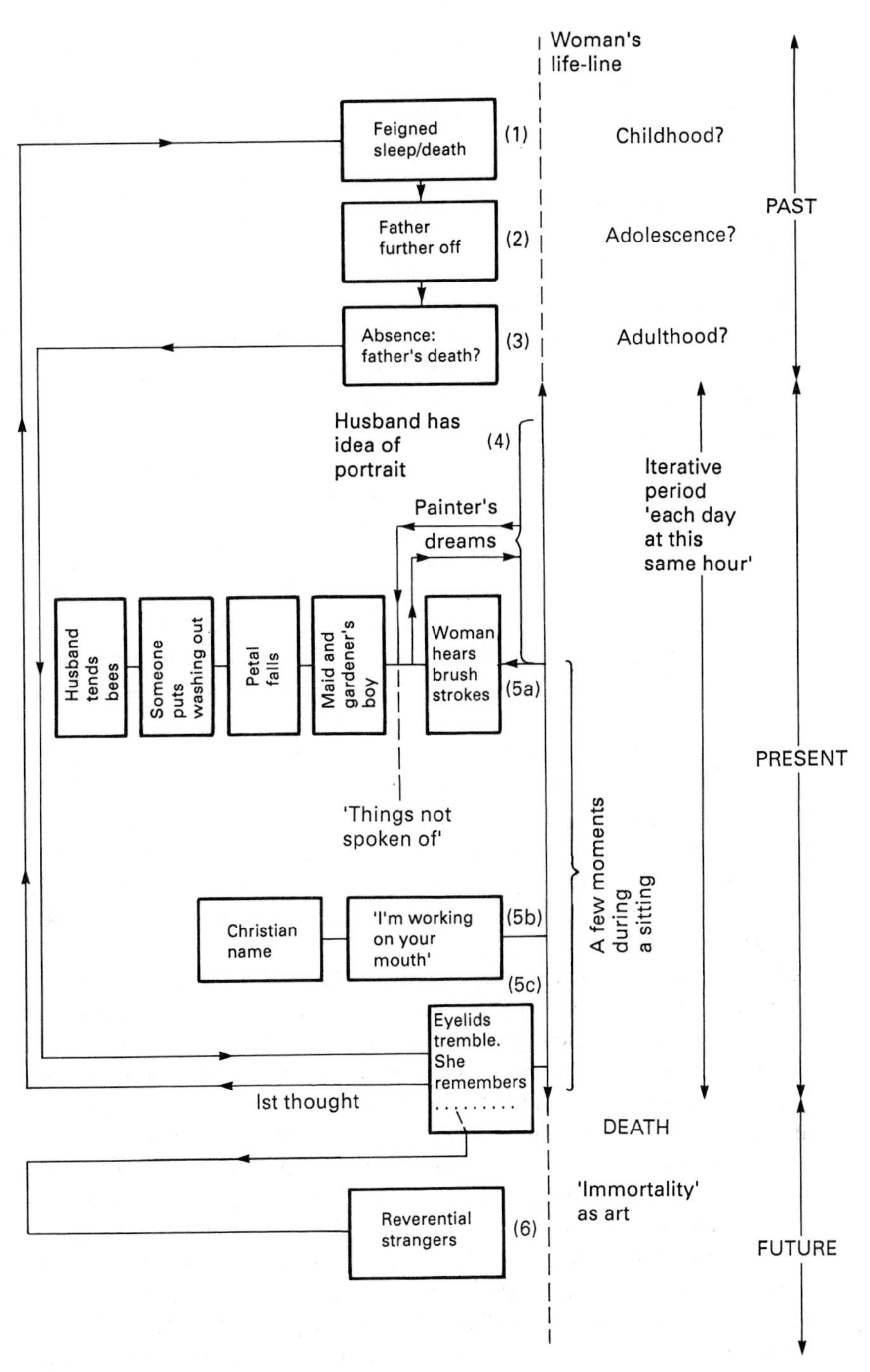

Figure 10.4 A narratological analysis of '*Siesta*', by Gareth Owen

of her father's face filling her entire vision to a 'middle-distance' image where the entire form is in view.

3 The 'distance' becomes an absence (father's death?) as further time passes. The woman recalls the absence frequently, and the loss is painful to her. The 'visits' that the woman takes to this period of time with its accompanying heartache are imaged by the omniscient narrator in terms of a place to which she goes.
4 At an unspecified point later, her husband suggests she has her portrait painted. This suggestion is of a different status from the other events in that it is the only one outside the iterative present that is more than a memory.
5 During the iterative period when the painter calls daily to continue with his work, three separate moments in time are captured.
   (a) In the first, which implicitly occurs some days into the work, the woman in her sleeping pose hears the brush-strokes of the painter: there is a suggestion that at this moment, as often before, the painter is aware of the all-pervasive effect that her countenance has upon his consciousness; the narrator observes that he says nothing about this. Simultaneously, outside, the maid and the gardener's boy trade 'amorous gossip', a petal falls, someone puts out washing and her husband tends to his bees.
   (b) Moments later during this sitting, the painter tells the woman he is working on her mouth; and she realizes that she does not know his christian name.
   (c) As her eyelids tremble, she recalls the similar pose of feigned sleep in 1 and this in turn prompts her to remember 2 and 3.

Here, then, we are closing in on the *poem's* 'frozen moment', but, as yet, there are three moments in time, all in one 'sitting', in which the whole landscape of consciousness is unfolded – primarily that of the woman but with hints at the state of mind of the painter and the husband through the interpolations of the omniscient narrator.

6 As a consequence of the combined memories 1, 2 and 3, the woman imagines the future, with this moment's feigned sleep/siesta captured on the painter's canvas for strangers to view. The mock sleep/death has been transformed into a 'reality' which, paradoxically, is a painter's illusion. It is this transformation that finally focuses us upon the 'frozen moment' of the poem; the idea that it encapsulates is a familiar one – the ability of art to capture a changing reality in relative permanence. The art of this particular illusion is rather like the well-known figure/ground pictures mentioned in Chapter 9, where we cannot see both images simultaneously. It is carried out with cunning 'sleight of language' in lines 29–30. Here, having lulled us into the plausibility of his narrative ('the landscape of action' in Bruner's phrase), Owen effects a slick transformation. His narrative illusion of following the thought-track of the woman is maintained to the end as she imagines herself transformed into a painting; yet, simultaneously, the final four lines project her thoughts and ours

into the future when the canvas is completed and she is fixed, 'like one already dead', as a painted image to be viewed by 'lines of curious, reverential strangers'. In the 'landscape of action', the order in which these events is recorded in the text is out of sequence, reflecting the 'time-free' nature of thought. In effect, the style of the poem embodies the quality of thought itself, rather than merely describing it.

The density and subtlety of this narrative contribute in large measure to the beauty of the poem. The most straightforward way to involve students with the text is to have them work in pairs on two tasks: firstly, to list the eight individuals or groups of people mentioned in the poem and what we know about them; and, secondly, to construct a time-line of the woman's life from the information given or implied in the poem. Both activities send them back inside the poem to look at that interior painting that Gareth Owen's words create in the mind's eye.

Students' final discussion of the painting and the poem

What did the four students make of the paired painting/poem? You will recall that, after their initial individual responses to the painting, they worked in pairs. They read the poem, annotated it and listed the explicit and implicit details about the people mentioned in the text. The final group discussion shows them moving easily between reading the painting and reading the poem; each invests the other.

The first phase of the discussion focuses on the poem and the fact that the past, present and future of the woman's life is each dominated by a different male figure.

Extract 1

Rachel: I think this is her train of thought – yeah?

Susie: Yeah. And, em, the main characters are men, and . . .

Rachel: But also there's the same amount of reference to her husband as there is to the maid and that.

Susie: So he doesn't play an important, a major role in her life.

Sarah: Her father's got the biggest part, hasn't he?

Rachel: And the painter.

Susie: Yeah. That's what I said, the painter – the same thing you . . .

Sarah: Yeah, but she doesn't . . . make any reference to him herself in her thoughts; she doesn't say anything like, you know, I feel much better now because this bloke's painting me.

Susie: No but she's not . . .

Ben: I think she means more to help the . . .

Susie: No but I think he means more to her, the painter, than her father because . . . most of all to her husband because she's still living with him at present; whereas her father was past and the painter could be future.

Rachel: Yeah.
Sarah: The tenses involved?
Rachel: Yeah but do you think – em . . . so do you think that there's any kind of, like, plot to do with the painter, because her husband hired the painter, yeah, . . . and he's painting her and basically that's all she is in the marriage anyway, something to look at.
Susie: The picture suggests the plot 'cos I thought it's set up like a scene – like a stage scene, isn't it?

The concluding idea, identified in both painting and poem, that suggests that the woman, in Rachel's words, is just 'something to look at' is developed a few minutes later to explore their feeling that this role is highly restrictive. This refinement arises at the point where all four become excited at the patterns in the painting.

Extract 2
Susie: Yeah there's a lot of pattern involved isn't there?
Rachel: Yeah, networks.
Rachel: Also, right in the painting, you know this latticework business here.
Susie: Um.
Sarah: Right, this is very important.
Rachel: It's all over the painting.
Sarah: What is? The . . .
Rachel: It's not just on the walls – it's on the floor, it's on the couch.
Sarah: What?
Rachel: There's the lattice stuff, the squares . . .
Ben: Yes.
Susie: Yes . . .
Rachel: Everywhere.
Sarah: And also it shows very . . . maybe that means the fact that it's all very symmetrical.
Rachel: It's also to do with nets . . . When you say her husband's behind the net and she's back in all the . . . but she can't . . . but she's restricted.
Susie: Yeah – a cage . . . it's almost a cage.
Sarah: It's not an obvious cage with bars . . . it's very faint. It's a cage she can't actually identify.

The lattice screens and their shadows in the painting merge in the imagination with the husband's bee-keeping net in the poem, and together they become a metaphor for the barely perceptible cage of the woman's existence which Sarah mentions at the end.

Shortly afterwards, it is Sarah again who focuses the group on the colour of the woman's lips, and this leads to a series of exchanges where their responses to the painting and the poem become fully integrated.

Extract 3

Sarah: I don't think so, I think can we go back to the colour? . . . The lips . . . the fact that the lips are very red is . . . When he says, 'I'm working on your mouth' – so, they become very red don't they? They're a very important part of her . . . mouth . . .

Ben: Yeah. The fact that they're a deep red in the picture and also mentioned in the poem . . .

Sarah: . . . must mean that they're significant.

Susie: And also, when he says about the mouth she becomes very self-conscious and her eyelids tremble . . .

Sarah: Yeah, she does become self-conscious and embarrassed as if . . . Maybe she's ashamed . . . of her lips and the inside of her dress because that can be quite . . .

Ben: I don't think that's really surprising, because he's having to paint her in a lot of detail and really study her facial features and she might become frightened cos they're not perfect . . .

The sensuality that invests this portrait of a woman in both media is made explicit here; and, after some further talk about the significance of the fruit, the fan and the setting, the discussion finishes with some fine insights which draw upon their intimate knowledge of both the painting and the poem.

Extract 4

Sarah: Right. Can I say something about . . . If all the male . . . the men characters in her life . . . all the dominant characters in her life are men, OK, then she might be actually be afraid of her womanhood . . . which is the red lips and the red underskirt and the flowers which are feminine. Maybe she's actually afraid of that.

Rachel: Um. And also she seems to live in a sort of . . . I think it's probably that sort of . . . um . . . a long way before . . .

Sarah: I think she's really sort of decorative . . .

Rachel: And because she's got servants she's not considered even the housewifely type of person – just a decorative woman and that's all. So as soon as she, like the fruit, becomes rotten in this climate that's going to be it. That's why he's having her painted now . . .

Conclusions and classroom implications

When we stand back, as it were, from the detailed pictures of students' responses to paintings and to the poems written about them, they demand to be summarized separately because of the asymmetrical relationship between viewer/reader, painting and poem mentioned earlier. The following conclusions can be tentatively made.

Responses to paintings: what viewers comment on

Each of the four items can be expressed in two ways: as a 'determined' quality of the painting and as an 'undetermined' element of the viewer's response. This is intended to reflect the dialogic relationship that exists during the viewer's act of seeing-in. Viewers comment on the following:

Story
- The embedded narrative in the 'text' of the picture.
- The storying mode that viewers adopt to make meaning.

Significant details
- Images which the painter selects as emblems of an idea or feeling.
- The constructs that viewers make to interpret the details and subject matter of the picture.

Wandering viewpoint
- The painting's 'moment', which implies a past and a future outside the canvas.
- The viewer's shifting viewpoint during the time taken looking at the picture.

Formal composition
- The shapes, lines, colours of which the painting is made.
- The viewer's awareness of how the canvas space has been organized.

The first two items (which will assume central importance in Chapter 11 when we discuss narrative and emblem in Hogarth's works) account for much of the substance of viewer's stated responses and include the viewer's sense of the identity of the painter and the intentions behind the picture. The last two items indicate the conditions necessary for the dialogic relationship between painting and viewer to occur at all.

Responses to poems about paintings

Students' responses to the poems about the paintings they had looked at showed some characteristics similar to the reactions to pictures and, of course, to the elements of response to poetry discussed in earlier chapters of this book (Chapters 6 and 8); but there are also differences. In summary, readers are interested in the following.

- The stories created by the writers and the *viewpoint* from which the stories are told. Writers primarily engage with the paintings through narrative, as we have seen, in their attempts to situate the timeless present of the painting into a temporal sequence. The stance they adopt to do this – in the fictive time of the people in the painting (Owen, '*Siesta*') or in the real time of the viewer interpreting the artist's work (Longley, '*Man Lying on a Wall*') – is a source of fascination and of narrative viewpoints for pupils' own creative responses to the painting.

- The *voice* and *attitude* of the poet towards the painting and whether or not it agrees with their own. Readers come to the poem already armed with their views of its subject-matter; this can work either for or against the poem, as we have seen. Either way, it provides the students with a useful point of comparison and tends to make both poem and painting more accessible to comment and analysis.
- The *telling details*, the bit of information or the striking phrase, and their place in the whole poem. Their awareness of formal composition, especially the ways in which the detailed parts contribute to the whole, is less evident in respect of a poem than it is with paintings. With visual art, it seems the students are more conscious of dealing with a made object than they are with verbal art.

Classroom activities

There are many suggestions for classroom work in *Double Vision*, especially 'Ideas for coursework' (p. 14) and 'Making connections' (pp. 118–21), as well as in the approaches to particular pairs of paintings and poems throughout the book. A brief gloss upon some of the main activities is, therefore, all that is necessary here.

Gallery visit

This may be a first visit for many students, and it is worth spending some discussion time afterwards on the context of seeing paintings in a large public building. It may be appropriate to talk about the fact that, hung in a gallery, some paintings are now far from their originally intended contexts in a grand private home, or a church, or a town hall or civic centre. An initial visit can be focused best by asking students to identify, say, three paintings they like and to list a few points about each; subsequent visits might involve the use of simple, hand-held tape-recorders to help students recall their impressions in front of the originals for later playback and discussion in school.

Individual painters

Encourage students to find and develop an interest in particular artists by gathering together and displaying reproductions and information. Focus the work by demanding both commentaries and creative responses in relation to the pictures.

Points of view

The narrative stances that writers assume in reading paintings vary greatly. Narratives may be told as third-person accounts, as first-person reflections of the poet, as the thought-tracks of painter or sitter, as dialogues between depicted figures, as the interior monologue of the viewer, . . . A selection of paintings, some with poems representing one or two of these stances, is sufficient stimulus to generate discussion of narrative viewpoint and a range of writing.

Anthology-making

This is the simplest, most personal and one of the most effective ways of encouraging a lively and developing interest in both arts. Choice implies commitment; and deciding to write out this poem and buy a postcard of that painting to go into a personal collection is the crucial first step in acknowledging to yourself and to others that you have an interest in the subject. A scrapbook-style anthology of paintings, poems, factual information and the student's own writings can quickly become a valuable resource both for the individual and for the class.

11 William Hogarth: the artist as author and educator

Introduction: a literary artist

Hogarth is the most popular artist in English literary history. His esteem with the literary world – one he himself sought and cultivated during his lifetime – is a mixed blessing, for, while it lends his work a wider artistic and cultural reference, it also deflects attention from his qualities as a painter. Indeed, Hogarth's image with the public is equally mixed – made up of graphic journalist, pictorial historian, engraver, painter, cartoonist, moral satirist and someone who told stories through pictures.

The two works which have come to represent the extremes of his art are *Gin Lane* (1751 – Figure 11.1), his fierce attack upon the widespread addiction to gin, the cause of so many of London's evils at this period; and the carefree, joyous picture, sketched with a sense of delight in exploring pure form, in which he caught the smiling features of *The Shrimp Girl* (mid-1750s – Figure 11.2). The one is an engraving by a man with a strong social conscience moved to create a satirical nightmare out of London's streets; the other is an oil sketch of the face of a bright, optimistic young woman, animated as if to respond to a passer-by or to break into her fishmonger's cry in those same London streets. The engraving is heavily documented with details which the viewer is expected to read, mark, learn and inwardly digest. The painting is simply a head and shoulders, with no contextual background apart from the hints of her occupation in the clothes and tray of fish, where the viewer is invited to enjoy – through what Hogarth himself described as 'the coarse, bold stroke' – the form, colour and texture of the paint with which he conveyed 'the action and the passion' of his subject.

Yet, at least as well known as these two images are his anecdotal series, or 'pictur'd morals' as David Garrick called them, principally *A Harlot's Progress* (1732), *A Rake's Progress* (1735) and *Marriage à la Mode* (1745). Here Hogarth is not only an artist in two media, painting and engraving (though, sadly, the

Figure 11.1 *Gin Lane* (1751), by William Hogarth

paintings of the first series were lost in a fire in 1755), but a storyteller with a purpose. His famous declaration of his aims (1833: 8–9) confirms his intention:

> to compose pictures on canvas similar to representations on the stage . . . I have endeavoured to treat my subject as a dramatic writer: my picture is my stage, and men and women my players, who by means of certain actions and gestures are to exhibit 'a dumb show'.

These stories are to be told in the language of simulated speech and mimed movement through the still, silent medium of paint. Their subjects are the

Figure 11.2 *The Shrimp Girl* (1754?), by William Hogarth

manners and morals of the age, treated with a satirical eye that ranges from light raillery at prevailing fashions to trenchant attacks upon social inequalities and the conditions of the poor.

Hogarth's reputation as a literary artist is compounded by his reference to himself as 'the author' of many of his works, as well as by his turning to specific literary texts as sources for his pictures. His twelve illustrations (1725–6) for Samuel Butler's satiric poem *Hudibras* (1663–78), and his frontispiece for an edition of Pope's *Rape of the Lock* (1715), show an early interest in mock-heroic narrative, but it was the popular theatre of the day that was to be the more significant influence on the style and conception of Hogarth's art. He designed the frontispiece for Henry Fielding's farce *Tom Thumb* (1730) and painted *Falstaff Examining his Recruits* (1728).

However, the turning-point in Hogarth's artistic development was triggered by the production in January 1728 of John Gay's *The Beggar's Opera*. He made a pencil sketch on the spot, and over the next year he produced at least six paintings of the climactic scene in Act 3, scene 2, set in Newgate Prison, where Macheath's two 'wives', Lucy Lockit and Polly Peacham, plead with their fathers to save the highwayman from the gallows. The particular significance of the composition (Figure 11.3) is, firstly, that Hogarth has pointedly placed some spectators, either side of the actors, on the stage. He thus gives visual form to the dramatic concept that the audience themselves were being satirized by Gay and were implicitly part of the action. To signal the point, he hangs over the stage the inscription '*Velute in speculum*' ('Even as in a mirror'). Secondly, Hogarth also took delight in portraying well-known people in the audience, so his painting encompasses a double drama: that of celebrated actors and actresses playing fictional roles, and

Figure 11.3 *The Beggar's Opera* (1729), by William Hogarth

that of recognizable notables among the spectators responding to actors as real people. Thus, on the far right of the painting, Hogarth shows the Duke of Bolton staring fixedly at Lavinia Fenton playing Polly, his mistress in real life, while Lavinia/Polly is shown with her back to her stage lover and her gestures and gaze ambiguously linked to the figure of her real lover. In case we miss the idea, Hogarth has the statue of the satyr on that side of the stage pointing downwards towards the Duke of Bolton with its index finger. In these two ways, as well as through the circumscribed space and sense of enclosure in the setting, the psychological interplay between the figures, the delight in detail, the theatrical lighting and the eye-level position of the implied viewer, *The Beggar's Opera* anticipates the character and style of the moral cycles to come.

Hogarth's associations with the theatre continued and were reflected directly in his paintings of *Garrick as Richard III* (1745) and in portraits of actors like James Quin and Lavinia Fenton. He associated with literary people and met Richardson, Goldsmith and Dr Johnson; but, if the stage in the form of *The Beggar's Opera* was the single most important influence upon his compositions, it was with the period's greatest novelist, Henry Fielding, that Hogarth found his greatest affinity in terms of his narrative satires.

Both Hogarth and Fielding saw themselves as innovators. Hogarth (1833) speaks of 'painting and engraving modern moral subjects, a field not broken up in any country or any age'; Fielding regards himself as 'the founder of a new province of writing' (*Tom Jones*, 1749) who is initiating 'a species of writing . . . hitherto unattempted in our language' (Preface to *Joseph Andrews*, 1742/1962).

Clearly, they regarded each other as kindred spirits artistically, as well as valuing an acquaintanceship which dated back to the early 1730s and was to continue until Fielding's death in 1754. Fielding's celebrated Preface argues that Hogarth had created a new art form which was both uplifting and yet true to nature, one which lay between the classical depictions of gods and humans in traditional 'history painting' and the comic distortions of 'caricature'. This middle way was the portrayal of 'character' – the ability to show the whole person as a thinking and feeling human being. Fielding said of Hogarth, 'It hath been thought a vast Commendation of a Painter to say his Figures seem to breathe; but surely, it is much greater and nobler Applause that they appear to think' (1742/1962: xix). In turn, Hogarth produced a subscription ticket for *Marriage à la Mode* called *Characters and Caricaturas* (1743) in which, above a bottom row of three character heads by Raphael and four caricature heads by Leonardo and others, he engraved over a hundred faces intended to show the variety of nature and establish the merits of his position 'between the sublime and the grotesque'. Beneath, he directs the reader/viewer: 'For a Farther Explanation of the Difference Betwixt Character and Caricatura See ye Preface to Joh Andrews.' Both innovators needed to establish their positions in relation to classical precedent and to the prevailing taste of the times. The difficulties of doing so perhaps account for the strained phrases that Fielding used to describe their work, calling Hogarth a 'Comic History-Painter' and labelling his own *Joseph*

Andrews as a 'comic epic in prose'. None the less, it is in their notions of narrative and in their shared sense of the serious nature of comedy, one that can educate as well as entertain, that both painter and novelist held a common vision which profoundly influenced the development of both their arts.

It is no surprise, then, that in subsequent centuries the critical tradition has reinforced the view of Hogarth as a literary artist. Indeed, it seems almost as if literary critics have been keener to write about his work than have art historians. Charles Lamb (1811) places Hogarth next to Shakespeare and discusses *A Rake's Progress* through analogies with *Timon of Athens* and *King Lear*; Hazlitt (1818/1907) includes Hogarth in his *Lectures on the English Comic Writers*, and Thackeray's (1853) essay on 'English Humourists' sees Hogarth in the company of Swift, Pope and other writers. More recently, Dobson (1893), Sitwell (1936), Moore (1948), Quennell (1955), Praz (1956) and others have continued the literary line. The trend runs through to the present day: the standard life is by a Yale professor of English (Paulson 1971), and books by Cowley (1983) and Dabydeen (1987) are, similarly, by scholars whose prime professional work lies within literature.

Given this creative background and critical inheritance, it is appropriate to consider Hogarth's pictures from two points of view: as offering a unique challenge to read visual narrative and as providing a lively and provocative example of education through art. Both perspectives immediately bring us up against corresponding issues today; for example, in the reading of comic strips and in the ways visual media can be employed to portray and explore feeling and motives. Both perspectives, too, face us with some of the basic questions addressed in Chapters 9 and 10, and which were implicit in my comments on *Gin Lane* and *The Shrimp Girl*; in particular, the viewer's stance in relation to the paintings as distinct from the engravings. Paulson (1975: 40) remarks, 'I cannot emphasize too greatly the difference in the *reading* of a Hogarth print and the *seeing* of a Hogarth painting;' and he goes on to point out that engravings themselves are a form of reproduction whose purpose is to communicate – their intention is primarily to speak a message, not to embody a feeling or idea. Their literalness, Paulson suggests, makes the engravings the more direct medium for telling the stories; conversely, with the paintings, we can enjoy both the fiction and the subtle qualities of line and colour from which these Hogarthian worlds gather their density and their sense of the texture of daily living.

In the following discussion of *Marriage à la Mode*, two factors have meant that we will be looking at the engravings, not the paintings: firstly, the practical one that with full colour unavailable here the reproductions of the paintings lose much of their power whereas the more defined lines of the engravings make details clearer; and, secondly, as the copper-plate production process for the engravings meant that the engraved prints would appear as mirror images, laterally the reverse of the paintings, the reading of the events in the depicted narrative is significantly affected. The paintings tend towards the balancing of figures through the use of colour and the merging of forms, thus understating the

Figure 11.4 *Marriage à la Mode* (1745), by William Hogarth
Plate I: The marriage contract

Plate II: Shortly after the marriage

Plate III: The visit to the quack doctor

Plate IV: The Countess's morning levee

Plate V: The killing of the Earl

Plate VI: The suicide of the Countess

story-line; by contrast, the engravings tend to lead the eye through an easier viewing sequence where the figures are causally related from left to right in the way we are used to when decoding a written text. Hogarth was acutely aware of this fundamental issue of reading associated with making engraved copies from paintings. (Paulson suggests that from the outset it was Hogarth's intention to create the paintings for *Marriage à la Mode* with the engravings in mind.) It demonstrates that the literary quality of Hogarth's works is not simply a matter of superficial description but is integral both to the process of composition and to the reader's response.

Marriage à la Mode: reading the narrative

First, the plot. As a way-in to what is commonly regarded as Hogarth's best series, spend a few minutes studying the six pictures (Figures 11.4, Plates I–VI) in sequence and try to reconstruct the story.

There is a long tradition of commentary on Hogarth's pictures, beginning with that sanctioned by the artist during his lifetime (Paulson 1975: 201), which draws upon the evidence in the pictures for the names of many of the characters.

Plate I

The narrative begins with the concluding negotiations for an arranged marriage. The father of the bride-to-be, the merchant in the centre, scrutinizes the settlement while the bridegroom's father, Earl Squanderfield, receives a redeemed mortgage and cash as a dowry and points proudly to his family tree. The betrothed couple sit together in the background: the Viscount more interested in his own reflection in the mirror than in his intended; the merchant's daughter more interested in the attentions of the young lawyer, Silvertongue, than in her future husband. The seeds of dramatic conflict are sown: the intrigue and ultimate downfall of the main characters derive from both the dictates of commercially minded parents and the inherent weaknesses of the bride and groom.

Plate II

The young marrieds are in their own rooms early one afternoon. Breakfast is still on the table and lights are still smouldering in the chandelier. The husband wears his hat, and his broken, undrawn sword lies at his feet. A small dog sniffs inquisitively at a woman's cap in his coat pocket. We are to infer that the husband has been out on the town and has recently returned exhausted. His wife, meanwhile, has apparently been at an all-night card party held in the further room; she stretches with sensual robustness as she casts a knowing sidelong glance at her husband. The steward, carrying a sheaf of unpaid bills and only one receipt, has been dismissed and leaves with an ambiguous gesture of disgust at his employers and mock benediction towards the implied viewers. The marriage is at the point of disintegration; the scene prepares us for the separate lives of the couple in the next two pictures.

Plate III

The young nobleman is now seen in the laboratory of a quack doctor. With him is a sad young girl, a child prostitute dressed in adult finery – perhaps the owner of the mob-cap in his pocket in the previous picture. The subject of the scene is syphilis. With a show of bravado in his grin and the brandishing of his stick, the Viscount suggests he does not take this 'nobleman's disease' too seriously, as he holds out a box of ineffectual pills. Either this complaint or the raised cane, or both, produces a look of momentary annoyance on the face of the tall woman, thought to be an ex-procuress, who acts as the quack doctor's assistant.

Plate IV

There has been a considerable passage of time between the events depicted in this picture and the preceding ones. The old Earl has died (his coronets are above the mirror and the bed), and the young Countess is now a mother (a child's comforter hangs from the back of her chair). The Countess is at her toilette, having her hair done, while Silvertongue reclines on a sofa in the easy manner of a frequent and privileged visitor; he points to a picture of a masquerade on a screen and, tickets in hand, invites the Countess to accompany him to one. Behind the lovers is a mock-heroic altar, reminiscent of Belinda's dressing-table in Pope's *The Rape of the Lock*, surmounted by drapery arranged ironically like a bridal veil around the mirror. In front of them the black boy gleefully points to the horns of Actaeon, sharing the joke of incipient cuckoldry directly with the implied viewer. The gathering is being entertained by an Italian castrato, whose performance is being received with everything from ecstasy and delight to indifference and sleep by his audience.

Plate V

After the masquerade (signified by the masks and witch's hat on the floor), the Countess and Silvertongue spend the night at a Covent Garden bagnio. Meanwhile, her husband has learnt of the assignation (perhaps through the hairdresser in the previous scene) and, surprising the lovers, has challenged Silvertongue to a duel. The dramatic moment represented is just after the fatal sword thrust that kills the nobleman, because Silvertongue has had time to make his escape out of the window. The commotion has roused the proprietor of the house, who enters the room with a constable to find the Countess on her knees pleading for forgiveness from her dying husband as both he and his sword fall to the floor.

Plate VI

The Countess has now returned to the sparsely furnished home of her father on the Thames waterfront near Old London Bridge. The plot is resumed at the point when she has just received news of the hanging of Silvertongue at Tyburn for murder. (His 'Last Dying Speech' lies at his mistress's feet.) The Countess has committed suicide by taking poison just as her father was about to have lunch. The apothecary berates the half-witted servant, presumably for conspiring to buy the poison; the physician leaves in the background, unable to revive the Countess; and, seeing that his investment in the marriage contract in scene 1 has not paid off, the merchant cuts his losses by retrieving the ring from his daughter's finger before rigor mortis sets in. The only sign of real sorrow comes from the old nurse who lifts up the crippled child with its heavy leg-iron to kiss its mother. In the confusion, the house dog eats its master's lunch.

There is, of course, more to reading the narrative of *Marriage à la Mode* than simply reconstructing the plot. My remaining comments upon this series fall into the four areas discussed at the end of the previous chapter: story, significant details, wandering viewpoint and formal composition.

The *story-telling* potential of the six pictures operates in two complementary ways: *within* each image and in the gaps *between* the images. The dominant movement of the narrative from left to right, from past to future and from cause to effect is created both by the main events of the *plot* as we have deduced them from the subjects of the six pictures and by the particular *anecdote* depicted individually in each scene.

The time-scale of the narrative is subtly organized. The light in scene 1 (together with the data of 4 June on the steward's receipt in scene 2) suggests the marriage contract was made in late spring or early summer; the duel (scene 5) occurs on a night wintry enough to need a large fire; and the final picture shows another day warm enough for the windows to be wide open on to the river. One seasonal cycle is clearly insufficient; just how many years elapse depends upon the viewer's own estimate of the age of the child in the last scene. Story-time and discourse-time are cleverly handled: the first impression is of a discourse comprising a rapid sequence of events, culminating in the tragic deaths of the protagonists; once the 'indeterminacy gaps' between and, to a lesser extent, within the scenes are filled in by the viewer, the more extensive chronology of the story becomes apparent.

The setting of the narrative shows a downward progress in a different manner from that of Hogarth's earlier series. We begin in the Earl's grand mansion in West London and end in the bare Thames-side house of the merchant in East London; the incidents in between take place at different locations in central London. Each scene is set as on a stage; the action takes place within six different rooms, the figures spread across the bottom half of the picture each time, with the floor depicted in the immediate foreground and the walls and ceiling above and behind. Open windows, open doors, open archways, open curtains appear in every scene, increasing rather than diminishing the claustrophobia, since the main characters usually have their backs to them and their attention focused within.

The ways in which time and place are organized leave the viewer of the series much to do. Connections are inexplicit, the emphasis in each scene is upon the dramatic moment, and the gaps in time and place are often large ones to bridge. All this puts a heavy interpretive demand upon the viewer but, such is Hogarth's skill at enticing the implied viewer to become a *reader*, the story seems to grow out of the mass of significant details connecting each scene to the others through factual information and recurring metaphors.

The weight of *detail* in the series is far too great to deal with here, but a number of principal features deserve comment since they give the narrative its density and point. (An exhaustive analysis of the series is given in Cowley (1983).) There are several general aspects of the use of detail which Hogarth developed in his earlier work, such as *The Beggar's Opera*, *A Harlot's Progress* and *A Rake's Progress*. He looks for opportunities to portray real people: in scene 4, for example, the Italian castrato is a composite of two in real life, Carestini and Farinelli; the flautist is the German Weidemann and the ecstatic lady is usually taken to be one Mrs Fox Lane, who was notorious for her passion for Italian opera. Hogarth pokes fun at prevailing tastes for foreign music by the way he presents this group of figures. His use of body language, too, throughout the series is dramatically suggestive of mood and feeling, especially in scene 2. The positions, gestures and implied movements of the figures are more than a *tableau vivante*: they describe character and hint at personal histories or half-hidden wishes. In this series, as in the Progresses, fictional names are given to the characters with Jonsonian aptness: Moll Hackabout, the harlot, and Tom Rakewell, the rake, are here followed by Earl Squanderfield and Counsellor Silvertongue. However, there are three features which signify in a more fundamental way: Hogarth's use of recurrent metaphors, emblematic objects and 'interpictorial images'. A brief explanation of each is appropriate.

The dominant metaphor of *Marriage à la Mode* is disease. It runs through the series, from the old Earl's gout and his son's beauty patch on his neck to hide a sore which would be venereal (scene 1), through the dissolute, debilitating lives shown in scene 2 to the unsavoury sight of the diseased Viscount and his child mistress, both with their box of pills at the quack doctor's at the heart of the series (scene 3). Diseased relationships infect the fashionable lifestyle of the Countess's levee (scene 4); adultery and murder follow (scene 5); and the sad progeny of the marriage is depicted in the crippled child with its inherited deformities in the final scene. The diseases of these individuals both extend from parents to children in time and spread through the social structure.

Subsidiary running metaphors are those of money and the enclosed room. Monetary dealings – investment, payment, debt, redeeming losses – infect the series almost like a form of disease. Money initiates the narrative in the contract (scene 1) and closes it with the merchant's retrieval of his dead daughter's ring (scene 6). In between, there are unpaid bills (scene 2) and the suggested squandering of money in pursuit of fashionable pleasures: the Viscount's outlay for pills (scene 3), the Countess's for musicians and the adornments of high life (scene 4) and Silvertongue's for the masquerade and the hire of the bagnio (scene 5) are all one to Hogarth's satirical eye. Similarly, the enclosed rooms in which the drama is played out themselves take on a metaphorical status. A sense of airlessness is pervasive, despite the frequency of open doors and windows, which in these boxlike settings, crowded with figures and furniture, suggests the narrow self-interests of the protagonists and the stifling environment in which all the characters conduct their lives.

Whereas the metaphors are pervasive and reflect the underlying themes of the series which often operate 'unseen', as it were, at the general contextual level, emblems are particular objects which may occur once or more in the pictures to symbolize a significant idea. The bonnet in the Viscount's pocket (scene 2) and the masquerade tickets tempting the Countess (scene 4) are emblems of their respective infidelity, just as the figurine of Actaeon in the latter scene symbolizes cuckoldry. The overturned chairs (scenes 2 and 6) suggest moral disorder; the mirrors (scenes 1,4,5) point to the vanity of the characters and, by extension, of those viewers who harbour similar vanities in their own lives; and the chained pairs of dogs (scene 1) – one stamped with the Earl's coronet – provide an ironic emblem of the young couple being shackled in the marriage contract.

Finally, 'interpictorial images' are a major feature of the series. Over thirty pictures decorate the six rooms of *Marriage à la Mode*, most of which are accurate copies in miniature of works by known artists. Paulson (1971, 1975) and Cowley (1983) give detailed accounts of these, but even a cursory inspection of these interior paintings reveals that their subject-matter makes a pointed commentary upon the scenes which Hogarth is depicting. Images of murder, torture and martyrdom hang above the heads of the characters in scene 1, indicative of the violence that is being done to human relationships in sealing the contract. Silvertongue's seduction of the Countess (scene 4) is reflected in the scenes in the paintings above them; but perhaps Hogarth's sharpest authorial comment is in the bagnio scene. Here, on the wall behind the tragic couple, he has painted a picture of a prostitute (thought to be based on Defoe's *Moll Flanders*) and shown it hanging in front of a mural of a soldier whose burly legs protrude below the frame. The handle of the harlot's parasol dangles suggestively in front of her skirts. The result is a crude parody of the sexual act in a composite image which itself comments upon the adultery that is the subject of the scene. These interpictorial references might seem, at first, like sophisticated 'in-jokes' to be shared with the visually literate, but they are more than this: they are Hogarth's way both of giving artistic cohesion to the whole of a scene and, more pointedly, of satirizing the taste of those very connoisseurs who might catch themselves laughing at the joke before realizing that they are partly its target.

The third general area for discussion is that of the *wandering viewpoint*. Two aspects invite comment. Firstly, the implied viewer's position is that of the playgoer in the front row of the stalls, looking at eye-level scenes enacted, as it were, within the proscenium frame. Hogarth exploits this position, as we have noticed, by occasionally having one of his characters make a theatrical connection with the spectators by crossing the proscenium boundary. The black boy's gesturing (scene 4) is the clearest example in this series, but the steward's leave-taking (scene 2) is partly for the onlooker's benefit, and even the recumbent chained dog (scene 1) appears to be casting a knowing eye towards the audience!

The second aspect of this viewpoint relates to the manner in which the viewer 'reads' the picture. One of the main elements of reading fictional narrative in books is, as we have seen (Chapter 1), the process of anticipation and retrospection. The reader's response is directed in significant measure by the dictates of the single line. Anticipation of what happens next is the motor that drives the reading. The narrative mode of Hogarth's picture sequence places the emphasis upon the other half of this process, encouraging the reader/viewer to take a retrospective, ruminative stance. Predicting about the future of the characters is much less important than piecing together the past and present moments: the reader/viewer is drawn to interpret causes rather than to hypothesize about future effects. In this respect, coming to terms with a Hogarthian series offers a useful reading lesson to complement those learned from verbal texts.

Fourthly, there is the question of *formal composition*. Within these theatrical stage sets, Hogarth's basic means of visual organization are, to some extent, predetermined. Two principles appear to operate: a vertical one of grouping figures and objects in triangular shapes and a horizontal one of connecting these shapes by a waving line, usually discernible in the line of the heads and/or the arms and hands of the characters. In the former, there are often main and subsidiary groupings, clearly evident in scenes 1, 4 and 6; in the latter, the waving line, often across the middle of the picture (scenes 1, 3, 4, 5 and 6), is visually two-dimensional and tends to be apprehended as a flat plane. Compositionally, it draws together, separates, overlaps the triangular building blocks; psychologically, it indicates the direction of interest of each figure and connects it with the simulated dialogue of the scene. The exception to these general principles is scene 2, and the reason is that the visual organization properly echoes the theme of the disintegrating marriage: hence we have no groupings to unify the picture, but four individuals each presented as isolated in his or her own thoughts with distinctive, disconnected gestures, expressions and body language.

Despite our distance in time from Hogarth's mid-eighteenth-century world, reading one of his visual narratives can become a fascinating series of discoveries; his fictions are polysemic texts with layers of meaning, just as are the novels of his fellow innovator Henry Fielding. In practical terms, Hogarth acknowledged the different levels of reader response his fictions provoked by creating both paintings and engravings; but, within both media, he also allowed for the sophisticated audience which could pick up the artistic and cultural references and for the general one which focused on the basic plot. Neither can escape the general thrust of Hogarth's satirical purpose, summed up by Paulson (1975: 38):

> *Marriage à la Mode* embodies two themes: the struggle between the values of money and blood, the merchant and the aristocrat; and the heavy weight of the past, of one generation on another.

Prints and progresses

The Progresses – *A Harlot's Progress* and *A Rake's Progress* – of the 1730s and, particularly, the prints from the few years after *Marriage à la Mode* are the clearest examples of Hogarth's concern to edify as well as to entertain the public. Not that his social conscience and his economic self-interest were ever far apart. His engraved prints, although relatively cheap (single prints were commonly available via subscription at one shilling (5p) or a little more), were far beyond the pockets of the London poor, but Hogarth was well aware that it was the multiple copies of the engravings which would make money rather than the sale of the original paintings he did for the three major series. Yet his motives for creating his 'modern moral subjects', as he called them, did include a genuine desire to use his art for what would now be termed personal and social education. He realized that among those who controlled and organized society's institutions there was a ready market for pictures of topical, slightly risqué, satirical scenes and stories and that, through reaching this clientele, he might indirectly improve social conditions and personal morality.

The two Progresses are moral in two senses: they deal with both morality and mores. Their titles deliberately echo Bunyan's *The Pilgrim's Progress*, the most widely available book in the country after the Bible, and their themes are primarily about the moral and spiritual journeys of a symbolic protagonist: Moll Hackabout and Tom Rakewell are the ignoble, seedy descendants of Bunyan's Christian. Detailed analyses of these two series are unnecessary here: most books on Hogarth contain a commentary on them, of which Bindman's (1981) is probably the most readily available. Most of the points about narrative, significant details, viewpoint and composition that were discussed in relation to *Marriage à la Mode* could be made equally well about the earlier series. The brief accounts which follow are simply to indicate their moral and educational purposes.

The six pictures which take us through *A Harlot's Progress* show how Moll, still an innocent country girl from York, is met off the London wagon by the notorious procuress Mother Needham, probably acting for the equally notorious libertine Colonel Charteris, who is hovering in the background (scene 1). Moll soon becomes a woman of the world, the mistress of a rich Jewish protector, with a young lover and the customary black boy as a servant (scene 2), but her fortunes fall rapidly and soon she has exchanged the lifestyle of the fashionable courtesan for that of a common prostitute, when we see her on the point of being arrested (scene 3). She is committed to Bridewell Prison, where something of her lost innocence still shows against the leers and toughness of the inmates (scene 4). Some years then elapse, for she has given birth to a little boy. She is now in desperate circumstances. The diseases of her profession have caught up with her and she huddles by the fire, wrapped in loose garments, dying in pain while the two quack doctors argue and the nurse steals her few remaining possessions (scene 5). The series ends with her funeral, attended by her former associates and the pathetic figure of her child dressed up as chief mourner. The inscription on the coffin reads, 'M. Hackabout. Died Sepr. 1731 aged 23.'

The overriding feeling is that it is the utter wastefulness of a young life and the despoiling of innocence by the corruptions of a sick society that have provoked Hogarth's indignation, rather than any intrinsic wickedness on Moll's part. She is the victim of her own weakness, but she retains our sympathy because the forces against her are so powerful. The present-day parallel of the friendless, vulnerable provincial teenager arriving in London is inescapable, and it is as well to remember that Hogarth was a graphic social satirist before the days of illustrated journalism. His and others' prints were the only pictorial rendering of the flow of events, fashions, social attitudes and political comment – providing the service that newspapers and television do nowadays. The popularity of this series meant that the message it carried reached a significant audience and had the potential at least to affect the moral climate of the period.

There are other modern messages, too. As Dabydeen (1987: 130–2) argues, Hogarth's intentions in satirizing both the exploitation of women and the demeaning role of blacks in society were ahead of their time. He claims that:

> *A Harlot's Progress* makes seminal connections between race, class and gender; Hogarth gropes towards an understanding of the female (black and white) experience of subjugation, he senses solidarity between blacks and lower-class whites which overrides racial division, a solidarity of peoples victimized by an economic system controlled by the moneyed class.

Despite the suspicion that Dabydeen makes too strenuous a case for Hogarth's sympathies, based partly upon the inclusion of a black woman deep in the background of the Bridewell scene, his is a fascinating study which makes the viewer look again at Moll's serving boy, the two black servants at the Countess's levee (*Marriage à la Mode*, scene 4) and the one waiting on the tables at the Sheriff's banquet in *Industry and Idleness* (scene 8), and at the black whore in the tavern scene in *A Rake's Progress* (scene 3). He is incorrect to claim (1987: 9) that other recent commentators have been guilty of 'colour-blindness' and have not even made 'token acknowledgement' of the presence of blacks in the pictures: Cowley (1983: 109 and 119) and Paulson (1975, plate 79) both do so. None the less, his insights do make the roles of black figures in the pictures considerably more visible. He effectively highlights, too, the ironic commercial juxtaposition in the period of trade in young black slaves rubbing shoulders with trade in what Hogarth called 'old black masters' – imports of Continental paintings which were then in vogue. Dabydeen puts it tartly: 'Buying blacks was as much an investment as buying art' (1987: 88).

A Rake's Progress is a more loosely constructed story than its predecessor. Tom Rakewell inherits his miserly father's fortune, and the dramatic moment Hogarth chooses is when Tom is attempting to pacify with cash the tearful girl, Sarah Young, whom he has seduced and made pregnant, and her angry mother (scene 1). The next two pictures show him sampling the high life at his levee, surrounded by artists and experts of all sorts (scene 2), and the low life of drunken brawls and late-night orgies in the Rose Tavern in Covent Garden (scene 3). He is arrested for debt but saved from prison by the timely intervention of the still faithful Sarah, who pays off his dues from her meagre earnings as a milliner (scene 4). To boost his fortunes, he marries an old, ugly but wealthy woman while, at the back of the church, Sarah, with child in arms, and her mother try to stop the ceremony (scene 5). The rake's decline is then rapid, from the gaming house where he loses his second fortune (scene 6), to the Fleet Prison where insolvent debtors were incarcerated (scene 7) and, finally, to the infamous 'Bedlam' – Bethlehem Hospital in Moorfields for the incurably insane (scene 8 – Figures 11.5 and 11.6). His madness is seen developing in these later pictures, and the ever-loyal Sarah is shown with him both in prison and in Bedlam.

The emphasis of this morality tale is a little different from that of *A Harlot's Progress*. Where Moll was presented more as a victim of circumstance, Tom is destroyed by the greedy pursuit of his own indulgences. His progress from wealth, social pretension and dissolute living in the early scenes into ultimate penury, depravity and madness is offset by the presence of Sarah in no fewer than five of the pictures. She plays the part of the good angel, an embodiment of virtue to balance the rake's vices. She represents a moral integrity that rises above her exploited innocence and survives even in the horrors of the Fleet and Bedlam.

Figure 11.5 *A Rake's Progress*, by William Hogarth – scene 8 (painting)

Figure 11.6 *A Rake's Progress*, by William Hogarth – scene 8 (engraving)

The message is encapsulated in the final image where, amid the manic tragi-comedy of fashionable ladies laughing at the antics of the inmates, Sarah supports and weeps over the crazed figure of Tom. The allusion to a *pietà* in this portrayal is clear, particularly in the painting (Figure 11.5).

If Hogarth's purposes and emphases in these 'modern moral subjects' are fairly clear, we can be less certain about their effects – though, in the estimate of one well-informed sympathizer, their impact was great. Henry Fielding, writing in *The Champion* (Antal 1962: 8), says:

> I esteem the ingenious Mr Hogarth as one of the most useful satirists any age has produced . . . I almost dare affirm that those two works of his, which he calls the Rake's and the Harlot's progress, are calculated more to serve the cause of Virtue, and the Preservation of Mankind, than all the Folios of morality which have ever been written.

The tenor of Hogarth's prints in the five or six years after *Marriage à la Mode* changed noticeably: to the moral messages are added the voice of protest and a more overt concern for the education of the young. Hogarth's sense of audience is a greater determining factor in the twelve pictures of *Industry and Idleness* (1747), *The Four Stages of Cruelty* (1751) and the pair of prints *Beer Street* and *Gin Lane* (1751). Instead of first being created as paintings to be engraved afterwards by other hands, these pictures were not painted at all but were drawn specifically for engraving, with the intention of conveying their messages with simplicity and directness.

Writing about *Industry and Idleness*, Hogarth (1833) was explicit that the series was 'calculated for the use and instruction of youth, wherein everything necessary to be known was to be made as intelligible as possible'; he was equally clear, too, that the cost of prints should be 'within the reach of those for whom they were chiefly intended'. The story of the two apprentices whose careers follow different paths is based on Lillo's popular play of the period, *The London Merchant* (1731); in Hogarth's hands it becomes another morality series, as though vice and virtue, symbolized in *A Rake's Progress* in the characters of Tom and Sarah, have now polarized into two oppositional and, in the end, dramatically entwined 'progresses' – those of Tom Idle and his industrious counterpart Goodchild. The pair are together at their weaving looms in scene 1 and then follow their separate careers, each stage being contrasted until they meet again in scene 10, when Idle the criminal is brought before Goodchild the magistrate. One ends on the gallows at Tyburn, the other as Mayor of London at the Guildhall. As Bindman (1981) has pointed out, there is a ballad-like character to the series; and the simple, readable message is underlined by quotations from the scriptures beneath each print. Everything points to stark, uncomplicated moral alternatives.

Simplified drawing and cheap editions of each print also indicate Hogarth's educational motives in the harrowing series *The Four Stages of Cruelty*. His aim is less artistic than humanitarian. 'The leading points were made as obvious as possible,' he wrote, 'in the hope that their tendency might be seen by men of the lowest rank . . . The prints were engraved in the hope of, in some degree, correcting the barbarous treatment of animals . . .' (1833). The four pictures chart the career of a young sadist, Tom Nero. We see him first as a delinquent charity-school boy who enjoys torturing dogs (scene 1); then in his job as a hackney coachman, where he is shown maltreating his injured horse (scene 2). His 'cruelty in perfection', as Hogarth entitles it, is to murder a maidservant whom he has seduced, made pregnant and persuaded to rob her mistress (scene 3); the 'reward of cruelty' is to be hanged and subsequently laid out for dissection on the anatomist's slab in the lecture room of Surgeons' Hall. Even as the corpse is being disembowelled and having its eyes cut out, Hogarth cannot resist a touch of black humour in the suggestion that it can still feel the pain. Tom Nero's progress is depicted with unrelieved power in scenes that are unpleasant, even repulsive, to examine. Educating the young through such visual shock tactics is a doubtful enterprise. To modern eyes the prints are perhaps more comprehensible as protest pictures than as the serious and well-intentioned attempt to change behaviour that Hogarth had in mind.

Beer Street and *Gin Lane* arose out of another of Hogarth's campaigns to educate the poor about a particular social evil: alcohol addiction, especially to gin. By 1748 the novelist Henry Fielding was also magistrate for Westminster and knew at first hand the devastating toll that cheap gin was having on the population. Employers sold gin to their workforce and even paid their wages in the form of drink. Fielding estimated that gin was the principal sustenance of more than 100,000 Londoners at this period. The extent of this addiction is difficult to comprehend in a city where gin was seen as the safest, cheapest and most plentiful liquid to consume. It may well have been that Fielding enlisted the help of his friend Hogarth to counter this evil, since they shared a common desire to control the trade and its effects.

Hogarth's response to the situation was typically robust and uncompromising: British beer, the national drink, is good for you; gin kills. Hence, in *Beer Street*, all is prosperity and cheerfulness: foaming tankards, baskets of food and rounded paunches are in abundance. In *Gin Lane*, violent deaths and macabre horrors fill the streets, and the foreground is dominated by two figures on some stone steps: an emaciated gin-seller and a drunken mother too besotted to prevent her baby from falling head-first into the alleyway below. This perversion of the image of the Madonna and Child is yet another example of Hogarth's allusions to Christian iconography in order to give his message power and authority. *Gin Lane* has a 'sick humour' comparable with that of Swift's *A Modest Proposal*: it is more desperate than amusing. It is, perhaps, the most lethal attack ever made in protest at the social evils of eighteenth-century society.

Classroom activities

Clearly, in deciding how and when to use any of Hogarth's pictures, the teacher needs the same acute sense of audience that the artist himself showed when creating them. In most cases this implies older classes (GCSE and above), where the students' historical sense is sufficiently developed and their interest in social and political issues can be engaged. There are opportunities here for cross-curricular work; liaison involving English, History and Art teachers could produce a rich resource pack of teaching materials tailored to the needs of particular students. The account of Hogarth's work in this chapter has indicated some of the lines that such a unit of study might take; further ideas could be incorporated from the list of classroom activities below. The following material is arranged in two parts: (i) Information and Resources and (ii) Teaching Ideas. The aim is to give confidence to those whose previous knowledge of Hogarth's work is slight, on the principle expounded by another literary acquaintance of Hogarth, Dr Johnson, who said that there are two sorts of knowledge – you either know a thing or you know where to find out about a thing!

Information and resources

Chronology of Hogarth's main works mentioned in this chapter

1697	Born, Smithfield, London.
1713	Apprenticed for seven years to a silver-engraver.
1720	Starts his own business as an engraver.
1724	Joins Thornhill's art academy in Covent Garden.
1726	Twelve illustrations for Butler's *Hudibras*.
1728	*Falstaff Examining His Recruits.*
	The Beggar's Opera.
1732	*A Harlot's Progress.*
1735	*A Rake's Progress.*
1742	*The Graham Children.*
	Fielding's *Joseph Andrews* published.
1743	*Characters and Caricaturas.*
1745	*Marriage à la Mode.*
	Self-Portrait with Pug.
	David Garrick as Richard III.
1747	*Industry and Idleness.*
1751	*Beer Street* and *Gin Lane.*
	The Four Stages of Cruelty.
1753	*The Analysis of Beauty*, Hogarth's treatise on aesthetics, published.
1754(?)	*The Shrimp Girl.*
	The Election series.
1764	Died, Chiswick, London.

Original works

'Original' is an ambiguous term where Hogarth's works are concerned. Many of his paintings are in London galleries only a few miles apart. The engravings are, by definition, for mass production where the usual concept of 'an original' scarcely applies. One of the real bonuses for teaching purposes is that it is easy and legal to photocopy Hogarth's prints from books and obtain good reproductions for study purposes. The following London galleries hold Hogarth's main paintings:

The National Gallery	*Marriage à la Mode*
	The Shrimp Girl
The Tate Gallery	*Self-Portrait with Pug*
	The Graham Children
Sir John Soane's Museum	*A Rake's Progress*
	The Election series
The British Museum	Prints of all major works

Note: Colour slides of the main paintings are available from the galleries.

Books
The three books below are the most useful and accessible books for teachers. Other publications mentioned in this chapter are listed in the general bibliography at the end of the book.

D. Bindman, *Hogarth*, Thames and Hudson, London, 1981.
R. L. S. Cowley *Marriage à la Mode: a Review of Hogarth's Narrative Art*, Manchester University Press, 1983.
R. Paulson *The Art of Hogarth*, Phaidon, London, 1975.

Teaching ideas

Gallery visits
The National, The Tate, and Sir John Soane's Museum have small selections of Hogarth's paintings. (The latter is worth visiting for the delightful tiny picture-gallery alone: its walls unhinge like the pages of a book). It is necessary to prepare for and focus upon particular paintings. Depending on time and energy, work on Hogarth's paintings could be incorporated into the activities suggested under the same heading at the end of Chapter 10.

Paintings/engravings
Comparisons of Hogarth's work in these forms can illuminate both the nature of the two media and the relationship of his intentions to his audience. *A Rake's Progress* is a particularly useful series to highlight these points – especially scene 4, where the Rake is arrested for debt, and scene 8, in Bedlam. Students list the differences in details, the portrayal of the characters, the definition of the images and so on, and discuss Hogarth's purposes in the two versions.

Sequencing
Using shuffled packs of photocopies of the six pictures of either *A Harlot's Progress* or *Marriage à la Mode*, students work out the order of the narrative and write a sequence of brief captions to tell the stories, including details of the settings and the time-scale of events.

Comparison
Students study *Beer Street* and *Gin Lane* closely and make two lists, one for each picture, of all the details they notice about shops, buildings, people, activities and so on. Ask, 'What's the message of this pair of prints?' Discussion could lead into a written comparison.

Comic Strip
Hogarth's anecdotal series tell their stories without using words in speech/thinks bubbles as later graphic artists such as Gillray and Cruikshank were to do. But

what *might* Hogarth's characters be saying and thinking? Students take one series and add their verbal texts to Hogarth's visual sequence.

Up-date

Newspapers and television are not short on stories similar to the ones enacted by Hogarth's characters: teenagers arriving alone in London; inherited fortunes 'blown' in a few weeks; shocking accounts of the living conditions of the poor and homeless; cruelty to animals; sensational murders; fashionable affairs; . . . The overall standard of living has vastly improved, but the problems which provoked Hogarth's moral indignation remain much the same. Students either rework Hogarth's stories 'in modern dress' or take a modern news story and retell it in Hogarthian terms as a series of pictures with a written commentary to express a particular message.

Protest poster

Students design a poster to protest about a particular social issue on which they feel strongly. The poster should include either a detail from a Hogarth print and/or a similar image from a newspaper as well as verbal slogans.

12 Working with picture-books

Five varieties of picture-book

When does a picture-book cease to be a picture-book and become a book of pictures, with or without captions? Or become a book of stories and poems with illustrations? As Hunt (1990) has pointed out, the visual aspect of children's literature is a remarkably unconsidered area, remaining until recently on the periphery of both literary and graphic-art criticism. Yet illustration of children's books has a rich and fascinating history over the past two centuries and, particularly in the picture-books of the past twenty-five years, has 'grown up' into a more sophisticated art form capable of social and political comment and showing all the subtleties of a mixed medium in a media-conscious age. However, we still have no coherent means even of describing the range of picture-books and illustrated texts; and we know still less about how young readers (or any readers, for that matter) understand such books, despite some recent notable efforts in both these respects (Moebius 1986; Meek 1988; Graham 1990).

My present purposes are not to attempt to remedy such deficiencies but simply to provide some working definitions in this area, and to discuss the relationship of the visual and verbal elements as a context in which to consider the implications for teaching and learning.

Categorization of literary texts is an imprecise and, in most cases, superfluous task: the works of art we tend to value resist all attempts at pigeon-holing – which, in part, is why we value them. Yet, in order to provide a context in which to talk about picture-books, a few basic distinctions help to answer the questions posed at the start of the chapter. The following discriminations, therefore, are made more tentatively than the numbered descriptions suggest. Five types of visual/verbal relationship seem to exist in the range of books in which both pictures and words appear together. In the absence of any other means of distinguishing between their characteristics, they can be described in a sequence which moves progressively from visual to verbal dominance:

1 *Books where the visual predominates as an autonomous art object; words, if present at all, are separate from or integrated within the visual design*
Examples include *Anno's Alphabet: An Adventure in Imagination* by Mitsumasa Anno (1974), with its paintings of the letters of the alphabet planed and jointed into a continuous Escher-like *trompe-l'œil* and framed by borders in which the eye has to play hide-and-seek to find the objects beginning with the particular letters. Heidi Holder's *Crows. An Old Rhyme* (1987) is a different example. Here the Rackham-style paintings each incorporate four or five words of a counting rhyme which act as titles to the images. 'One is for bad news/Two is for mirth/Three is a wedding/Four is a birth . . .' Crows are the inspiration for this counting rhyme and provide twelve left-hand-page pictures; the right-hand pages portray the fortunes of a faithful mink and an adventurous weasel. Overriding the sequential nature of these pictures is the way in which the abstractions of the rhyme – joy, love, sorrow and so on – are depicted and symbolized in the paintings. Different again, but still with autonomous pictures, is *Under the North Star* (1982) where Leonard Baskin's paintings can be appreciated independently for their power and beauty while also acting as a complement to Ted Hughes's poems.

2 *Books where visual art dominates as an independent mode of expression but is enhanced by actual or implied narrative structures, or verbal 'captions', as prompts to the pictures*
Compared with the books in the first group, wordless picture books like Shirley Hughes's *Up and Up* (1979) or Raymond Briggs's *The Snowman* (1978) rely for their effects less upon their qualities as painting but more upon visual design and narrative sequence. A different example is Peter Spier's *The Great Flood* (1978), which places the poem of the Noah story on a separate page and has brief captions in the endpapers; the rest is pictorial – humorously detailed and with some striking changes of perspective.

3 *Books where the visual and verbal elements are interdependent: the pictorial images reflect the words, the words complement the pictures as an integrated whole*
Many of the best-known modern picture-books come into this group: Maurice Sendak's *Where the Wild Things Are* (1967), *In the Night Kitchen* (1971) and *Outside Over There* (1981); Raymond Briggs's cartoon picture-books with their questioning, sympathetic probes into the received wisdom of everything from our views of Father Christmas to the values and lifestyle of contemporary society and the double-standards that prevail in times of war. In *Rosie's Walk* by Pat Hutchins (1970), *Come Away from the Water, Shirley* by John Burningham (1977), *Gorilla* by Anthony Browne (1983) and *The Jolly Postman* by the Ahlbergs (1986), the verbal and visual elements relate to each other in different ways, but in no case can the one stand without the other.

4 *Books where the verbal text dominates as an independent work of art but where illustrations, comprising a visual parallel to the text, show a distinctive interpretive freedom of style and thought*
An example here is Charles Keeping's illustrations for Alfred Noyes's poem *The Highwayman* (1981). Noyes's romantic tragedy has been known to generations of schoolchildren since its publication in 1913 but, seventy years on, Keeping's black and sepia pictures reinterpret the whole narrative afresh for the reader/viewer, heightening the moods of love, jealousy, terror and violence upon which the story turns. Anthony Browne's modern illustrations for *Hansel and Gretel* (1981) constitute a similar visual reworking of a familiar text. The fairy tale is, literally, in modern dress: father in jeans and donkey jacket, his wife in a garish leopard-spotted coat and high boots with enough money to spend on earrings, make-up and cigarettes, while the children wear shabby clothes. The same interpretive freedom and consistency of style are shown in a quite different vein by Quentin Blake in illustrating Russell Hoban's *How Tom Beat Captain Najork and his Hired Sportsmen* (1974), where the text remains of prime importance but the pictures achieve a continuous, zany humour of their own in response to the story.

5 *Books where the verbal text, usually fiction or poetry, is autonomous; illustrations are subservient, incidental or perhaps just decorative, and aim to give a visual version of an aspect of the text, maybe tied to an actual quotation*
Examples are scarcely necessary here, since this is the conventional way in which children's fiction and poetry have been illustrated over the years. With some popular 'series' texts, illustrations can gain the status of familiar imagery, as happens, say, with the pictures in Hugh Lofting's Dr Dolittle books (e.g. 1922) and in Enid Blyton's *The Famous Five* (1950), but the visual remains of minor significance compared with the verbal narrative and never aspires to more than a few snapshots of particular incidents.

So much for working definitions; no more is claimed for these five groupings than that they provide a rough and ready means of describing the sorts of texts we are dealing with. The majority of what is customarily meant by the phrases 'illustrated books' or 'picture-books' fall within the middle three groupings. Readers/viewers may argue about whether the above examples are appropriately placed, but quibbles over the assignment of particular books are less important than the fact that, in all these three groupings, the picture-book gets the best of both media: it exploits both the impact of visual simultaneity and, in direct or implied form, the continuous enticement of verbal linearity. From the point of view of literature and learning, it is this interplay that requires exposition in respect of particular texts and exploration through appropriate classroom activities.

Visual and verbal

Some books are born as children's books, some achieve this status through social usage and some have it thrust upon them by the serendipity of publication. This is as true of the history of picture-books and illustrated books for children as it is of the fiction and poetry written for them.

The black humour of Heinrich Hoffmann's *Struwwelpeter* (n.d.) designed 'not to horrify, but to entertain in grotesque exaggeration of the ordinary stricture books of the time' (Feaver 1977: 12) remains memorable for its pictures of shock-headed Peter with hair like some marine plant and nails of painful length, and for the scissored stumps of little Conrad's thumbs, rather than for the verses that carry the 'warnings' about dishevelled hair, long nails and thumb-sucking. Like so many other children's writers and illustrators, Hoffmann created the books for a real child – his own son. Similarly, the zany pictures which Edward Lear drew to complement his limericks and nonsense poems (1846/1947) were also created for particular children – the family of Lord Derby in this case. Clearly, the majority of children's picture-books were conceived and born as such, from those invested with genius, like Blake's *Songs of Innocence and Experience* (1796/1970), to the more mundane curios in the museum of nineteenth- and twentieth-century illustrations.

The clearest example of the influence of social and cultural usage is in the illustration of traditional tales from oral literature. Books of fairy stories, tales of Robin Hood or King Arthur, myths and legends from around the world, all provide popular subject-matter for picture-books. Such stories were told, remembered, repeated and eventually recorded in print not just for children but for the whole communities from which they sprang. Yet, gradually as Tolkien (1938) and others have shown, these traditional tales were appropriated by the nursery. In mid-Victorian times, particularly, the major illustrators turned to such stories and from then on the visual appeal of Crane, Caldecott, Greenaway and, later, Arthur Rackham compounded the successful take-over bid that children's literature made for these tales.

The unpredictable world of publishing has, of course, also affected the status of children's picture-books. As Hogarth was producing his educational prints to encourage industry and criticize idleness in the young, and to admonish a generation of Tom Neros for its cruelty to animals, so John Newbery began to publish his Juvenile Library in the 1750s with edited versions of *Gulliver's Travels* and *Robinson Crusoe* in which the pictures played a major role. How many childhoods have been imprinted with the image of Crusoe in his goatskins staring at the footprint in the sand? Or of Gulliver with his hair staked to the ground and swarming with Lilliputians or, later, towing the Blefuscan fleet like toy ships? These images, often from Victorian editions, derived from Newbury's publishing innovation, which originated in the same few years as those of his better-known contemporary innovators, Hogarth and Fielding. Today, the constraints of publication are such that a picture-book's life may well be under one year unless it appears in paperback. Commercial considerations haunt the visual even more strongly than they do the verbal.

The importance of this inheritance cannot be exaggerated: picture-books and illustrated books for children have a distinguished history and, thankfully, the works of all the artists mentioned remain available in modern editions. There is ample guidance for those who wish to explore this inheritance (Feaver 1977; Townsend 1987; Whalley and Chester 1988; Nodelman 1988). The present focus must, of necessity, be narrower. Three books, all of which have been popular within the last ten years, will enable us to observe how the visual and verbal elements complement each other and to assess the interpretive power of the image placed within a narrative setting. The three books are *Up and Up* (1979) by Shirley Hughes; *Gorilla* (1983) by Anthony Browne; and *The Highwayman* (1981) by Alfred Noyes, illustrated by Charles Keeping. These three examples are taken one from each of the middle three groupings described in the previous section. Together, they allow us to explore some of the differences in reading these three types of text, as well as to identify the visual character of three distinguished artists in this medium. With the wordless picture-book, we are reading the pictures for their revelation of plot and character; with the picture-book proper, we are reading the pictures for their amplification of the verbal story currently unfolding; with the illustrated book, we are reading the pictures for their interpretation of a known story. Adapting the principles of image analysis (Bisson and Hart 1990), we need to keep in mind the elements of composition, light and colour, framing, the grouping of figures, the *mise en scène*, the focus and the body language of the figures when making a 'reading' of these texts.

Up and Up is a wordless cartoon story about a little girl who, after some amusing false starts, manages to fly round her neighbourhood. The events of the plot are told with subtle image repetitions and innovative framing devices; the story of the girl's fluctuating disappointments, fears, delight and sheer sense of mischief is conveyed through her changing facial expressions and body language. That all this is achieved only with black and sepia colours throughout is remarkable and places great importance, in turn, upon the varied use of different perspectives, viewing angles and frame shapes to give both depth to the image and momentum to the narrative.

The opening endpapers provide a double-page spread of the whole landscape of the story to come, with a small, lonely girl (at bottom left) looking skyward at the birds and the implied viewer/reader. The story opens, comic-strip style, with the slapstick humour of some predictable but none-too-serious accidents, as the would-be flyer attempts a running jump at the sky, a 'bird-girl's' take-off from a step ladder and an ill-fated balloon ascent. The arrival of a large chocolate Easter egg, which she climbs inside and steadily eats her way through, signals her transformation from mere earthling into the mischievous flyer. Thereafter, the framing of the pictures lengthens into columns to capture her aerobatics at home, and into horizontal strips as she zooms over the heads of a startled bus queue.

Figure 12.1 'Capture by the balloonist', from *Up and Up*, by Shirley Hughes

The sense of movement and the girl's *joie de vivre* are perfectly harmonized. She is protected by the birds against the humans trying to catch her; but, in her later adventures, her cheekiness and tendency to show off increase as she teases the local balloonist, until she finally comes down to earth once more in his punctured balloon (Figure 12.1).

The way the eye is manipulated produces a range of effects in which the viewer collaborates. Some sequences are 'read' conventionally from left to right where the pace might be, either slow so that expressions can be interpreted, or fast to create the speed of her flight. Other images tempt the reader to turn the book round to follow the mazy movements; we read some pages from top to bottom down open sides of buildings, others from bottom to top, following the gaze of the onlookers peering at the girl aloft. The turning-point of the plot is signalled by a circular image of the balloonist superimposed upon a rectangular one of the girl flying away above the crowd. Details break the frames to carry the momentum of the story, and there are constant shifts of perspective as the focal point of the images alters with the demands of the plot. The groupings of the figures become increasingly complex as the book proceeds and the number of onlookers increases; sometimes we are at a distance, at other times we are members of the crowd. Reading the details of this sepia-distanced setting is one of the delights of the book: the suburban roads, the Victorian buildings, the schoolroom where chalk, blackboards and easel are still in use, the bric-à-brac of the rooms and lofts upon which we eavesdrop – all provide visual entertainment and lend depth and character to the narrative. *Up and Up* needs no captions to tell its story: the reader/viewer is drawn in to participate in the telling by being required to interpret movements, feelings, hidden thoughts, body language and repetitive details from a variety of stances.

The surreal appeal of *Gorilla* starts on the cover. Here, behind the images of the protagonists, the silhouetted rooftops of the town have several figures (including King Kong), an up-ended fork, a snail and a wine-bottle tower; there is a window of noughts and crosses, one with a pair of dangling feet and another with a pair of inquisitive eyes. The cover effectively catches the tone of Anthony Browne's story of Hannah, apparently the only child of a one-parent family, whose father is always too busy with his work to talk to her or take her out. Hannah becomes obsessed with gorillas in books, pictures and drawings, although she has never seen a real one. For her birthday, she asks for and gets a gorilla as a present, and her imagination does the rest. The toy is transformed into the father-gorilla of her dreams, who takes her on a night-ride around the town, to the zoo to see the real gorillas, to the cinema to see superman-gorilla, to a café to eat a midnight feast far more inviting than that of the cold breakfast table she shares with her father each morning, and finally to late-night dancing on the garden lawn. The next morning Hannah awakes to find the toy gorilla next to her, and her father, with a banana in his jeans' pocket, ready to take her on a birthday treat to the zoo.

The landscape shape of the book allows Anthony Browne to use the right-hand pages for single large-scale pictures and the left-hand pages for the text plus one or more smaller, framed images. As in his *Hansel and Gretel*, one of the compositional features is Browne's interplay of vertical and horizontal lines, suggesting variously both the stability and the isolation of Hannah's life. Her empathy with the caged primates is hinted at early in the vertical bars of the wallpaper, chair and curtains of her father's study; the staircase, and the brass bedstead in her bedroom (Figure 12.2) – a motif which is later taken up when she visits the zoo. There is some humorous interpictorialism, too, in the plethora of gorilla pictures within the pictures. There is Mona Gorilla framed on the staircase, King Kong on the bedroom wall, a Cézanne gorilla by the door; Superman, Charlie Chaplin and John Wayne gorillas at the cinema; and Che Gorilla on a fence poster on the way home! In all, then, there are four varieties of primate represented – the birthday toy, the dream-father-gorilla, the real ones in the zoo and these decorative images interpictorially present in many pictures. Their interplay creates much of the bitter-sweet tone of the book and helps orchestrate the fluctuating emotions which invest it.

Browne's concern to create mood and explore relationships is evident, too, in the emphasis he places upon a strong sense of design in the pictures. The

Figure 12.2 'Gorilla at the end of the bed', from *Gorilla*, by Anthony Browne

perspective is consistently full frontal, giving a diagrammatic feel to many of the images; pictorial space is flattened into a number of interconnecting geometric shapes, where pattern is more important than the creation of a believable three-dimensional landscape for the figures to inhabit. This can be seen most clearly in the first large picture of Hannah and her father at the breakfast table, where triangles and rectangles help to create the sterility of the relationship. Colour, too, plays its part, and there is a marked contrast between the cold blues and creams of this picture and the warmer browns, reds and greens which dominate the later ones with the gorilla.

The visual and verbal interplay is carefully deployed to exploit both the linear movement of the words and the reflective 'filling-out' offered by the pictures. The text is in simple, short sentences which relate directly to the small, framed images above them; the right-hand pages provide a visual amplification of the already stated theme of each spread. Words and pictures complement each other, together creating an exploration of a father–daughter relationship with a metaphoric power derived from its central memorable image.

Charles Keeping's pictures to accompany Alfred Noyes' poem *The Highwayman* provide the example of an illustrated book. Arguably, the pictures heighten the dramatic impact of this romantic tragedy to a degree that puts it beyond the young readership who might otherwise enjoy the poem for its own sake. This, alone, is testimony to the interpretive power of Keeping's art. He has produced a framed visual narrative, with the highwayman on the front cover and the ghostly lovers on the back. Closed wooden shutters appear in both endpapers, and there are two double-page spreads repeated at the beginning and end of the poem, the first to introduce Bess, the highwayman and their story, the second, in negative, to create their ghosts. Throughout, Keeping uses only two colours, black and sepia, but the range of moods and the variability of light at different times of day and night are richly evocative. Love, jealousy, betrayal, sexuality, violence, suicide, assassination and ghostly hauntings pervade this tale and, in Keeping's interpretation, resolve into an opposition of high romance and base nature. The two lovers are idealized at the outset: Bess is presented as pure, innocent, naïve, trusting; the highwayman as the romantic and debonair lover. The charm of their relationship is reflected in the love knots carved in the casements and in their body language as he doffs his cap and Bess leans from the window, her hair cascading over him. Opposing these star-crossed lovers are the images of base nature as portrayed in the figures of Tim, the ostler, and the gross, leering soldiers – Calibans all!

In an interesting study of Keeping's art, Lopez (1991) comments on the role of the soldiers when they use Bess as bait to trap her lover, showing how the unsavoury subtext of the poem is given explicit visual impact by Keeping.

> This portrayal of them as facially leering, lecherous, pimply louts certainly exaggerates any textual reference to their behaviour. Indeed, the gagging scene [Figure 12.3] is tinged with intense sexual perversion. Here, the expressions of the

Figure 12.3 'Gagging scene', from *The Highwayman*, by Alfred Noyes, illustrated by Charles Keeping

soldiers as drawn by Keeping reveal what he wants us to see as their true natures. The eyes of the two soldiers in the foreground seem to be looking inwards, as towards a mirror, furtively enjoying what their fellows are doing to Bess. The shaded intensity of their eyes gives way to the open-mouthed and evident excitement of these men as they tie Bess to her bedpost. Immediately after this, the illustration of the two thin-lipped soldiers stylistically holding out their muskets, while two others press themselves with threatening eyes and cruel lips against the helpless Bess, all go to symbolize a rape scene of considerable distaste.

The final pictures of Bess and the highwayman stress their tragic fate rather than the romantic adventure of their story. Bess is depicted at the point of death and straight afterwards, where the symbolism of her sacrifice to warn her lover is caught in her resignation and the icon-like appearance of these final images. The horror of realization is depicted in the highwayman in the pages that follow, until he too is gunned down in a bloodied image which the reader/viewer looks at from a high vantage point, effectively foreshortening the figure and intensifying its impact. Throughout, Keeping's interpretation of the themes of the poem add a dimension to the text which few readers would otherwise realize from the buoyant rhythms of the poem alone.

Picture-books in school

The above are just three examples from an area where visual literacy is clearly of major concern to the teacher of literature. How can this rich resource be best exploited in the school context?

The single most useful source of information is Elaine Moss's excellent annotated book guide, *Picture Books For Young People 9–13* (1985). The most useful resource – indeed an obligatory one – is a collection of forty or fifty picture-books. Ideally, these can be bought as a permanent resource for the school (for no more than a set of thirty course books) but, failing that, could be borrowed from the local library. Below are some teaching ideas using such a resource, most of which are appropriate for two or three periods' work. These are followed by details of an extended project on picture-books carried out in a Hampshire secondary school; this received wide circulation in the county and proved readily transferable to other secondary and junior schools.

Teaching ideas

The first three suggestions are geared towards highlighting the qualities of the middle three groupings discussed at the start of the chapter.

Storytelling

Using either a wordless picture-book or one where the verbal content is minimal, pairs of pupils tell the story together, perhaps turn-taking a page at a time.

An alternative is for one pupil to read the picture-book to the other; then, without having seen the book in any detail, the second pupil retells the story to the first.

Words and pictures

Slides of a picture-book (purchased from Weston Woods, Henley-on-Thames, or made, say, at a local teachers' centre) are viewed by the class as the story is read aloud. Note-making and discussion might focus upon:

- how the pictures and the text relate;
- the position and size of figures; repeated figures; the placing, size and typeface of the text;
- perspective – the construction of the image; sense of depth etc.;
- framed and/or unframed pictures; design of the pages; how words relate to the framing/design;
- line – the use of verticals/horizontals; straight/wavy lines;
- colour – the main tones; any changes as the story proceeds; association with mood or feeling; colour of printing of text;
- repeated motifs or shapes; visual symbolism or imagery; the style of the story or poem in relation to the pictures.

Visual interpretation
Pupils work on a selection of six or eight illustrated books – enough for a different book for groups of four. The task is to describe your book to the rest of the class and, in particular, to say *how* the artist has interpreted the story or poem. Groups draft a one- or two-sentence statement which summarizes their view of the illustrations, plus a list of particular points or examples of the artist's style in preparation for their presentations.

Sequencing
Photocopied pages of the pictures and/or text of a picture-book are shuffled and distributed to groups of no more than three or four pupils. Their task is to reconstruct the book in its proper sequence and explain their reasoning to another group.

Display
Exploit the visual nature of this genre by making pin-board space available in the classroom for a changing display of picture-book images. A particular book or artist/author could be featured each month, with pairs/groups of pupils responsible for mounting and maintaining the material.

Individual artists/authors
Encourage pupils to explore the work of particular artists/authors who appeal to them. Among those in modern times who have developed a substantial enough body of work to repay careful study are Maurice Sendak, Anthony Browne, Raymond Briggs, Charles Keeping, John Burningham, Shirley Hughes, Michael Foreman, Colin McNaughton, Mitsumasa Anno and Janet and Allan Ahlberg. And, of course, look for opportunities to promote the work of earlier illustrators – Kate Greenaway, Randolph Caldecott, Walter Crane, Arthur Rackham and Beatrix Potter. Studies of individual artists/authors should be seen as a natural complement to pupils' work on particular writers and poets.

Picture-book project

Introduction

This is a brief, basic and essentially practical guide to a project undertaken at a Hampshire secondary school during a Summer Term. The project stemmed from concern that picture-books are given scant attention in the secondary phase of education and the belief that such books can be exploited more fully than at present with older children. This guide was compiled by Mark Dawkins, the English teacher in charge of the project.

The project

The goal was to produce a picture-book suitable for reading to children of eight or nine. The class involved in the project were aged twelve to thirteen, generally able and well motivated.

Aims and objectives

These tended to expand organically as the project developed, but in retrospect turned out to include the following:

1 To encourage concentration on the process of writing through drafting and redrafting, with all its implications for quality of content as well as technical accuracy.
2 To encourage self-evaluation and the critical exchange of views on each other's writing.
3 To provide genuine audiences for the work at all stages of development.
4 To foster a sense of purpose and cooperation – for example, meeting real publication deadlines externally imposed, which served to divert attention from the authorial function of the teacher, who could then work as an adviser/team member.
5 To gain the satisfaction of producing a near perfect product, professionally bound and laminated.
6 To foster links between a variety of 'agencies'.

The participants

	'Agency'	*Role*
(a)	Southampton University, School of Education	Acted as a catalyst for the start of the project and supplied a large number of picture-books as the initial stimulus. Involved later in making the videotape of work in the Junior School.
(b)	Hampshire County Library Service	Supplied a selection of picture-books for classroom use.

(c) Parents/peers	Both were encouraged to be active in the drafting and illustrating.
(d) Teachers' Centre (Educational Development Centre)	Provided expertise/machinery for binding and laminating.
(e) Local Junior School	Provided an audience for the completed books, plus invaluable advice.

The programme

It should be noted that the class had five lessons of English per week, each lesson lasting thirty-five minutes. Every week a double lesson was used for the project, and the numbers below refer to this sequence.

Time	*Activities/Comments*
Before project began.	Contacted all the 'agencies' involved to 'set up' the project.
Lesson 1	Topic announced to class, and time given for thought. Knowledge of the subject-area was given in advance, on the premise that pupils cannot avoid preparing for a demand they know will be made.
Easter holiday	Period for gestation of ideas, note-making and first tentative illustrations.
Lesson 2	Examined a range of picture-books (suitable for two- to fourteen-year-olds). Discussed style, content, narrative lines, presentation, integration of pictures etc. A session enjoying the books.
Lessons 3–7 (plus six homeworks)	Devising a picture-book for use with eight- to nine-year-olds. In the following sequence of work, interim deadlines were agreed on an ad-hoc basis.

1 Draft the story, read it to peers and/or parents and redraft as necessary.
2 Plan pictures, illustrations and captions (consider cartoons, paintings, photos, collage etc).
3 Embody the concept in a mock-up booklet to anticipate the difficulties

	and 'iron out the bugs'. Following this, further redrafting. 4 Using A5 or A4 format, copy up – printing or typing. Produce illustrations. Leave a 2 cm margin for spiral binding. 5 Produce cardboard covers. 6 Peripheral activities – introduced to sustain interest or seized as opportunities for learning – included pupils writing about themselves as authors, naming the publisher and printer of their book plus the owner of the copyright, the ISBN number, writing a publisher's blurb, and listing other books by the author.
Whitsun holiday	Pupils collated the book in its final form.
Lesson 8	Books collected and taken for laminating and binding.
After publication	Books taken to the Junior School for staff there to give advice on their suitability and usefulness, followed by joint planning of the Junior School session.
Lessons 9 and 10 (plus two homeworks)	Pupils exchanged completed books and read them. Minor adjustments were made using Tipp-Ex fluid! Plans were evolved for using the books in the Junior School. Each Secondary-school pupil was briefed to: (a) Prepare a reading of his or her book for two eight- to nine-year-olds; (b) Based on the book, organize a fifty-minute lesson for the two younger children. Lesson organization and content were discussed, and open-ended activities were preferred. Among tasks planned by the Secondary pupils were cloze-test procedures, additional illustrations, collage work, word searches, treasure-hunt maps, crosswords and quizzes. At

	this stage every pupil was offered duplicating facilities.
Lesson 11	The Secondary pupils were transported by minibus to the Junior School, where they were allocated to one of five separate rooms and given time to organize the furniture appropriately. The Junior pupils were then brought in and introduced to their Secondary partners. The lessons then began, each room supervised by Junior or Secondary School staff. As organizer, I shuttled around the rooms ironing out problems. Meanwhile a member of the University staff made a video recording of the event for future use. The lessons were well prepared and extremely business-like, rendering the staff almost redundant!
Lesson 12 (plus one homework)	Secondary-school pupils discussed the project and mounted a display of work from the Junior School. Some tape-recordings made by pupils of work in progress were played and the videotape was viewed. A brief report and evaluation of the topic was then written.
After the project	The books were loaned to the Junior School library, then put on display at the Secondary School. All pupils received a 'Course Criticism'. The experience gained will be used for curriculum development and further liaison with Junior Schools.

Evaluation

There was a considerable degree of success in realizing the aims and objectives of the project. The pupils clearly grew in confidence and ability throughout the topic. It was especially pleasing to note the emphasis that they placed upon the process of learning and the drafting of their work. The necessity of exposing their writing and drawing to a variety of audiences induced a sense of purpose, and the critical element of this process contributed to some superb books. It was also worthwhile in terms of liaison between schools, and the marvellous atmosphere of cooperation here was mirrored by the enthusiastic response of parents when encouraged to become partners in the business of educating their children.

Afterword

Good English teachers know the art of eavesdropping. They establish a tacit understanding with their pupils that listening-in is a matter of trust. Their classrooms are organized around talk; discussion of books figures prominently in their practice. They become expert listeners, moving round the classroom, tuning in to how different groups of pupils are coping with a text or proceeding with a task. Typically, this demands a 'bifocal awareness' – one which enables them to concentrate for a time on one group while simultaneously surveying and managing the whole class. Reading pupils' journals, jottings and essays is another form of eavesdropping, allowing the teacher to overhear their 'written voices' and to assess their literary competencies with a range of texts and a variety of assignments. In developing oracy, the art of eavesdropping entails a willingness to listen to pupils' talk in order to build upon their perceptions, as well as to initiate and to direct. In developing literacy, it entails a willingness to become a responsive reader of pupils' writings in order to reach the writers behind them, as well as to assess and to mark.

These emphases are nowhere more important than when dealing with poetry, fiction and the visual arts. If we accept Auden's view quoted as the epigraph to this book, then the secondary worlds that readers and viewers explore become the essential substance of literature lessons: they are the actual phenomena with which teachers work. Enabling pupils 'to make new secondary worlds' of their own and 'to share in the secondary worlds' made by others are the fundamental activities of good literature teaching. Enabling teachers to become confident in these areas has been my purpose in this book: taken together, an understanding of the theoretical principles which permeate classroom methods and an awareness of what is appropriate for particular groups of pupils should provide that confidence. When in doubt, the key question for self-appraisal in literature teaching is, 'Does the work I am doing honour both the integrity of the text and the integrity of the readers?'

The question, of course, brings me back to where I started, for it focuses attention directly upon the central tenet of reader-response theory – that text and reader must complement each other in action for the experience of literature to exist at all. My emphasis upon process, upon teachers developing and monitoring pupils' responses to literature and the visual arts, builds upon this tenet on the basis of two convictions: firstly, that good literature teaching is generally carried out by reflective professionals who accommodate the notion of the teacher as enquirer as a vital part of their work; secondly, that, in school, good literature learning is generally experienced when critical appreciation is founded upon shared knowledge of how individual pupils read and respond. Given these principles, for both teacher and taught the making and sharing of secondary worlds become sources of both intellectual curiosity and continuing pleasure.

Bibliography

Abbs, P. (ed.) (1989). *The Symbolic Order: A Contemporary Reader on The Arts Debate.* London: The Falmer Press.

Abse, D. and J. (eds.) (1986). *Voices in the Gallery*. London: The Tate Gallery.

Adams, P. (ed.) (1986). *With a Poet's Eye*. London: The Tate Gallery.

Ahlberg, J. and A. (1986). *The Jolly Postman or Other People's Letters*. London: Heinemann.

Anno, M. (1974). *Anno's Alphabet: An Adventure in Imagination*. London: Bodley Head.

Antal, F. (1962). *Hogarth and his Place in European Art*. London: Routledge & Kegan Paul.

Arcimboldo, (1987). *Arcimboldo Poster Book*. Berlin: Taco Verlagsgesellschaft & Agentur.

Auden, W. H. (1968). *Secondary Worlds*. London: Faber.

Auden, W. H. (1969). *Collected Shorter Poems*. London: Faber.

Auden, W. H. (1970). 'Freedom and necessity in poetry: my lead mine'. In Tiselius, A. and Nilsson, S. (eds.). *The Place of Value in a World of Facts, Nobel Symposium 14*. Stockholm.

Auden, W. H. (1973a). 'Afterword – George MacDonald'. In *Forewords and Afterwords*. London: Faber.

Auden, W. H. (1973b) 'How can I tell what I think till I see what I say?' In Bagnall, N. (ed.). *New Movements in the Study and Teaching of English*. London: Temple Smith.

Auden, W. H. (1975). *The Dyer's Hand and Other Essays*. London: Faber.

Bacon, F. (1625/1890). 'Of studies'. In Reynolds, S. H. (ed.) (1890). *Bacon's Essays*. Oxford: The Clarendon Press.

Bakhtin, M. (1981). *The Dialogic Imagination*. (Trans. C. Emerson and M. Holquist). Austin: University of Texas Press.

Balaam, J. and Merrick, B. (1987). *Exploring Poetry: 5–8*. Sheffield: National Association for the Teaching of English.

Barnard, P. and Fox, G. (1990). *Cascades Coursework Folder 14–16*. London: Collins.

Barthes, R. (1970). *S/Z*. (Trans. R. Miller). London: Cape.

Barthes, R. (1976). *The Pleasure of the Text*. (Trans. R. Miller). London: Cape.

Baskin, L. and Hughes, T. (1982). *Under The North Star*. London: Faber.

Bennett, J. and Chambers, A. (1984). *Poetry For Children*. Stroud: The Thimble Press.

Benton, M. (1974). 'Detective imagination'. *Children's Literature in Education*, **13**, 5–12.

Benton, M. and P. (eds.) (1988). *Touchstones Vols. 1–5*. London: Hodder & Stoughton, 2nd edition.

Benton, M. and P. (eds.) (1990a). *Double Vision*. London: The Tate Gallery and Hodder & Stoughton.

Benton, M. and P. (eds.) (1990b). *Examining Poetry*. London: Hodder & Stoughton.

Benton, M. and Fox, G. (1985). *Teaching Literature 9–14*. Oxford: Oxford University Press.

Benton, M., Teasey, J., Bell, R. and Hurst, K. (1988). *Young Readers Responding to Poems*. London: Routledge.

Benton, P. (1986). *Pupil, Teacher, Poem*. London: Hodder & Stoughton.

Berger, J. (1972). *Ways of Seeing*. London: BBC and Penguin.

Bindman, D. (1981). *Hogarth*. London: Thames & Hudson.

Bisson, A. and Hart, A. (1990, rev. edn). *The Cinema Pack*. Southampton: Southampton Media Education Group.

Blake, W. (1796/1970). *Songs of Innocence and Experience*. Keynes, Sir G. (ed.). London: Oxford University Press.

Bleich, D. (1978). *Subjective Criticism*. Baltimore: Johns Hopkins University Press.

Blyton, E. (1950). *The Famous Five*. London: Brockhampton Press.

Booth, W. (1961). *The Rhetoric of Fiction*. Chicago: University of Chicago Press.

Briggs, R. (1978). *The Snowman*. London: Hamish Hamilton.

Britton, J. N. (1977). 'The role of fantasy'. In Meek *et al.* (eds.) (1977).

Britton, J. N. *et al.* (1975). *The Development of Writing Abilities, 11–18*. London: Macmillan.

Browne, A. (1981). *Hansel and Gretel*. London: Julia MacRae Books.

Browne, A. (1983). *Gorilla*. London: Julia MacRae Books.

Brownjohn, S. (1980). *Does It Have To Rhyme?* London: Hodder & Stoughton.

Bruner, J. (1962/1965). *On Knowing: Essays For the Left Hand*. Harvard: Harvard University Press.

Bruner, J. (1986). *Actual Minds, Possible Worlds*. Cambridge, Mass.: Harvard University Press.

Bryson, N. (1991). 'Semiology and visual interpretation'. In Bryson *et al.* (eds.) (1991).

Bryson, N., Holly, M. A. and Moxey, K. (eds.) (1991). *Visual Theory*. London: Polity Press.

Bullock, Sir A. (1975). *A Language For Life*. London: HMSO.

Burningham, J. (1977). *Come Away From The Water, Shirley*. London: Cape.

Butler, S. (1663–78). *Hudibras*. London.

Calvino, I. (1982). *If on a Winter's Night a Traveller*. (Trans. W. Weaver). London: Picador.

Causley, C. (1979). *Figgie Hobbin*. Harmondsworth: Puffin.

Chambers, A. (1983). *Introducing Books to Children*. London: Heinemann.

Chatman, S. (1978). *Story and Discourse. Narrative Structure in Fiction and Film*. NY: Cornell University Press.

Chukovsky, K. (1963). *From Two To Five*. (Trans. M. Morton). Berkeley: University of California Press.

Coleridge, S. T. (1798). 'The Rime of the Ancient Mariner'. In *The Lyrical Ballads*. London.

Coleridge, S. T. (1817/1949). *Biographia Literaria*. London: Dent.

Collinson, D. (1985). 'Philosophy looks at paintings'. In Deighton, E. (ed.). *Looking at Paintings*. Milton Keynes: Open University Press.

Cooper, C. R. (ed.) (1985). *Researching Response to Literature and the Teaching of Literature*. Norwood, NJ: Ablex.

Corcoran, B. and Evans, E. (eds.) (1987). *Readers, Texts, Teachers*. Milton Keynes: Open University Press.
Cowley, R. L. S. (1983). *Marriage à la Mode: A Review of Hogarth's Narrative Art*. Manchester: Manchester University Press.
Cox, C. B. (1989). *English For Ages 5–16*. London: HMSO.
Craig, G. (1976). 'Reading. Who is doing what to whom?' In Josipovici, G. (ed.). *The Modern English Novel*. London: Open Books.
Culler, J. (1975). *Structuralist Poetics: Structuralism, Linguistics and The Study of Literature*. London: Routledge & Kegan Paul.
Culler, J. (1983). *On Deconstruction*. London: Routledge & Kegan Paul.
Cumming, R. (1979). *Just Look*. Harmondsworth: Kestrel.
Cumming, R. (1982). *Just Imagine*. Harmondsworth: Kestrel.
Dabydeen, D. (1987). *Hogarth's Blacks: Images of Blacks in Eighteenth-Century English Art*. Manchester: Manchester University Press.
D'Arcy, P. (1973). 'The reader's response'. *Reading For Meaning, Vol. 2*. London: Hutchinson.
Day Lewis, C. (1948/1961). *The Otterbury Incident*. Harmondsworth: Penguin.
Dias, P. and Hayhoe, M. (1988). *Developing Response to Poetry*. Milton Keynes: Open University Press.
Dobson, A. (1893). *William Hogarth*. London.
Doonan, J. (1986). 'The object lesson: picturebooks of Anthony Browne'. *Word and Image*, **2** (2), 159–72.
Farr, D. *et al.* (1987). *Impressionist and Post-Impressionist Masterpieces: The Courtauld Collection*. New Haven and London: Yale University Press.
Feaver, W. (1977). *When We Were Young: Two Centuries of Children's Book Illustration*. NY: Holt, Rinehart & Winston.
Fielding, H. (1730). *Tom Thumb*. London.
Fielding, H. (1742/1962). *Joseph Andrews*. London: Dent.
Fielding, H. (1749). *Tom Jones*. London.
Fish, S. (1980). *Is There A Text In This Class? The Authority of Interpretive Communities*. Cambridge, Mass.: Harvard University Press.
Fish, S. (1989). *Doing What Comes Naturally*. Oxford: Oxford University Press.
Fowles, J. (1977). 'Notes on an unfinished novel'. In Bradbury, M. (ed.). *The Novel Today*. London: Fontana.
Fox, G. and Merrick, B. (1981). 'Thirty six things to do with a poem'. *The Times Educational Supplement*, 20 February.
Freud, S. (1908/1970). 'Creative writers and day dreaming'. In Vernon (ed.) (1970).
Freund, E. (1987). *The Return of the Reader*. London: Metheun.
Fry, D. (1985). *Children Talk About Books: Seeing Themselves As Readers*. Milton Keynes: Open University Press.
Frye, N. (1957). *The Anatomy of Criticism*. Princeton, NJ: Princeton University Press.
Garner, A. (1973/1975). *Red Shift*. London: Collins.
Gay, J. (1728). *The Beggar's Opera*. London.
Genette, G. (1980). *Narrative Discourse*. Oxford: Blackwell.
Ghiselin, B. (ed.) (1952). *The Creative Process*. NY: Mentor.
Gombrich, E. H. (1962). *Art and Illusion*. London: Phaidon.
Gowing, L. (1971). *Hogarth*. London: The Tate Gallery.
Graham, J. (1990). *Pictures on the Page*. Sheffield: The National Association for the Teaching of English.

Graves, R. (1961). *Robert Graves. Poems Selected By Himself.* Harmondsworth: Penguin.
Greene, M. (1989). 'Art worlds in school'. In Abbs (ed.) (1989).
Hackman, S. (1987). *Responding in Writing.* Sheffield: The National Association for the Teaching of English.
Hall, J. (1974). *Dictionary of Subjects and Symbols in Art.* London: John Murray.
Hagstrum, J. (1958). *The Sister Arts. The Tradition of Literary Pictorialism and English Poetry from Dryden to Gray.* Chicago: University of Chicago Press.
Harding, D. W. (1962). 'Psychological processes in the reading of fiction'. *The British Journal of Aesthetics*, **2** (2).
Harding, D. W. (1967). 'Considered experience. The invitation of the novel'. *English in Education*, **1** (2).
Harding, R. (1948) *The Anatomy of Inspiration.* London: Heffer & Sons.
Hardy, B. (1975). *Tellers and Listeners: The Narrative Imagination.* London: Athlone Press.
Havelka, J. (1968). *The Nature of the Creative Process in Art: A Psychological Study.* The Hague: M. Nijhoff.
Hayhoe, M. and Parker, S. (eds.) (1990). *Reading and Response.* Milton Keynes: Open University Press.
Hazlitt, W. (1818/1907). 'On the works of Hogarth'. In *Lectures on the English Comic Writers.* Oxford: Oxford University Press.
Hesketh, P. (1988). *Netting the Sun: New and Collected Poems.* Petersfield: The Enitharmon Press.
Hirsch, E. D. (1969). *Validity in Interpretation.* New Haven: Yale University Press.
Hoban, R. (1969). *The Mouse and His Child.* London: Faber.
Hoban, R. (1974). *How Tom Beat Captain Najork and His Hired Sportsmen.* London: Cape.
Hoffmann, H. (n.d.). *English Struwwelpeter.* London.
Hogarth, W. (1754/1955). *The Analysis of Beauty and Autobiographical Notes.* Burke, J. (ed.). Oxford: Oxford University Press.
Hogarth, W. (1833). *Biographical Anecdotes of William Hogarth.* Nichols, J. B. (ed.). London.
Holder, H. (1987). *Crows. An Old Rhyme.* London: Simon & Schuster.
Holland, N. (1968). *The Dynamics of Literary Response.* NY: Oxford University Press.
Holland, N. (1975). *Five Readers Reading.* New Haven: Yale University Press.
Hughes, S. (1979). *Up and Up.* London: Bodley Head.
Hughes, Ted (1957). *The Hawk in the Rain.* London: Faber.
Hughes, Ted (1967). *Poetry in the Making.* London: Faber.
Hughes, Thomas (1856/1971). *Tom Brown's Schooldays.* Harmondsworth: Penguin.
Huizinga, J. (1949/1970). *Homo Ludens.* London: Picador.
Hunt, P. (1990). *Children's Literature. The Development of Criticism.* London: Routledge.
Hutchins, P. (1970). *Rosie's Walk.* London: Bodley Head.
Iser, W. (1974). *The Implied Reader.* Baltimore: Johns Hopkins University Press.
Iser, W. (1978). *The Act of Reading. A Theory of Aesthetic Response.* London: Routledge & Kegan Paul.
James, H. (1896). 'The Figure in the Carpet'. In Edel, L. (ed.) (1964). *The Complete Tales*, **IX.** NY.
Kermode, F. (1975). 'How we read novels'. Southampton: University of Southampton Press.
Kingman, Sir J. (1988). *Report of the Committee of Inquiry into the Teaching of English Language.* London: HMSO.

Knight, R. (1989). 'Trivial pursuits'. *The Times Educational Supplement*, 12 May.
Koch, K. (1970). *Wishes, Lies and Dreams*. NY: Harper & Row.
Koch, K. (1973). *Rose, where did you get that red?* NY: Vintage Books.
Koestler, A. (1975a). *The Act of Creation*. London: Picador.
Koestler, A. (1975b). *The Ghost in the Machine*. London: Picador.
Kris, E. (1952/1964). *Psychoanalytic Explorations in Art*. NY: International Universities Press Ltd.
Lamb, C. (1811). 'On the genius and character of Hogarth'. In *The Reflector. A Collection of Essays . . . On Literature and Politics*, 2 vols. **II**, 61–77. London.
Langer, S. (1953). *Feeling and Form*. London: Routledge & Kegan Paul.
Langman, F. H. (1967). 'The idea of the reader in literary criticism'. *The British Journal of Aesthetics*, **7** (1), 93–4.
Lawrence. D. H. (1961). 'Preface' to *Chariot of the Sun*. Macdonald, E. D. (ed.). *Phoenix*. London: Heinemann.
Lear, E. (1846/1947). *The Complete Nonsense of Edward Lear*. Jackson, H. (ed.). London: Faber.
Lesser, S. O. (1957). *Fiction and the Unconscious*. NY: Beacon Books.
Lewis, C. S. (1961). *An Experiment in Criticism*. London: Cambridge University Press.
Lillo, G. (1731). *The London Merchant*. In Hampden, J. (ed.) (1928). *Eighteenth-Century Plays*. London: Dent.
Lister, R. (1985). *The Paintings of Samuel Palmer*. Cambridge: Cambridge University Press.
Little, R. *et al.* (1989). *GCSE Contexts*. London: Heinemann.
Lodge, D. (1990). *After Bakhtin: Essays on Fiction and Criticism*. London: Routledge.
Lofting, H. (1922). *The Story of Dr Dolittle*. London: Cape.
Lopez, R. (1991). *The Moral Odyssey of Charles Keeping*. Unpublished M.A. (Ed.) dissertation. Southampton: Faculty of Education, Southampton University.
McEwan, I. (1980). *The Cement Garden*. London: Picador.
McKeller, P. (1957). *Imagination and Thinking*. London: Cohen & West.
MacLeish, A. (1963). *Collected Poems*. NY: Houghton Mifflin Co.
Mark, J. (1980). 'William's Version'. In *Nothing To Be Afraid Of*. Harmondsworth: Kestrel.
Martin, D. (1980). *The Telling Line*. London: Julia MacRae Books.
Meek, M. (1988). *How Texts Teach What Readers Learn*. Stroud: The Thimble Press.
Meek, M., Warlow, A. and Barton, G. (eds.) (1977). *The Cool Web: The Pattern of Children's Reading*. London: Bodley Head.
Michelangelo (1961). 'Sonnet XV'. *The Sonnets of Michelangelo*. (Trans. E. Jennings). London: The Folio Society.
Miller, M. (1989). '*The Mouse and His Child: a reader-response study*. Unpublished M.A (Ed.) dissertation. Southampton: Faculty of Education, University of Southampton.
Moebius, W. (1986). 'Introduction to picturebook codes'. *Word and Image*, **2** (2), 141–58.
Moore, R. E. (1948). *Hogarth's Literary Relationships*. Minneapolis: University of Minnesota Press.
Moss, E. (1985). *Picture Books For Young People 9–13*. Stroud: The Thimble Press, 2nd edition.
Nochlin, L. (1991). 'Women, art and power'. In Bryson *et al.* (eds.) (1991).
Nodelman, P. (1988). *Words About Pictures: The Narrative Art of Children's Picture Books*. Athens, Ga: University of Georgia Press.
Norton, M. (1958). 'Paul's Tale'. In Reeves, J. (ed.). *A Golden Land*. London: Constable.

Noyes, A. and Keeping, C. (1981). *The Highwayman*. Oxford and London: Oxford University Press.

Opie, I. and O. (1973). *The Oxford Book of Children's Verse*. Oxford and London: Oxford University Press.

Oppé, A. (1948). *The Drawings of William Hogarth*. London: Phaidon.

Parker, R. and Pollock, G. (1981). *Old Mistresses: Women, Art and Ideology*. London: Routledge & Kegan Paul.

Paulson, R. (1971). *Hogarth: His Life, Art and Times*, 2 vols. New Haven and London: Yale University Press.

Paulson, R. (1975). *The Art of Hogarth*. London: Phaidon.

Pearce, P. (1975). 'Writing a book': *A Dog So Small*'. In Blishen, E. (ed.). *The Thorny Paradise*. London: Kestrel.

Pirrie, J. (1987). *On Common Ground*. London: Hodder & Stoughton.

Podro, M. (1991). 'Depiction and the golden calf'. In Bryson *et al.* (eds.) (1991).

Poe, E. A. (1846/1963). 'The philosophy of composition'. In Gibson, W. (ed.). *Poems in the Making*. Boston: Houghton Mifflin.

Pope, A. (1715). 'The Rape of the Lock'. Butt, J. (ed.). *The Poems of Alexander Pope*. London: Methuen.

Price, M. (1971). 'Irrelevant detail and the emergence of form'. In Hillis Miller, J. (ed.). *Aspects of Narrative*. NY: Columbia.

Protherough, R. (1983). *Developing Response to Fiction*. Milton Keynes: Open University Press.

Praz, M. (1956). 'Introduction. Genre painting and the novel'. In *The Hero in Eclipse in Victorian Fiction*. (Trans. A. Davidson). London: Oxford University Press.

Purves, A. and Rippere, V. (1968). *Elements of Writing About a Literary Work*. Urbana: National Council of Teachers of English.

Purves, A. and Beach, R. (1972). *Literature and the Reader*. Urbana: National Council of Teachers of English.

Quennell, P. (1955). *Hogarth's Progress*. London: Collins.

Read, H. (1943). *Education Through Art*. London: Faber.

Redgrove, P. (1960). *The Collector and Other Poems*. London: Routledge & Kegan Paul.

Reynolds, Sir J. (1789). *Discourses*. London.

Richards, I. A. (1924). *The Principles of Literary Criticism*. London: Routledge & Kegan Paul.

Richards, I. A. (1929). *Practical Criticism*. London: Routledge & Kegan Paul.

Richards, I. A. (1943). *How to Read a Page*. London: Routledge & Kegan Paul.

Roberts, T. J. (1990). *An Aesthetics of Junk Fiction*. Athens, Ga: University of Georgia Press.

Rosen, H. (1982). *Stories and Meanings*. Sheffield: National Association for The Teaching of English.

Rosen, M. (1981). *I See A Voice*. London: Hutchinson.

Rosenblatt, L. (1938/1970). *Literature As Exploration*. NY: Modern Languages Association.

Rosenblatt, L. (1978). *The Reader, The Text, The Poem. The Transactional Theory of the Literary Work*. Carbondale: Southern Illinois University Press.

Rosenblatt, L. (1985). 'The transactional theory of the literary work: implications for research'. In Cooper, C. R. (ed.). *Researching Response to Literature and the Teaching of Literature*. Norwood, NJ: Ablex.

Rushdie, S. (1990). *Haroun and the Sea of Stories*. London: Granta Books.

Ryle, G. (1949). *The Concept of Mind*. Harmondsworth: Penguin.
Sampson, G. (1921/1970). *English For The English*. Cambridge: Cambridge University Press.
Sampson, G. (1946). 'A boy and his books'. In *Seven Essays*. London: Cambridge University Press.
Sartre, J.-P. (1972). *The Psychology of Imagination*. London: Methuen.
Scholes, R. (1985). *Textual Power. Literary Theory and the Teaching of English*. New Haven and London: Yale University Press.
Sebestyen, O. (1987). *Words By Heart*. London: Hamish Hamilton.
Sendak, M. (1967). *Where The Wild Things Are*. London: Bodley Head.
Sendak, M. (1971). *In the Night Kitchen*. London: Bodley Head.
Sendak, M. (1981). *Outside Over There*. London: Bodley Head.
Sitwell, S. (1936). *Conversation Pieces. A Survey of English Domestic Portraits and Their Painters*. London: Batsford.
Skelton, R. (1978). *Poetic Truth*. London: Heinemann.
Slatoff, W. (1970). *With Respect to Readers. Dimensions of Literary Response*. Ithaca, NY, and London: Cornell University Press.
Smith, F. (1971). *Understanding Reading*. NY: Holt, Rinehart & Winston.
Spalding, J. (1979). *Lowry*. London: Phaidon.
Spender, S. (1946/1952). 'The making of a poem'. In Ghiselin (ed.) (1952).
Spier, P. (1978). *The Great Flood*. Tadworth: World's Work.
Spilka, M. (ed.) (1977). *Towards a Poetics of Fiction*. Bloomington and London: Indiana University Press.
Squire, J. R. (1964). *The Responses of Adolescents to Four Short Stories*. Urbana: National Council of Teachers of English.
Stephens, K. (1990). 'Peepo ergo sum? Anxiety and pastiche in the Ahlbergs' picture books'. *Children's Literature in Education*, **21** (3), 165–77. NY: Human Sciences Press Inc.
Sterne, L. (1767). *Tristram Shandy*. London: Pocket Library (1959).
Stevens, W. (1963). *Selected Poems*. London: Faber.
Storey, E. (1982). *The Dark Music*. Peterborough: Annakin Fine Arts Press.
Styles, M. (ed.) (1989). *Collaboration and Writing*. Milton Keynes: Open University Press.
Styles, M. and Triggs, P. (eds.) (1988). *Poetry 0–16*. London: Books for Keeps.
Suleiman, S. and Crosman, I. (eds.) (1980). *The Reader in the Text: Essays on Audience and Interpretation*. Princeton, NJ: Princeton University Press.
Thackeray, W. M. (1853). 'Hogarth, Smollett and Fielding'. In *The English Humourists of the Eighteenth Century*. London: Dent (1904).
Tolkien, J. R. R. (1938/1964). *Tree and Leaf*. London: Unwin Books.
Tompkins, J. (ed.) (1980). *Reader-Response Criticism: From Formalism to Post-Structuralism*. Baltimore: Johns Hopkins University Press.
Townsend, J. R. (1987). *Written for Children*. Harmondsworth: Penguin.
Vernon, P. E. (ed.) (1970). *Creativity*. Harmondsworth: Penguin.
Warnock, M. (1972). 'Introduction'. In Sartre (1972).
Warnock, M. (1976). *Imagination*. London: Faber.
Weir, R. (1962). *Language in the Crib*. London: Mouton & Co.
Wellek, R. and Warren, A. (1949). *Theory of Literature*. London: Cape.
Whalley, J. and Chester, T. (1988). *A History of Children's Book Illustration*. London: J. Murray.
Whitehead, A. N. (1975). In Auden, W. H. *The Dyer's Hand and Other Essays*. London: Faber.

Whitehead, F. *et al.* (1977). *Children and Their Books*. London: Macmillan.

Wimsatt, W. K. and Beardsley, M. (1954/1970). *The Verbal Icon: Studies in the Meaning of Poetry*. London: Methuen.

Winnicott, D. W. (1974). *Playing and Reality*. Harmondsworth: Penguin.

Witkins, R. (1974). *The Intelligence of Feeling*. London: Heinemann.

Wollheim, R. (1980). *Art and Its Objects*. Cambridge: Cambridge University Press, 2nd edition.

Wollheim, R. (1987). *Painting as an Art*. London: Thames & Hudson.

Woolf, V. (1925). 'Modern fiction'. *The Common Reader, 1st series*. London: The Hogarth Press.

Index